You Call This Living?

By
Bill Kingsley

You Call This Living?

International Standard Book Number: 978-1-938911-44-6

.

Printed in the United States of America

William (Bill) Kingsley
seabed999@yahoo.com

TABLE OF CONTENTS

Affectionately inscribed to Bill Frost,
The fountainhead of inspiration
From the University of Dayton, Ohio;
Cheers to my mentor and friend.

CHAPTER 1

The Problems People Face
On Your Mark, Get Set: Thieve Away!

You're watching the greatest theft in world history—right now. Since the turn of millennium, I have debated this idea with any fellow travelers who seemed to listen. But over the years I have begun to question if the average person even cares. People seem to understand it at an intellectual level, but they view Wall Street bailouts and corporate wrongdoing from a distance, as if the events are happening to someone else. It's as though they feel that if no one is rifling through their pockets at the moment, they aren't affected. But where do you think they get the money for these bailouts? What other ridiculous ways does money *disappear* when corporate functionaries lose risky trades and ventures? It is not surprising public trust in government and corporations is very low. Theft is nothing new—it's just now on a grand scale, unimaginable to past generations. The list of suspects include multinational corporations, financial institutions, lobbyists, special interest groups, drug cartels, weapons dealers, government officials and others that operate or rule by fiat. Some authorities believe this unprecedented thievery is due to the spiritual deterioration of society.

The Time Magazine Person of the Year for 2011 was *The Protester* in recognition of dissent against authoritarian leaders in Tunisia, Egypt, and other countries. In the same year, the *occupy movements* across many U.S. cities were raving for economic justice.

Today, around the world, people still reeling from homelessness, poverty, foreclosures, and economic inequality are taking action. The continuing protests seem to coalesce with other subjects of dissent such as movements against globalization and the World Trade Organization (WTO). The environmental organization, Greenpeace, continues to protest a variety of concerns from nuclear power to whale slaughter. Some spectators have a gut feeling that these particular movements represent pursuits with some validity or justification. There is a smoldering presentiment that the boat is rocking against the status quo, and we wonder about the fine line between anarchy and impassioned dissent. The protest movement reminds us of the 1976 movie *Network* in which Peter Finch screams, "I'm as mad as hell, and I'm not going to take this anymore!"

At some point in your life, you wake up to reality, and by that time you realize you have been slapped into awareness and wonder, "What am I doing here? What is the point of my life and of living in this space-time?" It can be a lonely world out there. Beyond our own self is termed—"out there" because we often do not feel a part of what's going on around us.

There are times when we sense life is passing us by, or that we are passively watching the world go by. We are born in the warm and fuzzy protection of our mother's womb and slapped into the harsh world of reality. From then on, the animal world fights for survival. Charles Darwin informed the cognoscenti about it in his book *The Origin of Species* (1859), with the insight "survival of the fittest" as coined by Herbert Spencer.

Humans strive to survive, but better yet, we are programmed to endure and pass on our biology, the genes or hereditary substance that is one of the purposes of sex. There is this dance going on around us, among the flowering beds, euphemistically called "the birds and the bees." It is restless, this thing called life, swarming after its initial start about 3.5 billion years ago. And since the planet is 4.5 billion years old, life evolved on Earth within the first billion years, from tiny bacteria to recently, humans with consciousness.

We seem to be robots or like the lower animals that instinctually react to stimuli and not always in tremendously enlightened ways. Perhaps the description is more akin to "entranced" as in some hypnotic, somnambulant state, crawling around like ants—but at least *they* seem to have a purpose. The reason for this anomaly is the origins of human behavior are biological and this evolution of mankind occurred over a period of three to five million years.[1] In contrast, ants have lived for over 100 million years and show surprising social behavior to include slavery and suicide.

Humans were riding with horse and buggy just some few years ago, so is it any wonder technology has brought us far but too fast in the rat race we call civilization? Like the crawling ants, we may be seen to have a purpose but what about the question of meaning? If you ask 100 people "what is the meaning of life?" you may not be surprised by the kaleidoscope of answers.

It amazes me to observe the geniuses of the intellectual world muddling along with their $50 words. They want to impress the rest and gain their 15 minutes of fame with printed accounts of how they know it all. And they suavely insert foreign words or phrases to really show off such as doppelganger. But in academic or literary circles, you cannot get published unless you thoroughly confuse the hell out of people. For example, take a random quote from the eminent physicist, David Bohm:

> *"The experience of reality includes the projection of representations into what you see. But it is not entirely that, because if your mind is working right you have to take into account that the whole thing is incoherent. Then is loses its hold and you begin to change. Is that clear?"*[2]

Hopefully the tone of this book will steer clear of that kind of wordiness. We appreciate and quote academics that do not reside in ivory towers.

In his book, *Why We Do It*, Niles Eldredge writes:

> *"Science, of course, doesn't deal with strictly philosophical questions, and even philosophers seldom wrangle anymore over life's meaning or purpose. Meaning-of-life issues*

have long since been relegated to the provinces of received doctrine in organized religion and college dormitory bull sessions."[3]

As Johnny Carson used to say: I did *not* know that! You see how the *experts* are so knowledgeable; you don't even have to ask a specific question about the meaning of life.

In *Rocks of Ages*, Stephen Jay Gould advocates that Science and Religion have their separate domains or *magisterium*. Many readers know that the giant of evolutionary biology was a paleontologist and intense writer whose credits include essays in the magazine, *American Museum of Natural History*. Brilliant people can be prickly as porcupines—and the record shows many of his contemporaries are just like the rest of us, highly capable of sniping at one another. Stephen wrote as follows:

> *"Science tries to document the factual character of the natural world, and to develop theories that coordinate and explain these facts. Religion, on the other hand, operates in the equally important realm of human purposes, meanings, and value—subjects that the factual domain of science might illuminate, but can never resolve. Science studies how the heavens go, and religion how to go to heaven."*

Stephen Jay Gould's point is that science and religion should not be in conflict since they each cast their nets on different fishing grounds. There can be mutual respect between the two. However, I am a bit more cynical than the referee cited above. I can see the relevance of scientists with their Ph.D.s, but I don't agree that the department of religion should necessarily be the arbiter of human purpose and moral values. On what basis, other than faith do the operators of the various religions lead the faithful? There are no mathematical formulas, data processors, or verifiable experiments employed.

Adventurers Ahoy!

Who out there is adventuresome? There may be a few but certainly not the majority. Evolution and human history has taught us that, when we step outside the cave, we'd better have a sturdy club in our hands or else we might be attacked or bamboozled. This is obviously the case in the animal world, hence the expression "it's a dog-eat-dog world." No wonder there are few takers for the adventure-bound life. You step outside the boundary of your camouflaged existence and you might find yourself in the nasty sites of some loathsome villain. Therefore it is easier to go with the flow, however stagnant, to march to the tribal beat, and keep your head low to avoid incoming fire. And so it is no wonder the average person does not want to stand out in a crowd or think outside of the box—conformity is the norm from kindergarten onward to the end.

All of us defend self-preservation throughout our lives. It becomes our goal in life, to buttress the body and ego against outside assault even if we have to resort to camouflage or retreat into the armored shell. There are circumstances that compel conformity such as Boot Camp or the cubicle, where anonymity may be the logical strategy.

However, I contend that it is a good idea to get *out of line* and choose your own path in life. There is no irrevocable reason to be coerced into a mundane existence. A famous saying, mistakenly attributed to the circus manager (P.T. Barnum), proclaims, "There's a sucker born every minute." Of course that is absolutely right, but we don't *have* to be one of them.

This book is an attempt to awaken the senses, stimulate thinking, and hopefully entertain as well. The aim is to identify the crucial challenge for humanity in the near future; how to raise global educational awareness in order to combat the effects of rising populations and deterioration of environments.

Most people travel through life as walking idiots, contriving to get in your way at every opportunity. Wind them up at the start of the day and off they go, careening in every direction in a helpless or hopeless manner until they wind down and drowsily fall back to their dreaming state. It's the same old story—"forgive them, for they know not what they do." This isn't because people are unintelligent. It's a matter of programming. People lack awareness and live their lives in a robotic manner, doing the same things day after day.

In my Catholic school, they proclaimed that the "age of reason" was seven years of age. I guess the toddler is officially culpable or capable of sinning when he turns seven. It seems impractical to me, but then the power of brainwashing is effective. Obviously there is not a lot of awareness going on at age seven. And when an older person reflects back on his life and says, "What have I been doing the past 10 years?" there is not a lot of awareness going on even then.

I hear people say they hate their lives and want out of the rat race. Can things be so bad that you would admit to living like a rat? Or they say, "I gotta get out of this ditch." However, people who have a keen awareness are on a higher rational level than the commoners, and scientific studies indicate that awareness is one of the many attributes which differentiates humans from most other animals such as the chimps, chumps, and other endangered creatures.

Awareness may be characteristic of human nature, but it appears to be superficial in most cases. If the world's population were all running around Gandhi-like, that might be awareness running amok (the opposite of reality). To look back on your life and have regrets is normal—I should have been a lawyer and the spilt milk attitude. To have awareness is to say, "Yes, I could have been a lawyer, but for some reasons it didn't happen that way." Perhaps in the next life—who wants a next life? This is *it* pal! Actually, you could have been a lawyer, but you had to become a sturgeon.

When I looked at my wife, Luchia's, pictures from her past, I was in awe of her obvious beauty and wondered what I'd been doing for the foreseeable past. I surmised that my life had been fairly pitiful during those years. There was a lack of awareness since my outlook was somewhat provincial and rooted in a limited part of the United States.

Her story turned out to be amazing in that she sacrificed

all her energy to help her family of eleven. Luchia was married off at the age of 14 since her father knew she would otherwise be kidnapped. When she was as young as 12, Ethiopian men, including her teachers, were stalking her and trying to convince her parents to hand her over for marriage. Luchia had to be sent to another province to avoid kidnapping and her father finally consented to have her married as the lesser of two evils. Her older husband died in a trucking accident after three months, leaving her with an unborn daughter. She eventually endured a horrific 13-day walk with 26 other runaway students from the barbarous Ethiopian, socialist dictator, Mengistu. During his despotic reign, Mengistu directed the torture, hanging, and murder of ordinary citizens. It was standard business to leave murdered bodies on the street as a showcase of what the citizenry could expect. Luchia experienced a terrifying ordeal during her long journey, including bandits, attempted rape, and constant hunger and thirst. But she made it to the Sudan and credited her gentle upbringing by caring parents. Luchia thereafter made landfall in Saudi Arabia to work and support her large family in Eritrea as well as the daughter she left behind. It took her nine years to return for a visit with her daughter and family back home. You can imagine the tears at that homecoming!

Don't Blame Murphy

Everyone has life experiences and, since we are cruising in this *vale of tears*, we all have some good and bad ones. But these are relative terms. For example, pain is usually thought of as bad. But sometimes pain is a way to inform us we have a bodily problem that needs attention. When we burn our finger on a hot stove, pain is a signal to withdraw the finger quickly to prevent further injury. It's a defense mechanism.

Then there's Murphy's Law: *anything that can go wrong, will go wrong*. I know because Murphy has followed me around quite a bit in my time! But this Murphy's Law is actually one of the principles of science, the *second law of thermodynamics*, which is "the tendency of physical systems to evolve toward states of higher entropy."[5] That is, things have a tendency to become disordered and you are more likely to see an egg splatter rather than unsplatter. That explains why your bedroom was always messy and your toys were always breaking. Is this bad? It is simply nature's way—the physical *rules* of the universe. These are rules we barely understand, never mind being able to control.

But this is our problem. We always want to *control* things don't we? For example, some people are meticulous cleaners, and their house must always be spotless and neat with nothing out of place (a place for everything, and everything in its place). Another good example is money, money, money. Most people want to control their money. Not many would say "here is all my money and I trust you will take good care of it." But even animals are controlling organisms like the lions which have social hierarchies with dominant and controlling individuals (the male, naturally). The explanation of certain animal behavior is rooted in biology. For instance, an infant does not learn to cry—one initial slap on the fanny will do it. They are programmed to behave that way by heredity.

Many aspects of our life are predestined, for example, growing old. And it seems predestined that the Arabs and Israel will battle to the death (and probably take the rest of us with them). For now, we have no choice, at least about growing old. The opposite of predestination is the notion of 'free will' which means we call the shots and are therefore responsible for our actions. It may not surprise anyone that philosophers have been kicking around the idea of 'free will' for over two thousand years.

A more practical issue is the nature versus nurture concept. Does a man learn to become an alcoholic or do some people carry a hereditary gene that predisposes them to a problem with the sauce? We all have problems and no one is immune. Should I blame my parents if I am poor? Should I blame society if no one finds me likable? Should I blame myself if I am depressed? Well, who is at fault for all my problems and can I deal with every existential crisis?

But first, difficulties should be put in perspective because there are problems of varying degree, and trouble can seem never-ending if there is no differentiation between major and minor problems. For example, if you have no family or friends to speak of, that is not the end of the world. But if you're facing a physical or emotional crisis, you could use some help.

We see how *road rage* has ballooned into an explosive ordeal for many drivers. There is something going on behind the wheel that has nothing to do with traffic or another driver. Beware of wide-faced, Neanderthal-looking men because people are still holding primitive thoughts and behaviors. When you add modern stress and frustration to the mix, you have a recipe for out-of-control, raving lunatics. This road rage tendency is no laughing matter. It is serious business on the major roads in my area of the country. I don't see many ten-gallon hats around this town but plenty of horse's asses. A 2011 study had ranked Texas as having the third worst drivers in the U.S. They are just as bad as the Pakistani drivers with whom I competed in the Middle East—all fearless and reckless, perhaps because Allah was seatbelted in the passenger side for all I know. I normally drive like Jed Clampett, but within the speed limit, so as not to be a danger, but the drivers around me don't like it—and I can't just space out when surrounded by fools.

It seems to me that problems are always coming around the corner, straight at us. They're always cropping up. Murphy is constantly following us around. Sometimes life is like a country music song: "Lost my wife, lost my dog, and can't find my car keys." I used to say that the more types of music you like, the more open minded you are, but there are some exceptions. This may insult some kinsfolk, but it isn't meant to; it's just one of my prejudices. American country music is in its heyday and just as popular as Coca-Cola (well, almost). And the reason is nostalgia, for the way things "used to be" or the good old days. Whereas in the past, country music was for losers or "hicks" on the prairie, now it's as hot as sex in an oval office. As the old saying goes: Nothing wrong with opinions; they're like rear ends; everybody has one and they're all different! In order to improve our discourse and prospects, we should talk about our differences.

What's It All About?

It's not getting any easier in the melting pot of various cultures and languages, so we need to put our cards on the table in an effort to sustain harmony and mental health. Psychiatrists and shrinks get 100 bucks per hour for listening to troubled people's problems. Hell, I wouldn't charge you half as much. In fact, I usually tell my troubles to the guy who cuts my hair. He only charges ten bucks and I get a haircut out of the deal.

Seriously though, the trouble with life is all the small, ludicrous problems just add up like a bad country music song.

This Jewish guy goes to the doctor and says, "Doc, I seem to get up on the wrong side of the bed every morning."

Doc says, "Alright already pick another side."

The key to success in life seems to revolve around balancing the yin and yang of happiness versus turmoil or madness. Some problems can be eased with the medicine of laughter and humor but not every aspect of life if funny or humorous. Although I've noticed and envied the way some people are able to sneak a laugh or toothy smile into their conversation, it's not one of my specialties.

One way to look at personal problems that seem insurmountable is to employ fantasy. Imagine that you are able to board a space craft and rocket out 100 miles and then look down at earth. The farther you go, the smaller everything appears to be back on earth, and we are as small as ants. Human nature is not disposed to see our problems from this perspective, so we have to train ourselves.

Many years ago, I perused the famous book that is in many households: *The Power of Positive Thinking*. But when I reached a page with the word Jesus, I closed the book due to the realization that this shouldn't be the answer to all of life's problems. We can seek help but the answers reside either here in ourselves or there among our corporeal compatriots.

This book is instructive— hold the mustard and relish. As my last Jewish mother-in-law would say, "It's got everything in there—the clowns, the elephants, and the doves." The story begins with an examination of the familiar problems of the world. The narrative flows more like an oscillating sine wave, than the typical straight-line, formula writing of the dusty warehouse establishments. And I don't pretend to be a prolific writer along the lines of famous novelists of our time; "It's Wednesday, so I must be working on my 23rd book." That reminds me of a story from my brother-in-law, Dave Smith, who was in the insurance game in Baltimore. Many years ago, Dave and a colleague stopped by the house of another insurance associate. The man had papers all over the place and told them that he was writing a book. When the two visitors left the house, they giggled and shook their heads: "He's writing a book!" The writer turned out to be Tom Clancy, and the book: *The Hunt for Red October*.

A large part of *this* book explores the human propensity to conjure belief systems and cultural traditions against the backdrop of science and the pursuit of a rational psychology. We revel in various diversions such as sports and entertainment and waste valuable time on aliens and other futile illusions. Our own problems are a microcosm of looming clouds on a global scale.

In the final analysis, only a crash program to overhaul the system of education may prevent a spiraling decline of our living standard and healthful existence. It is not an extreme exaggeration to analogize to the Manhattan Project, which was a race to develop atomic weapons before Nazi Germany. From the days of the caveman to particle physics, we are at the point where only a major overhaul of education has a slight probability of righting the ship of state and staying a course with consciousness intact. Progress in our current environment is a mixed bag of beneficial and unpleasant consequences, and as we spin and wobble through the cosmos, the evolution of mediocrity becomes apparent. Therefore mankind cannot continue on a path of business as usual in order to survive with our collective sanity intact.

Many of us are brought up in a society which drills into our heads the idea that we have to play the game—compete or be left on the sidelines. We can't just do as we damn well please. We have to play by the rules—their rules—not ours. So what's the problem? Some people seem to have plenty, and many more have not. The earth now has seven billion people, unfortunately, and most of them are poor and clueless. In the words sung by Dionne Warwick, "What's it all about, Alfie?" What's it all about seven billion people?

CHAPTER 2

The Good Old Days
Brooklyn Real Estate is Outta Sight!

Did you know there are about 80,000 lawyers in New York City? And no, I'm not kidding!

Question: if you are stranded on a desert island with Adolph Hitler, Attila the Hun, and a lawyer, and you have a gun with only two bullets, what do you do?

Answer: shoot the lawyer twice.

Whenever things look bad and I am depressed about some or another mistake in life, I think of the remarkable idea that 2.5 million people live in Brooklyn! I know they have good pizza there but man does not live by bread alone. They have plenty of graffiti in the city and mainly on property that is not in motion (with the exception of subway cars and tattooed bodies). As in most cities worldwide, the young *puds* consider their scribbling "art" and need to do penance when caught. To most intelligent people, graffiti is an eyesore and you won't find this nonsense in the Irish or English countryside for obvious reasons—they don't have the wonderful diversity that spawns this despicable behavior. And no, this city wasn't built on rock and roll, no sir.

Another notable attribute in Brooklyn is sneakers hanging by the shoelaces over the power lines. Such artistry!

Nevertheless, I have known some very nice people there. I remember a lovely character by the name of Sid who was a kind of father figure to me. When New York changed the glass bottle law on deposits and returns, Sid immediately went to his local Waldbaum's with two soda bottles and requested his 20 cents. Although the law was effective on 1 July 1983, the store was not ready to comply with the returns and they refused to give Sid his 20 cents. In Saudi Arabia, we didn't have to concern ourselves with returns. Since booze was supposedly forbidden, we had bottle crushing machines to hide the evidence. Not to be denied, Sid returned home to call the chief executive at Waldbaum's to offer his two cents of advice and then some. Sid drove his point home, and then marched back to the local store manager, who had received a call from Headquarters to pay out the 20 cents. I also noticed that Sid would track the interest rates from various local banks, and if a higher rate was offered, even a quarter of a percentage point, he would transfer his funds.

This frugality, however, failed to rub off on me, because the five brothers in my family were mainly a mob of gamblers. I'll bet that we collectively squandered about a half million dollars on all kinds of foolish investments which never paid out. The casinos, horses, stocks, options, real estate—we failed to read the small print which evidently reads, "Warning: the first principle is that you must not fool yourself; and you are the easiest person to fool." (Richard Feynman). I should have paid closer attention to Sid.

My eldest brother helped me land a job at Monmouth Park Racetrack, in Oceanport, New Jersey. For five summer vacations during my youth, I was employed at the track by Sullivan Brothers from Lowell, Massachusetts, printing the racing program. It was a crazy crew of blue collar characters who lived in either South Jersey or Philadelphia. We used offset printing presses and the ancient linotype machine that was first introduced around 1884. Our printed program was sold at the track and was therefore used as a system of barter. When the presses were not running, a portion of my day was devoted to the role of gofer. I ran around the racetrack to exchange programs for ham and egg sandwiches from the Jockey Club in the morning. I brought pastries and milk from the cafeteria and submarine sandwiches and soda for lunch.

People would show up and drop off beer and cigarettes or perhaps a cheesecake. But I witnessed as a teenager how gambling on the horses is one of those vices euphemistically termed thoroughbred racing. It draws you in, like any addiction, until its clutches are firmly set. The atmosphere was a surreal cacophony of the tip-sheet hawkers simultaneously shouting: "Lawton — *Lawton! Racing Form — Race-sing Form!* Reilly — *Reilly!"* Men zip around or make a bee-line to the betting windows with the latest *tip from the horse's mouth*, smacking lips and blinking eyes of disbelief as they mutter "today is *the* day" to win at long last on the street of dreams. Like any house of ill repute, winners scramble to the payoff window while the more numerous losers toss their cigarette butts and losing tickets on the garbage strewn floors. It was a sad spectacle to watch the multitudes throwing good money after bad and cursing their ill fortune. And of least concern for the "Sport of Kings" was the stable area known as the backside, manned by illegal aliens, out of sight and out of mind, with the mistreatment of the animals, the drugs, the booze, and the fighting.

In the afternoons, I worked in the scullery of the Clubhouse restaurant, washing dishes as the lone white among a dozen or so African Americans from Camden, who like the men in the print shop, would move from racetrack to racetrack from one season to the next.

Brooklyn has a number of high-rise residential towers that always sparks my imagination as to all those people living there. For instance, there is Warbasse Houses, a Mitchell-Lama housing cooperative located on 26 acres with five, 24 storey buildings and 2,585 apartment units. When the elevator stops and opens, you can smell all the cooked foods from every apartment on that particular floor. Mrs. Holzman is cooking leg of lamb; Mrs. Medoff is doing roast duck, and every floor has a smorgasbord of menus. But as to the pigeons on the Coney Island boardwalk, I can do without, and besides, it's scary to drive over the Guinea Gangplank (Verrazano-Narrows Bridge) especially if you have a problem with heights. Cruising near Brooklyn always fills me with wonderment—the idea that 2.5 million people choose to live there as a slice of the Big Apple.

There are worse places to live such as Ethiopia, where in the capital of Addis Ababa, you could walk around with all your pockets turned inside-out and still be confronted by local pick-pockets on the street. While living in Saudi Arabia, I recall with fondness a planned visit to my fiancée's home in African Eritrea. Quite a few African guys from different countries advised me to skip where I was going and detour to a place notable for their brothels. Why would I even consider visiting the fiancée's family? Go to Addis. By the way, if you were thinking of touring in Ethiopia, beware of Montezuma's revenge.

Do You Remember When?

Over a span of time, we exchanged one lifestyle for another. In the good old days you pulled on something, you got fresh milk. Today you buy a box of doughnuts and the ingredients read like you just found the Chinese-stolen secrets from Los Alamos nuclear laboratory. Take for instance the ingredient list for a popular spongy snack below. Note the parent company filed for bankruptcy in 2012 (deservedly) because consumers are eating less junk and the unions drove the enterprise off the cliff. But there are competitors today who manufacturer even cheaper junky snacks.

Enriched Wheat Flour - enriched with ferrous sulphate (iron), B vitamins (niacin, thiamine mononitrate (B1), riboflavin (B12) and folic acid), Sugar, Corn syrup, Water, High fructose corn syrup, Vegetable and/or animal shortening—containing one or more of partially hydrogenated soybean, cottonseed or canola oil, and beef fat, Dextrose, Whole eggs, It also contains 2% or less of: Modified corn starch, Cellulose gum, Whey, Leavenings (sodium acid pyrophosphate, baking soda, monocalcium phosphate), Salt, Cornstarch, Corn flour, Corn syrup solids, Mono and diglycerides, Soy lecithin, Polysorbate 60, Dextrin, Calcium caseinate, Sodium stearol lactylate, Wheat gluten, Calcium sulphate, Natural and artificial flavors, Caramel color, Sorbic acid (to retain freshness), Color added (yellow 5, red 40). Yum!

The problem with progress is that it comes with a price tag which can seem too expensive in terms of a cost/benefit analysis. What is the point of accumulating more and more material possessions in a society with loss of both personal roots and health? And watching the world go by while motoring from traffic light to traffic light? California is experiencing a substantial cost-benefit situation of environment versus power generation and quality of life with the invasion by illegal Mexicans. As an idealist, I tend to favor keeping a semblance of a semi-normal environment in lieu of the following negatives:

☐ Lack of local and regional planning which is a major factor for environment degradation.

☐ Over population and over development, which if left unchecked will heighten problems.

☐ Failure to stop illegal and unwanted aliens (thieves in the night) is courting disaster.

☐ Overuse of energy and lack of conservation is indeed piggish.

Just look at the mammoth, gas-guzzling vehicles on the road. I don't expect consumers to tailgate or imitate, but I have owned a tuna can on wheels for many years. Generally there are a few reasons why people prefer large vehicles—such that in 2013, SUV sales accounted for more than one-third of the U.S. auto market. This will come as no surprise to readers if I mention that men want to bully the roads and metaphorically extend their private part.

Noise, there's a lot of noise in the city. You become more sensitive to noise as you get older because the sense of (good) hearing decreases over time. And part of the abuse of hearing is due to man-made hazards like loud rock music or drilling equipment. In Cairo, Egypt, the overwhelming noise in the streets makes people shout to be heard.

Silence is golden.

Going back to Eritrea, when you visit a place with no electricity or running water, everything seems so quiet. I can hear a faint tinkling in the air as my hard-working father-in-law maneuvers a team of oxen in the fields. I see billions of stars (Carl Sagan) at night, sparkling in the rarified air, and I imagine how generations have viewed the same for thousands of years. These are all attributes becoming lost to lights and air pollution. They have a donkey that roams at will and returns to the compound, knocks at the metal perimeter door and farts in the breeze. That's poetic.

The younger generations grew up with the boob tube (TV) as friend and babysitter. And no wonder silence seems awkward to those who expect conversation from a box. People live their lives reacting to the box, imitating its force-fed fodder which creates our culture—or, more accurately, dictates the attitudes of society, along with the favorite saying of the week. At one time it might have been, "Not only is there no God, but try getting a plumber on the weekend." (Woody Allen). That's brilliant as the British would say. But today's usual palaver is more like, "I'm loving it," or "My bad." Great use of the English language!

And the irony of text messaging is lost on the online crowd— saying as little as possible with as few words and abbreviations as feasible. With social media, the masses can parrot the same expressions endlessly until some new prodigy of popular culture gets hatched onto the scene. The homogenized news networks mimic one another and use pundit-speak. The word 'yes' is not good enough; every affirmative requires the rejoinder "absolutely." All topics and controversies are fraudulently convincing with the Jack & Jill journalists:

"*Clearly*, Jack, the situation is worsening."

"*Absolutely*, Jill, and time will tell."

"*Do you believe in Reverend Pappy's prediction of the coming Armageddon, Jack?*"

"*Now that's a great question, Jill.*"

There's nothing new under the sun besides boredom. Although time washes away the fads and fashions of the here and now, it's a simple delusion to follow trends. The clothes now in vogue seem grand and important, but they become outdated. Is everything in the present time already scheduled for the dust bin? Laughable in the wake of the future? (I'm not sure if I was in Amsterdam when this was written). That sentence is just as poor as "I'm loving it," and if this book is ever translated into Mandarin (don't scoff—you never know), the sentence will probably read, "His chicken-feet soup is especially good today."

Will my hairstyle be laughable ten years from now? (Probably, if there's any left). Think about other hairstyles such as the beard. Where do you see bearded fellows these days? They are limited to throwback locales like the Muslim world, since Sharia Law sanctions a long beard, and the moon-shining hills of West Virginia. Some things are called classic that serve as a standard or model like Elvis or the old Hollywood movies such as the portrayal of integrity by Jimmy Stewart in realistic Westerns which place you in the scene as you watch the action. What makes that perception different than the wearing of a bow tie? Shouldn't just poodles wear a bow tie? In recent years, men wear running shoes whether they run or not. It's the fashion. What is the difference between classical music like Mozart versus rap? Is it really simply a matter of taste or is there some discreet and deep difference in perception of good versus inferior? Keep in mind that people have been listening to the works of Mozart for almost 250 years, and yes, there is a difference between a piano concerto and the kazoo or washboard. Young Mozart composed his Symphony Number One at the age of eight in 1764.

I believe that businesses exploit the populace and their propensity to fall for advertising with a sales pitch. We don't seem to do a good job of filtering experience through our bullshit meter, assuming we have one, and detecting substandard culture for what it is—the senseless advertisement, the lousy fashion garment, or the awful movie.

If a comedian has a few *plants* in the audience who will laugh on cue, the group will follow suit, which is called the herd mentality. The masses can be fooled because people are gullible and open to suggestion. We live for TV commercials that should be an insult to our intelligence but we just accept them. In fact, during some periods the ads are almost as valued as the show itself. A 30-second commercial during the 1967 football Super Bowl was $42,000 and in 2013 the cost was $3,800,000! This championship football game is one time that the public is "onboard" with the advertisers since commercials are like academy award nominations. Otherwise, the viewer must put up with this peddling nonsense in order to watch the actual entertainment. It's much like putting up with the dentist's drill in order to have good teeth. The TV commercials are even planned to be annoying like a drill. It's effective because the annoying affect is riveted in the mind like the typical movie plot of good guy fighting the bad guy.

From your airplane seat at night, you can see the carbon footprint or light pollution radiating at all hours. For example, most of Saudi Arabia appears eerily dark, until your flight-approach to a city such as Riyadh that is lit up as if fuel is free (it is almost). The lights are burning all night in the major industrial countries on the planet resulting in global warming and pollution. This type of problem is complex and may require complicated and debatable solutions. Certainly there is a common-sense approach to most issues. But if there is a lack of awareness, common-sense cannot prevail. Just like national governments, we're all faced with varied issues and problems in our lives. I contend the government cannot fix all problems. The system has become too large and complex. Any State of the Union pronouncements that "all will be handled," are lies and self-serving propaganda.

Consider the following short list of issues:

> Poverty
> Terrorism
> Crime
> Pollution
> Failing infrastructure roads, bridges etc
> Population diversity stresses
> National defense and nuclear threats

These are too vast for any government to solve at all, let alone in a four-year term. And there are hundreds, if not thousands, of more problems that would make quite a long list indeed. I find it ironic that the *progressive* business interests constantly talk about *growth* in the economy. We must always have more buildings, more development, more expansion, more auto sales, and more money for more consumers to drive the cogs in the wheel of fortune. This "make and toss" mentality seems to be a headlong rush to pollute our homes and strip the land to the point of naked degradation. Meanwhile the eyes of the greedy are locked on the stock markets like vultures surveying the next prey. Call me naïve, but I am not an advocate for growth and expansion.

For example, London was quaint and endurable during periods of recession and can be insufferable when the economy is prosperous. Vacation spots such as Cocoa Beach are similarly less crowded and less expensive. Negative growth sounds gloomy but I want a jolly downturn for my money. Instead of the modern madness, I would advocate that less is more or at least less is better. Doesn't it make sense to live in less crowded communities where there is space to breathe and fresh air?

Consider some of the positive things we require but are losing rapidly:

> Close knit community
> Normal living space
> Air that is not polluted
> Water that is not toxic
> Less noise and light pollution
> Less urban sprawl

These basic amenities should be available for people to live a normal and healthful life. For tens of thousands of years humans have lived a more natural life without the artificial environment that comes with progress. Not to say that the good old days were pie in the sky. I'm not advocating that we bring back the Spanish Inquisition and whale oil. I rather contend that we are unbalanced and sadly out of touch with a healthy lifestyle. Humans have made it through some dark ages, leaped forward with technology, but may have advanced too fast. Like an adolescent discovering genitals, it appears that thinking is not being done by the average brain. The time is now when guidance can fill the void for both teenagers as well as societies. When there is no hand on the tiller, we're talking about boats now, the ship goes off course and the crew can become disoriented when lost at sea. Some believe there is an automatic pilot that steers regardless, in a metaphorical sense—but then sailors were always known to be superstitious. There is one possible solution to the human dilemma—educate the son of a gun!

Formal education is a relatively new occupation for the human citizen. In prehistoric times, there was no writing, and learning was handed along with grunts and gestures, followed by a primitive club or fist, depending on the mood. With the advent of language and writing, school was in-session, but only the rich and powerful were educated since the lower classes were occupied in supplying and serving grub for the ruling classes.

Throughout human history, unique individuals have stood apart as great intellects such as Aristotle and Einstein, people of obvious genius. It is not important here to chronicle the development of educational systems or the functioning of the human brain. With the stability provided by agriculture and domesticated livestock, societies were established that could maintain a limited schooling for the lower classes, typically termed on-the-job training in occupations handed down in trades such as pottery, metal shop, later to be found in England as the guilds and also the caste system in India.

The citizenry are not educated to be independent thinkers. According to Frans De Wal: "It's a safe bet that cultures are historically derived from the tribal way of living, where the individual is tied to the group for survival purposes."[6] Keep your head down to avoid unwanted negative attention. Play brain dead and you will be a success of sorts. To stand out from the crowd is either bravery or foolishness depending on whether you get to keep your head. Life's dichotomy then is a flow of experiences where the individual is propelled to swim against the prevailing current of society or join on-board the communal train that hypnotically rolls along the tracks as the conductor watches and intermittently checks your ticket. You get lolled to sleep by the rhythm of the ride on the journey to nowhere in particular.

The non-conformist is now romanticized as the proverbial loner who shuns all contact with the community, opting instead to live in the forest of Thoreau, or perhaps opening a beer brewery in Colorado. We occasionally find him face-to-face with other people, by accident, mischief, or necessity where he faithfully maintains his independence and innocence. Tarzan comes to mind, the unscratched hero, swinging from tree to tree on the vines of the forest. But this is not the kind of independence that is called for today. Even though it is praiseworthy to dream of escape to a log cabin in the wilderness, it is becoming less likely. No sooner do we escape, than the real estate developers come knocking on our door. They are carving up the forest floor for a retirement/golf community. Independence of thought is in short supply. Americans used to be known for this quality, due to the young country's vast expanse and westward moving, homesteading population. There was plenty of time to work the land with their own hands, and determination to carve a living by a God-fearing lot that was both practical and conservative.

Today's America is different in that the populace has moved from the territories to the non-rural habitats and become dependent on one another in many aspects of life. It is now the norm that most people do not provide their own food but obtain it from a shrinking percentage of food producers. The industrial corporations have weaned the public away from natural and sustainable agricultural practices and substituted fossil fuels and chemicals that redirect the focus to increasing productivity and profits. With so many different people, Americans do not have a single gastronomic ritual or tradition and therefore are susceptible to the whims of business.

Although America is quite diverse in respect of ethnic population, there is a system of smoothing out the differences through education and other government driven institutions that mold the consistency of *the American way*. Certain immigrants quickly take on typical American traits like shooting from the hip or straight talking. America has been perceived as the land of opportunity and consequently swallowed a goodly portion of the world's talent who are desperate to succeed and very often do. If success breeds success then the rich will get richer as you would expect and some of the population will be left behind. That dovetails with the evolutionary idea of survival of the fittest. If America has the best and brightest, it may be equally true that other parts of the world include the dumb and dumber. Through no fault of their own, they have been disadvantaged due to the reasons eloquently outlined by Jared Diamond in *Guns, Germs and Steel*. European-derived people obtained food production, and the resulting technology, that led to their domination of the world. It is not evident that the disadvantaged people in Africa are intrinsically dumb but rather circumstances have kept them in the dark so to speak.

America's educational system strives for mediocrity, but at least that's preferable to outright failure. This is no different from past kingdoms which had no incentive to smarten up the peasants because revolt is unpalatable to the movers and shakers of the enterprise. Remember, to keep our heads, we must generally keep them down, and since the eyes are the window to the soul, it helps to display a blank or dim countenance of face to support the notion. The planet has recently emerged from the dark ages, so mediocrity is really not that bad. People talk of the good old days but I don't think they had in mind the Black Plague of the 1400s. Some people believe there never were any good old days, but I deny that assertion. They say today are the good old days but that must mean tomorrow are also the good old days.

As Dickens said (*A Tale of Two Cities*, 1859) *"It was the best of times, it was the worst of times, it was the age of wisdom, it was the age of foolishness, it was the epoch of belief, it was the epoch of incredulity, it was the season of Light, it was the season of Darkness, it was the spring of hope, it was the winter of despair, we had everything before us, we had nothing before us, we were all going direct to heaven, we were all going direct the other way—in short, the period was so far like the present period."*

It's the old people who boast of the good old days; damn straight, they were good days, especially since life is a downhill, run-away affair when we reach the pinnacle of our roller coaster ride. There had better be some good old days remaining when we're 80, unless we care for trouble. Those were the good old days—presupposes the past. These are the good old days means the present, but how do you signify the future? Somehow, I don't foresee a lot of good old days in the future—things aren't looking up.

In his book *Physics of the Future*, the physicist, Michio Kaku, speculates about life by the year 2100. For example, nanotechnology will provide molecular replicators capable of creating anything. The devil loves a wealthy optimist. Granted the mob has forecasted the end of the world time and time again—but in the past, bird brains didn't possess nuclear weapons either. Imagine being a fly on the wall when FDR read the letter signed by Einstein on 2 August 1939 about the possibility of uranium being used to construct *extremely powerful bombs of a new type*. The Bomb has been used within the past 100 years and by a relatively benign Kingdom (the United States) but the next episode by a rogue nation or terrorist group might outperform the past catastrophe. Nuclear weapons can cause a lot of noise and confusion. Perhaps it's the fearful idea itself that prompts the gun-toting militia to escape the rat race for more isolated locales where they more-or-less drop out. But the crowds carry on business as usual with the faint hope that all will be well, that the good old days are still to be had—if only we could control the forces of evil. They should realize it's not evil but stupidity or insanity. Why else would somebody willingly strap on explosives and ignite unwitting bystanders? If they controlled a larger device, be assured they would use that as well for their ticket to Allah, or for any other *just cause*.

Good and Evil

As social and spiritual beings, people have a propensity to use labels for categories of behavior and perception like good versus evil, such that certain acts are viewed as bad or morally wrong and the antithesis of good. The term evil denotes an action that we consider wrong which is intentional and consciously perpetrated. For example, society decides that the name Charles Manson is synonymous with evil, although his behavior can be explained by a defective brain. And certain disasters such as floods and droughts might be considered evil manifestations of nature and yet they are only natural occurrences of the world we live in. Human nature has a need for this dichotomy of good versus evil to help explain the perception of reality, but there is no autonomous agent responsible for these notions.

For example, a certain species of wasp seeks another insect, such as a caterpillar, as a host for her young. The female wasp paralyzes the host and then injects her eggs which will feed from inside when the larvae are hatched, but very methodically, leaving the vital organs until the last in order to extend the fare.

In relation to issues of moral purposes and ultimate meanings, Charles Darwin commented in 1860 that he could not see as plainly as others do, evidence of design or beneficence on all sides of us; he could not believe that an omnipotent God would have designedly created the insect wasp with the express intention of their feeding within the living bodies of caterpillars. Obviously, the insect is not evil per se—the wasp is simply trying to perpetuate the species, but people attribute such grisly actions as despicable and wrong.

The concepts of good and evil are universal and very ancient. They may defy concise definitions, but we probably can all agree with Supreme Court Justice, Potter Stewart's comment in 1964 about hard-core pornography; it may be hard to define, but "I know it when I see it." Examples abound. If we see a child run onto a busy street, we automatically rush to prevent its harm and that is good. When we have a cheerful, young boy, and yes my brethren from India and other pathetic places, even a daughter, we rejoice in the good. On the other hand, a senseless and gruesome murder scene is viewed as evil. Throughout the ages, demons or devils were believed to be the source of evil. This belief was likely held to account for mental illness and abnormal and strange human behavior and resulting in the need for a shaman, medicine man, or priest. Different cultures deal with evil in various ways. For instance, the idea of *karma*, a fundamental doctrine in Buddhism, addresses the problem of evil by means of retribution. Every deed or action has consequences and most humans have uttered the phrase, "What goes around comes around."

The reason for concern is, that if we find it difficult to educate and civilize people in the developed world, how can we hope to touch the Great Unwashed? If we don't get our hands around the throat of these Muslim extremists, or magically transform them, we can say goodbye to our comfortable way of life—and we probably have less than ten years to do so. Another major explosion in New York City could devastate world economies and unleash waves of panic and anarchy. If the World Trade Center was a wake-up call, that will be our four-alarm fire. There exist other non-Muslim groups who pose a threat, but the former are front-and-center among the bad guys. Although we see the profile of these kooks, it is still considered politically incorrect to demand it's either us or them, and it ain't gonna be us. We can allow Islamic mosques in New York, Florida, and across America, but in Saudi Arabia (the defender of Islam) it is forbidden to have a church, synagogue, priest, reverend, or rabbi. Non-Muslims are strictly forbidden to enter Mecca and Medina, the two holiest cities in Islam. Can you think of anywhere else on Earth that is forbidden to travelers? In consideration of this and other unique Saudi traits, along with our presumed defense of the rascals, lends support to my saying, "We are whores for oil."

Black Gold – Texas Tea

In the 1930s, the Americans drilled for oil in Saudi Arabia and the rest is history. Since hitting the jackpot, the Saud family now numbering about 7,000 controls the desert country by a combination of force and the strict dogmatic religion of Islam. My wife and I worked in Saudi Arabia for a number of years and so we have some, hem, appreciation for the country. Men and women are rigorously kept apart. Women are covered in black from head to foot and cannot drive.

In 2011, the Saudis contended that, if women were allowed to drive, there would be no virgins left in the country and that would leave only homosexuals in their society. I couldn't make this stuff up if I tried.

It's ironic that many Muslim women are *encouraged* to cover up (head-to-toe) even in non-Muslim places such as the United States and England. Strangely enough many Muslim women defend these customs, and don't seem to view it as coercion, because brainwashing is very effective. To be fair, some of them need to cover their faces. Rodney Dangerfield said it best. "I knew a girl so ugly that she was known as a two-bagger. That's when you put a bag over your head in case the bag over her head breaks."

While in Qatar, I noticed that some of the older women wear a *batula*, an indigo-dyed cloth face mask that is pounded to give it a shiny, metallic appearance. It looks like a piece of tin over their face. One disadvantage of using indigo dye to color the *batula* is that it tends to rub off on the face, a problem which can be seen both under the cloth and when they are taken off. Suffice to say it is not an attractive sight, making the poor woman resemble Darth Vader. As you may have noticed, many Muslim women only show their eyes to the outside world; the rest of the anatomy is covered up with dark cloth. Yet, Holy Cow, what eyes! Shazam! But take off the veil, though, and roll the dice (Is it Grenada I see, or *just* Asbury Paaark?!...Frank Sinatra), *oy gaveld!* I recently visited a dental office that also performs cosmetic procedures. They have an advertising display which reads, "Eyelashes are the new breasts." Hello? What am I missing here?

By the way, if you have an interest in visiting Saudi Arabia as a tourist, you can forget about it. You wouldn't be welcome as an infidel. The country is dependent on foreign workers who must have a Saudi sponsor for employment. And you should be suspicious and circumspect about running a company for them because it would not be uncommon for Saudis to ship you out after successfully building the business. Most expatriates who have worked there consider themselves members of an exclusive club with hundreds of unbelievable stories. My wife was repetitively chased during taxi rides by Saudi drivers on her way to work and this was their typical reputation. I think she describes them as donkeys. I have a saying that applies to the male species generally: Young boys are kids and old men are goats. So if you hear that Billy is a dirty, old goat, there is some redundancy there. Saudi is a country of paradoxes. Unmarried men and woman are forbidden to mix or socialize, but it is not unusual to see two men walking down the street while holding hands. On the other hand, many single women gravitate to a lesbian lifestyle since normal relations are forbidden. Occasionally you might see a Saudi child with oriental features as a result of the wife playing around with their Filipino driver. You might see a doddering 80 year old Saudi with a toddler, but it could very well be his *son* rather than his grandson. And there are stories that an incapacitated wife in a hospital bed may be grist for the husband's mill, if you know what I mean. In 2013, A Saudi cleric called for all female babies to be fully covered by wearing the face veil or *burka*, citing reports of little girls being sexually molested.

Strangely, when I worked in Saudi Arabia, a certain U.S. Army general stated that we were there for *nation building*—what a joke! I almost spit out my bottled water but kept my mouth shut, of course, and thought, *Tell that to some other Rube.* He later got the boot for sexual harassment allegations.

Just as in Iraq, it's about the OIL… "Vat else?"

Question: What do call an active duty Army general?

Answer: Mum, because they forgo the truth and are silent

---

on issues of right and wrong in order to preserve their pension, perks, and the revolving door to the corporate boards and the media.

Living in Saudi as a foreigner is a very private affair. Everyone lives in a structure or compound surrounded by cement walls. Residences or businesses do not have street number designations. They only show or advertise a Post Office Box for an address.

Handicapped children or adults are kept behind closed doors. Viewing a magazine or a movie is a different experience as censors black-out any signs of cleavage, or other sexy parts. It is not unusual for the religious police (Mutawa) to remove Valentines Cards from the store shelves. The Mutawa are an influential group of roaming enforcers who actually have more power than the regular police, and in Gestapo fashion they routinely seek out the supposed morally blemished for incarceration, whipping, or worse. In the past, the Mutawa were recruited from the prison population, and the Al Saud (Saudi ruling family) would pay a stipend to those inmates who would convert to Islam.

You may have heard about the fire at a girls' dormitory in Mecca on 11 March 2002. The Saudi Mutawa refused to allow girls fleeing the fire to escape unless they were covered with the *abaya* and the *hijab*. Uncovered girls were beaten by the police and forced back into the burning building. At least 14 girls died in the incident and many more were injured.

The Mutawa career around the city of Riyadh in Chevy Suburbans and lurk around the shops and restaurants to catch unmarried men and women who are forbidden to be together. For example, our office workers went out to lunch and were approached by the lurking Mutawa (easily identifiable by their ugly puss, scraggly beard, and white *thobe* that is tailored slightly shorter than usual, around ankle length) and informed that we should not be eating lunch together. Since we were Americans, employed by the U.S. Army, we ignored the ugly one and he left for greener pastures or more exploitable prey.

In the Arab world, swords play a key role in ceremonial events and have symbolic status. You see them on the Saudi flag, for instance, and they are used as a metaphor in many phrases in the Arabic language. But in the history of the desert, they were likely used in a threatening manner during intra-tribal skirmishes. They would brandish the blade to take some of the other tribes' goats and women and run without any real intent on using it as a weapon.

If you want your expert slice and dice experts, you have to see the Japanese, who wield the steel expertly not only in the kitchen, sushi and hibachi style, but in the fields. During the time of the Samurai, a swordsman could sever a head clean from a body, before blinking an eye.

Arabs do not indiscriminately shoot people like the violent Americans, so the rich deploy expensive birds (Falcons) to kill prey as a popular sport. Most people associate this region with camels but actually the Saudis have camel races only once a year. My wife spoke to the young Sudanese jockeys and some are only about four years old. They are tied to the camels while riding and Luchia noticed that they don't have shoes so their bare feet are wrinkled like an old man.

The Third World and Other Strange Places

You may have noticed during your travels and airport stays, Saudis employ a substantial number of maids from the Philippines. At various times, quite a few run away from their employer to the Philippine embassy to escape abuse. The term skunks comes to mind. Only the clueless do not realize that slavery is alive and well in various parts of the world especially in Asia.

As an aside, the Philippines, with over 7,000 islands, is an interesting place to visit, although, because of the eroding values of youth, it can be a dangerous adventure. For example, their most popular means of public transportation is the Jeepney, a colorfully painted minibus originally made from U.S. military jeeps. I was warned that criminals might cut off a finger for a passenger's gold ring—if they were joking, they had me fooled and fearful. But the majority of the people are wonderful and quite unique. They tend to point with their lips and raise their eyebrows to answer 'yes' to a question.

The food is very good, although they consume some interesting tidbits. For instance, locust swarms in Saudi Arabia create an eating opportunity for Filipino workers who net the insects and fry them. Saudi Arabia's authorities warned their people in 2011 not to eat locusts as they could be poisonous after feeding on plants sprayed by insecticides. I always thought that poor countries generally consume peasant food, and yet the elite American gastronome considers their grub tantalizing challenges to the palate. My mother often said that the spices in Indian food masks otherwise bad meat in their curries. And what's so grand about Afghani food—a measly chicken specimen on rice. I don't need the buggy rice from Pakistan, Vietnam, or India. These people consume rice like a bum swills cheap wine. In Saudi Arabia, they feast on whole sheep and goats with metal platters so huge that you could easily use them for sledding down a snowy hill—and most of the food is wasted or thrown away.

You might be aware that insects now contribute to the diet of some 2.5 billion people worldwide.[7] Some of these delicacies include caterpillars, worms, fly maggots, crickets, and tarantulas. Bugs are now big business in the food industry. In the Philippines, Balut is a popular street snack and is essentially a duck egg with a fetus inside, typically between 17 to 20 days in gestation that is boiled alive. It is as customary a food item there as the hot dog or hamburger in the United States.

On one of my flights to the Philippines from Saudi Arabia, I was lucky enough to hold a diplomatic passport and the associated First Class ticket, on the upper deck of a huge Boeing 747. Since my companion was stuck below in Economy, I switched seats with her and was stunned by the cramped conditions for hundreds of Filipinos shoveling in their dinner with hardly elbow room. The experience almost makes you cry. And if you meet a Filipino (they reside in every country), you can say, "*Hindi ako mabuting mag-salita nang inyong wika,*" which means "I don't understand your language very well."

I have this love-hate relationship with languages, and can be a painful customer with a smattering of Arabic, Tigrinya (Eritrea), Tagalog (Philippines), and Spanish. Noam Chomsky might see languages as worthwhile but I have a problem with them. We live in a world of diversity like the Tower of Babel with everyone babbling in foreign tongues—no wonder we can't get along.

My unproven theory about children speaking dual languages indicates that it could be detrimental. For example, many Eritrean parents living in the U.S. will speak to their children in the native language rather than English. So the youngsters are able to speak both languages because the language-learning circuitry of the brain is more flexible in childhood than later on. While children are perfectly capable of acquiring two or more languages; in fact, in many parts of the world it is the norm rather than the exception. For children to grow up multilingual, educators must keep in mind that young children do not have a fully developed native language on which to base the learning of a second.[8] People generally believe that experience with various cultures and languages bring some spice to life. However, in view of the lack of hard evidence, it may signify a drawback to be immersed in several languages during childhood because the brain must work with competing interests. The monolingual English speaker is learning complex concepts that are not always compatible with another language. But the bilingual child has a larger mental load to handle and can be baffled by different vocabularies and vocalizations. This is not to be confused with linguistic relativity, or the Sapir-Whorf hypothesis, which holds that the grammatical structures of markedly different languages cause their speakers to experience and mentally represent the world in different ways. My belief is the learning of multiple languages is more advantageous to children of families with resources rather than poorer ones. In the former case it is a challenge whereas in the latter, it is a burden.

Although most of the world's population speaks more than one language, it is often by necessity. For example, my wife grew up in Eritrea and Ethiopia who speak Tigrinya, Amharic, and English; she also learned Arabic in Saudi Arabia. I don't want this to sound like linguistic chauvinism, but let's pay the rest of the world to speak English and forget the foreign aid otherwise.

It's a small world. Some years back, I was flying to England and a Filipina just happened to be seated next to me. She told me a joke by imitating a head-nodding Indian from the subcontinent: "My wife is dirty and I'm *dirty*-two."

So I asked her, "Do you know La-Lang (all Filipinos have nicknames) in Paranaque near Manila?

"Oh yes," she replied. "La-Lang is the one connected with the Soriano family, no?"

"Yes, that's right," I said. As they say in Walt Disney World, it's a small world after all. They have quite a network and you would be advised to watch your P's and Q's because you never know when you will meet a *kabayan* (Filipino countryman) with the connections to uncover or expose your anonymity.

Filipinos are very resourceful people. When I, uh, *lost track* of my Chevrolet SUV at a construction site outside of Riyadh, I had just enough wits to lose any incriminating evidence, such as forbidden alcohol, and hightail it out to the road before the Saudi police made the night any worse. I had no idea where this area was located, all the signs were in Arabic, and every square lick was under construction, so it all looked the same. The Saudis have so much money that they probably build, tear-down and rebuild just for the heck of it for all I know.

Anyway, I flagged a Pakistani taxi driver and asked him to take me home but pick me up next morning to return to the scene of the crime. He nodded and said, "OK boss," but of course he failed to show. Nervous? I'd lost track of my government-provided truck—just great. In desperation, I went outside at daybreak and flagged a Filipino taxi driver and explained my predicament. The SUV was somewhere and I could only recall some fledgling trees in the median on the street of dreams. He drove me around for several hours, and I finally recognized the trees in the median and stopped to survey the site. No SUV in sight! The taxi driver spoke in Tagalog to another Filipino working a backhoe who stated the police had just flat-bed trucked my vehicle away.

Well, at least I knew where it was which provided some relief, and I was able to stifle the grief in explaining some cock and bullshit story to the boss. In gratitude for his perseverance, I gave my Filipino friend 500 Riyals and a bottle of whiskey (God is great). I was at work when the SUV hobbled into the compound, gratis the Saudi military, and destined for the junkyard—made me want to cry, but I didn't receive any demerits for the experience.

My wife claims that you can leave your pocketbook or wallet on a store shelf in Saudi and it will still be there when you remember to retrieve it. I don't believe it is the fear of having your hand chopped off that accounts for this level of honesty, but the people are a religious group in general. In spite of this, the negative aspects of the society far outweigh any positive value. For example, both men and women will cut in line at the super-market checkout, or the restaurant waiting line, as if you weren't there.

The rich can be bold indeed. In 2012, a Saudi princess was stopped by police as she tried to sneak out of a luxury hotel in Paris at 3:30AM, along with her 60 servants and a mountain of luggage, leaving unpaid bills worth over seven million dollars.

When I worked in Riyadh, my co-workers informed me that they have a chop-chop square, where executions by beheading are performed. I was not able to observe these public events since by and large I would be sleeping late and the chops are few and far between. Beheadings do not occur every weekend and you might have to go there for some weeks before a chop-chop is actually done. They say it is something you will not soon forget. By the same token, my wife says that women often avoid the bathrooms at malls for fear of men disguised in the female black *abaya* to molest them.

Saudis and Catholics

There are some interesting parallels between my Catholic upbringing and the experience of working in Saudi Arabia.

Many poignant books have been written on the comic and tragic sides of each topic. And folks who have either attended Catholic schools or experienced life in Saudi Arabia are members of a convivial club. They have a lot of stories to tell and unforgettable memories, kind of like an adventure.

As the year 2000 approached, Pope John Paul II announced that penitents who do a charitable deed or give up cigarettes or booze for a day can earn an *indulgence* that will eliminate time in purgatory. Indulgences are an ancient form of church-granted amnesty that Catholics believe releases them from certain punishment in this life or the next. The medieval church sold indulgences as a shortcut to salvation.[9]

On the other hand, booze is supposedly forbidden in Saudi Arabia, though it is readily available for a price and there are many home brewers such as the author. Saudis drink primarily Johnny Walker Black scotch that is secretly imported by various embassies and wealthy princes. A bottle of the Scotch Whiskey sells for $150 or more on the black market. Some of the young Saudis drank perfume since it contains alcohol and the authorities banned certain brands for that reason.

Both Catholics and Arabs use a string of beads called a rosary and *misbaha* respectively. The string of beads is often referred to as 'worry beads' because people manipulate them between their fingers to keep their minds off the more mundane or worrisome problems, helping Arab gentlemen avoid tempting thoughts. During the French Revolution, when the guillotine was the darling of public life, a group of women became infamous for knitting while they watched the beheadings. The moral of the story is to keep your hands on the tiller, or otherwise busy, to reduce stress in your life.

Both of these groups pretend that sex is under cover, and you see how that works out! Catholics used to have large families and Ford station wagons while Saudis have large families and mammoth Chevy Suburbans which are a fertility symbol on wheels. The Catholics are better drivers as opposed to the former camel jockeys who obey the dictum of whichever nose stretches out farthest has the right of way. Although the West is experiencing a decline in family size, the rest of the world, almost without exception, will begin a conversation with a hello followed by "And how many children do you have?" The moral of *that* story: If you don't have children, pretend you do and go along to get along. Some on the far right teach sexual abstinence for teenagers. I call this the hands-off approach, and it's just as comical as, "No sex please, we're British." Both groups have a history that is dogmatic, fanatical, and intolerant, although the Muslims are way ahead in that game now.

I'll just say that you won't catch me again running a Chevrolet SUV through a Saudi construction fence anytime soon, *inshallah*. This Arabic word means "God willing." But it could have a reference to time. If you say, "I'll see you at the meeting at eight A.M. tomorrow," their response, "*inshallah*" might mean yes, maybe, or maybe not. There is a nice Arabic expression that we particularly like: "*Maffi Mouk.*" *Maffi* means none and *mouk* is brains—therefore the translation is brainless or stupid.

CHAPTER 3

The Business of Education
Trouble in River City

If education and poverty are leading us down the road to perdition, we had better redouble our efforts and include the have-nots with a missionary zeal. It seems absurd that the educators continue to drag along an outdated approach to education when the world has evolved with a quantum leap in technology and knowledge. Yet they still instruct the students with ancient techniques more suited to a bygone age. The system is as useful as cufflinks.

For example the current system of grades or levels is something like the following:

APPROXIMATE AGE	GRADE LEVEL
04	Pre-School
05	Kindergarten
06	1st. Grade
07	2nd. Grade
08	3rd. Grade
09	4th. Grade
10	5th. Grade
11	6th. Grade
12	7th. Grade
13	8th. Grade
14	9th. Grade
15	10th. Grade
16	11th. Grade
17	12th. Grade
18	College 1
19	College 2
20	College 3
21	College 4

The current trend is to propel infants into some kind of preschool or fast-track system so that the darlings can get a leg up on the potential competition. This is a scheme of the affluent sector that sees life as a game of poker with an eye to upping the ante—I'll see your summer camp and raise you a private tutor. The darling progeny are the pawns of the game. They espouse a goal that leads from the umbilical cord to the corporate board. Some of the more serious players even start with the fetus in the womb by playing classical music across the membranes and other exotic behaviors.

The preschool phenomenon is not from the good old days. It is a modern idea that research might discover to have negative consequences. Daycare is another debatable program. In essence these programs or institutions take a child from the home setting, which is the logical place for safe and secure play, and transfer the job to paid caretakers. To play is the obvious daily activity of the child who gains knowledge and experience within the trusting confines of home and there is no convincing substitute. For those who exist in the rat race, the job is often subcontracted out to strangers. This is quite different from previous decades when the job of most mothers was to stay at home and tend to their own, which is the way that creatures have lived for eons of existence. It is unfortunate but this time-honored practice should be a joy performed for the first few years and seems as logical and natural as breast feeding. Alas nothing is sacred in the contemporary world.

Since the modern inhabitants are no longer in harmony with the earth, they even lose basic common knowledge such as child rearing. The lowliest creatures do not need consultants—wolves, birds, and fish know how to raise their young instinctually, but the modern humans require professional help. For example, American society was changing so rapidly in the 1960s and 1970s that millions of parents found themselves somewhat at a loss to cope and desperately looked for answers in the books written by Dr. Benjamin Spock. The advent of technology, to include instant access to global information, has crept upon humanity in tantalizing steps and as enticing as a hooker in the window. But what good is it, if Johnny comes marching home with his tongue and cheek pierced?

They say the brain is the most amazing gadget in the known universe. The brain loves a puzzle and thus, being the grand machine it is, loves to put abstract ideas in categories or shelves. The neurons of the brain are arranged into specialized circuits running in parallel and very complex. The technical theories are not our aim here since they change over time. Nevertheless, I still remember sharing the scent and taste of the honeysuckle bush at the age of seven with my first girlfriend, Elizabeth, at Takanassee Beach Club on the Jersey Shore. My brain stored this sensory experience as a memory, so that to think of it today brings forth the honeysuckle, the dimpled beauty, and the feelings that accompanied the experience. Elizabeth, on the other hand, for all my doting and devotion, did not catch my genetic drift, and she grew shortly thereafter about a foot taller than the author. Oh well, maybe next time. The brain has enormous capacity but unfortunately we don't have the specifications or the owner's manual. Distinguished philosophers will debate semantics or the use and meaning of words, but we are using simple terms (Not trying to be Emmanuel Kant here). There are countless examples proving the human propensity to complicate or confuse issues. For example, just consider the titles of some U.S. Government offices:

☐ The U.S. Department of Labor—Employment Standard Administration—Office of Workers' Compensation Programs—Division of Energy Employees Occupational Illness Compensation.

☐ United States Permanent Mission to the United Nations Environment Program and the United Nations Center for Human Settlements.

☐ Joint Functional Component Command for Integrated Missile Defense (JFCC IMD) is a component of United States Strategic Command (USSTRATCOM). You get the idea.

In his book *Hitch-22*, Christopher Hitchens used the term "solipsism" several times but it's not a word that rolls off the tongue in everyday parlance and I wondered, *Who cares what it means?* Otherwise, he was an interesting personality and author. Some British are—well, you know what I mean. But the Brits speak "more better" English than Americans; I'll give them that. (For the curious, solipsism is the philosophical idea that only one's own mind is sure to exist. It is an epistemological or ontological position that knowledge of anything outside one's own mind is unsure. The external world and other minds cannot be known and might not exist).

One would suppose we need terms such as numismatist (something to do about coins) and pugilist (something about boxing) or perhaps one is ignorant of the etymology or word derivations from Latin. The average human can only consciously do so much at once and hence the joke, "he can't walk and chew gum at the same time." But the brain, like the Wizard of Oz, is the comptroller of many bodily actions, that don't require much active thinking such as breathing, blinking, and apparently driving in most countries. The brain engages both reflective thinking, for conscious decision making, and reactive thinking, hence the notion "he is among the walking unconscious." An example from the Neanderthal era would be the gnawing, empty stomach and the reaction of "Get ready to club an unsuspecting and slower animal species." There would be no need for the club without hunger (does not apply to civilized gun-toting hunters with canned spam and backpack).

Driving a car, playing a musical instrument, and typing are examples of *learned* action sequences whose performance is optimal only after the movements become *unconsciously* controlled. Zen-based systems of martial arts take advantage of this concept. They emphasize structured practice with endless repetition, and strict avoidance of conscious control while putting the techniques to practical use.[10] Active, conscious thinking takes energy and work, but up until very recently, most humans have been preoccupied (and controlled) with working to purchase a grave and pay the final bar bill.

What humans could afford the luxury to stop and think?

Who built the Great Wall of China? (800 million died on the job).

Who built the pyramids? (They certainly weren't union members).

Who lives in economic slavery and earn less than $1 per day? (Billions of people).

In order to shelve negative thoughts and dreams, we create diversions and cling to them like vines around the plant, or become preoccupied like squirrels with their nuts (we're talking about acorns here). These diversions include entertainment such as television and sports, as well as alcohol and drugs. Certain activities and substances, when employed in moderation, are satisfying and useful to a well-balanced life but have become an obsession of the stressed-out moderns who view them as the end game of existence.

Ordinary people contribute to paying hundreds of millions of dollars to individuals who throw, kick, and whack a ball or otherwise entertain the flock. We place jocks, boobs, and "pop tarts" on pedestals and worship them like the golden calf of biblical and pagan legends. If this is normal and acceptable, the state of our affairs is transparently pathetic. People can pay some imbecile to play games but many worthwhile endeavors are left for the dust bin to include poorly paid social workers and a portion of teachers. The scientists, pursuing unique work in a multitude of fields to include biology, physics, and astronomy are considered nerds or quirky substitutes for the first-round team of life's players. It's amazing that the populace will discount the work of science and humanities like a 'going out of business' sale. Observably, the dopers do that. Definition of doper: one who does not know he is a dope. Why are they this way? Not because of an innate lack of intelligence, but they are improperly educated or actually ignorant given their useless education. There are some people who do not believe that the United States landed on the moon, and no amount of logic or reasoning can change their mind.

Look at what sells today; a recent visit to a Manhattan bookstore revealed very few English Literature classics and some of the big outlets are loaded with volumes of "New Age" such as astrology & divination, reincarnation, witchcraft and other nonsense.

It is appalling to see the unadulterated crap on the history-type channels that passes for documented science—from 2012 apocalypse to aliens imparting innovative technology to humans, they provide work for obvious frauds and money-making charlatans. How many of us have seen the doctoral candidate for online theological studies, the Reverend Bible Belter, who is a charlatan and a hypocrite but likes to impress himself besides others?

I occasionally meet people, who divulge they have multiple academic degrees or double majors, which prompts my head nodding in response as I mentally conjure Groucho Marx with his arching, bushy eyebrows. When I enquire whether they believe in evolution; quite often, but not surprisingly, the answer is no. On the other hand, the average Joe is raised to be blissfully ignorant, and like the other creatures on the planet, will pass along those marvelous genes as best he can. It is apparent to me that Joe is schooled but not educated as he should be. In many locales, schooling is a babysitting service, taking the parental role of discipline and value engineering. Joe is just passing through as he accumulates the various rubber-stamps leading to release from monotony. It's an assembly line kind of schooling where people succeed in spite of the system. The excesses of the old despotic systems are forgotten now but can be refreshed by a reading of Dickens' 1839 tale of the boy schools in *Nicholas Nickelby*. Despotic schooling was not an anomaly but an ever-present reality well into the 1900s.

Catholic schooling is a notable example that has subjected pupils to various wretched experiences that affect individuals to the present day. It's incredible that a religion demands priestly celibacy (hello?) and thereby invites homosexual candidates that hide in a celibate lifestyle. For this reason, the church has been reeling in billion-dollar litigations which could finally bankrupt the institution. Worse yet are the Islamic schools that force memorization of their holy book, the Koran—in other words a lot of memorization and little learning. Of course the Jews have their Torah (mazel tov).

In many countries homeschooling is increasingly viewed as a decent alternative to the poor public school system. There are obvious positives to this approach such as superior outcomes due to homemade attention. And because homeschoolers generally have more education and resources than the average parent, that decreases the advent of *garbage-in, garbage-out.* Although a major reason for homeschooling invokes religious considerations, there is a good probability the parents can indoctrinate their children-pupils with more class than the taxpayer funded system.

There is a radio personality in Atlanta that contends that sending your children to public school is child abuse. Moreover, if you *do* send your children to private school, you are still on the hook to pay the taxes for public education. Many parents are subject to property taxes that pay for the public schools, and also sending Jane to Catholic high school at a cost of $11,000 per year! If that makes you laugh, it is not untypical to pay $160,000 for a college education, but there is a sucker born every minute.

More ludicrous is the recent instruction by computer. Think of the good fortune of Alexander the Great as a pupil under Aristotle. Now imagine if that mentoring was by computer screen. The process of learning requires interaction between student and teacher. Significant insights are not as likely found at home with mom or on a computer screen.

The educational establishment continues to have close similarities with the prison system. There are involuntary inmates and wardens, structured activities, confinement and punishment. In the United States alone there are two million people in prison at a cost of hundreds of millions. It's safe to say that the felons failed somewhere along the way, but can we not also blame the school system for its role in the criminal world? The blame game indicts schools, genes, and poverty, but solutions are wanted.

The business of education and child rearing are brainwashing propositions—we try to get other people to do as instructed or at least somewhat to that effect. This was doable in the good old days when the young population had a sense that, if things were not quite great, it will get better in the future, and of course the cane or whip didn't hurt the enterprise. Prospects don't look so bright for the younger generation and they know it or at least suspect it. The cost of education has skyrocketed while the job prospects have plummeted, and the world appears topsy-turvy. When the future is perceived as bleak, people have a tendency to rebel against the brainwashing and get out of control. For example, Africa is a basket case and generations have been literally mutilated in all senses of the term. If the problems aren't seriously attacked soon, we may have to start this game over from the beginning.

Thoroughly Modern Materialism

The status quo of the modern age was jarred with a loss of balance. Values and beliefs came to be questioned such as life's purpose, the existence of God, personal responsibility, and the roles of parent and child.

Due to the breakdown of the traditional family unit with the rising divorce rate, the primary authority and breadwinner (father) was somewhat displaced by various contenders, including the government, television and other media. The precious little quality time with the male role model was excusable due to his busy employment, but there was no question about the father's rule as absolute monarch of his domain. As described in Dickens' *Nicholas Nickelby*, women were not allowed to keep their own money until the 1800s. The father was someone to be respected and often feared. Legislative and other government actions, however, released his commanding grip, for good or ill, by women's rights for equality, voting, and equal pay.

After World War II, cash was king. Men's wallets were bursting with greenbacks. My eldest brother's trousers were filled with quarters, nickels, and dimes; if he'd fallen overboard, he would have sunk like an anchor for all the hard currency in his deep pockets. On the other hand, my wallet today is thin as a hungry crow and it occasionally contains a $20 bill, but not much more. The word credit used to be a trusty, upstanding noun but is now the blight of a foreclosed segment of the populace. You used to be able to detect a person's worth by the size or bulk of their key chains. In the good old days, my eldest brother, Howard, was a Chevy Corvette owner, and after a few rum and cokes, would toss his keychain to whichever broad was on the nearest bar stool, very subtle fellow.

The television had a major impact on the family and imprinted its programming, like duck and ducklings on the psyche of impressionable young and old viewers. Whatever soup of life was ladled out by the telly was lapped up by a mesmerized and voracious audience. Why not? Most previous entertainment required effort such as using the imagination in listening to radio programs, or the rare treat of finding money when a traveling circus rolled near town.

Not that entertainment was a priority in the good old days. Life for most people was a struggle and luxuries like china cups were few and far between. If you break a china cup today, you just run out and buy a new set. But in the previous century, mother used the china cabinet or hutch to store her precious items, which were handed down to the next generation, and therefore valued like a welcome partner in an otherwise austere household. The china cabinet is pointless today for the modern throw-away society whose whole policy is overindulgent materialism and maximal clutter in the house. Like those lovable and earthy Italian-Americans with their bric-a-brac and plastic butterflies hanging from the ceilings, like squirrels collecting and burying their acorns in various and sundry locations—although the squirrels make more sensible transactions. At a garage sale or high-end retail store, people will buy almost anything, whether they need it or not.

The problem with possessions is the squabble among

inheritors. For example, my mother bequeathed her antique china cabinet to her eldest of two daughters and there could have been some jealousy involved. Unfortunately, when my mother died, I was the last at her casket (gruesome terminology), before it was closed (cried the raven nevermore), and I forgot to retrieve her precious pearl necklace which should have been given to either one of my two sisters. That slip-up may have avoided further resentment, who knows.

Speaking of inheritance, in merry old England, the oldest son was the prime inheritor, but in my wife's country of Eritrea, the youngest son inherits the estate. I suppose they deem the youngest to be their best bet for care in old age.

Possessions clutter your life as they accumulate to unprecedented levels and the laws of supply and demand prevail. Consumers are persistently hounded by the material purveyors with the persuasive proposition that happiness can be purchased, and the retail displays of merchandise can be enticing like the windows of Macy's on Herald Square. People will buy anything for any price these days. For example, in 2011, a rare and pristine copy of the first issue of Action Comics, famed for the first appearance of Superman, set a record for the most money paid for a single comic book: $2.16 million. Frank Sinatra liked to quip, "He who dies with the most toys wins."

Materialism is broadcast by the deception of advertisements. For example, commercials propel the unaware women to desire/demand, and their intended partners to buy the obligatory diamond ring upon marriage. What I call Madison Avenue and the diamond cartel are able to make a slobbering Pavlovian dog of the average consumer with jingles such as, "a diamond is a girl's best friend" (and similar drivel) while laughing all the way to the bank. Potential and short-term mates dance to the farce like moths to the light. To place an expensive rock on the finger, as a symbol of true love, is an indication of conformity and perhaps naivety. I could understand this sentiment more if the rock held value but it doesn't. It actually represents a dubious investment. Snake oil sir? Yes, a full measure if you please as it goes down so well! You probably don't know that there is no such thing as a "used diamond," and so the rock that is purchased from the expensive jewelry retailer may have come from a pawn shop.

Shame on any man who should use his senses and doubt of the propriety and rationale for this tradition of wealth making for Belgium traders! He is obviously not in love or worthy of mating. It does not occur to him that some diamonds are associated with amputated arms and legs of poor Africans who get in the way of the diamond trade. That's why they are called blood diamonds. People have been enslaved and murdered as a result of the trade.

The gem business has ancient antecedents. Prehistoric creatures not only scraped and polished stone for tools but also as favors for females of the clan, to gain distinction and to clinch mating opportunities. Females inferred superior genes from males who could fashion unique and artistic manipulation of ordinary objects. The De Beers cartel has only followed the trend.

Gold on the other hand, as used in places such as India and Africa, is at least a viable and worthy medium of exchange or barter (your daughter for some gold) because it holds its value. But we don't mean that cheap 14-karat American favorite. It's shiny so it works for them.

Getting back to diamonds, it is difficult to detect a diamond as fake or real so why not buy the fake and save the funds for more practical purposes like an education for the potential progeny. Perhaps the ladies should endorse this idea and remove guilt from the mating ritual. There is a perception that "diamonds are forever," but with a high divorce rate, marriages are not everlasting. Unfortunately, the resulting effects of daycare and fatherless families must be striking indeed with repercussions for society as a whole. For example, almost 70 percent of black children are born to single mothers in the United States. That means that only 30 percent of African-American marriages are successful and though that is an extreme, the institution of marriage for the rest of us hasn't fared much better. So clearly, the diamond doesn't hold the marriage together forever. In fact, it has been revealed by research that materialists have unhappier marriages than couples who don't care much about possessions.

If you agree that values are in flux in some of the better neighborhoods, imagine the other side of the railroad tracks. But there are those who will not intuitively perceive their surroundings—just as the populations of Brooklyn (New York) and Calcutta (India) see nothing wrong in their midst. They know no better—their neighborhood is their normal. Bring back the good old days for surely there was a better time in Brooklyn, such as when my parents lived there in the 1930s. There are 2.5 million lucky souls who live there now and so it goes.

Mysteriously my dad's family moved at least ten times in New York City when he was a child—from Manhattan to the Bronx, to Brooklyn etc. He told us his mother liked a freshly-painted apartment, but his rich sister-in-law explained that in the early 1900s, renters received three free months when they moved in.

My parents relocated to the suburbs of New Jersey in 1941 and took a secret to their graves. They never told their seven children that our dad, Howard Kingsley, had changed his name from Howard Katzman. We learned decades later about another side of the family: The Katzmans were Russian Jews who emigrated from Odessa to New York in 1881. The patriarch, Samuel Katzman, my great-grandfather, progressed from cigar maker to an ostrich *feather merchant*. In her book, *The Pursuit of Plumes*, Sarah Stein writes: "You might imagine that few things could be less important historically, and less connected to Jewish life, than ostrich feathers. But it turns out that ostrich feathers have an important story to tell about the development of global commerce and the place of Jews in it. From the 1880s to the outbreak of the First World War, ostrich plumes were coveted items of adornment, their value by weight almost equal to that of diamonds."[11]

Interestingly, Old Samuel had a business connection with a man whose family would become extremely wealthy. Samuel was part of a real estate venture with Jonas Scheuer. Scheuer was a prominent Jewish real estate mogul in New York City. He was the President of the J. Scheuer Company and Director of the

N.Y. & Richmond Land Improvement Company as well as many other enterprises. Jonas Scheuer, a *feather merchant*, created the beginnings of the family holdings which later grew in retailing, textiles, and real estate. His grandson, James Scheuer, was a candidate for mayor of New York City during the 1960s. Jonas Scheuer's son, Simon "Sy" Scheuer sought to ensure his fortune would outlive him. It did, and then some of it wound up with Bernie Madoff. Sy Scheuer amassed an estimated $500 million from the 1920s to the 1970s, buying New York real estate during the Great Depression and later stocks he considered undervalued. He arranged before his death in 1979 at age 88 to bequeath his estate to some 27 descendants and a charitable foundation through trusts to be overseen by a handpicked group of directors. Born in 1891, Sy Scheuer sold most of his stock holdings before the market crash of 1929 and began investing in properties.[12] Sy first made money as a *feather merchant* (like his father Jonas) in Argentina and then real estate in New York. He started acquiring West Virginia Coal and Coke, once the privately owned business of the family of composer Cole Porter in the 1950s. Getty and Scheuer were two patient schemers who operated on a grand scale.[13] On his deathbed, Sy Scheuer was after Rouse Company, the Columbia, Maryland, firm that developed Boston's Faneuil Hall Marketplace. Rouse learned on 23 October 1979, that Scheuer had purchased a 7.5 percent stake in the company, only to receive a call ten minutes later advising management that the financier was dead, according to a Washington Post article published at the time.

My Great-Grandfather Samuel had three sons; the eldest, Adolph was a pharmacist and physician. Alexander also became a pharmacist, and my father's dad, Jacob Katzman, was a collection lawyer. I recently spent hundreds of hours on the internet in search of their past. Some of them seemed to be interesting characters. The eldest, Adolph the physician, entered bankruptcy in 1904 and was evicted from his rental house in 1921 for nonpayment of rent in the same year that my father's dad went bankrupt in the collection business. My internet search revealed they had various business enterprises to include pharmacies, real estate, and a "culture station" for the collection of specimens from cases of Diphtheria, TB, and Typhoid… operated for the Health Department at their tenement residence at 964 Second Avenue on the corner of 51st Street.

My dad was an electrical engineer and technical manager for the Army but also led a secret life of spying against Russian agents, and he traveled overseas for various clandestine engagements. His only brother, Robbie, on the other hand, who earlier agreed to the name change, would become very successful in the Esso/Exxon oil business, as well as the President of the Arts and Business Council in New York City. Dad did not marry into wealth and was on the backside of the military-industrial complex. As to the name change from Katzman to Kingsley, it may have been sparked by a fear of anti-semitism in the job market or the stigma of earlier bankruptcy in the family since that was associated with the word "thief" in the early twentieth century. Or it could have been distancing himself from the association with Communist sympathizers by his uncle, Adolph Katzman. In 1921, Adolph formed a corporation, for drugs and medicine, with Isaac Shorr and Joseph R. Brodsky, some of the most famous Communist and radical attorneys in the 20th century. Isaac Shorr, a Russian Jew, was a prominent attorney for the ACLU (American Civil Liberties Union), and merits the dubious distinction of the first person known to have made J. Edgar Hoover's enemies list.[14] Some of his "clients" were charged with conspiracy to blow up munitions factories in WWI. Joseph Brodsky was an attorney for the International Labor Defense, the Communist Party's legal arm.

I often wonder how this turn of events colored our self-perception, *oy vey*. During our childhood, we noticed our dad eating matzo crackers with butter, but we probably thought, *Well, go figure!* (Who knew?) Incidentally, my dad's father and mother were buried in the Gate of Heaven Cemetery, Valhalla, New York, in 1947 and 1972 respectively. They did not receive a headstone, presumably to keep the name change private. It is my understanding our three cousins (from the wealthy aunt mentioned above) have been *cogitatin'* for some years as to providing a headstone for grandfather and grandma. My silent rejoinder is that I have been busy re-reading (Dickens) *Our Mutual Friend* whereas the wealthy relatives have been busy reading *Our Mutual Funds*. I am not airing the dirty laundry but just the facts. When I get up there, Dad, you have some 'splaining' to do.

Love and Marriage Go Together Like…

Speaking of marriages, I met and married my wife, Luchia, in Saudi Arabia which is very unusual for two non-Muslims. I was swimming in the pool at her compound in *Al Yamamah* while she was sitting at a nearby table, watching her two charges in the pool. Luchia worked as a nanny for an American couple. In those days, I didn't think anything about wearing those skimpy Speedo swimsuits. I jumped out of the water, sat right next to her, and struck up a conversation. I gave her my business card and went on my way.

Days later, I jogged around the compound for several hours before meeting one of the little tikes, playing on the street. The little one showed me the villa where Luchia worked. For days afterward, I jogged along the streets by her home until I *accidentally* ran into her again. She was a sight to see after dark—a ready smile showed ivory white teeth, and gums of an iridescent violet.

During one of our evening walks, Luchia showed me her passport and I was somewhat relieved that her ostensible age was close to mine. Then she informed me she was actually younger; the Saudis don't want women to enter the country under the age of 30 and thereafter lead them into temptation. Luchia told them she was 31 on her entry form in 1983 when she was actually 19. We were married at the Eritrean embassy in Riyadh and I'm not sure whether Luchia got the short end of the stick, but I really don't view myself as the Master Cylinder (from the 1959, Felix the Cat cartoon), not really.

Before this point in time, I worked at an Army office building in Riyadh, Saudi Arabia, from 1991 to 1993. This later became the target of the first terrorist bombing in Saudi Arabia on 13

November 1995. It did not receive the press that the next attack in Dhahran would on 25 June 1996. The U.S. Air Force personnel were the target there. My office building was converted from a dilapidated apartment building and had minimal security measures. Although I was luckily not there at the time, my supervisor's face was blown-off and he later succumbed to his wounds.

Prior to my arrival in Saudi, I knew more of the Arabic language than most of the American Army personnel who had worked there for several years. It was just a matter of learning from the tapes supplied by the Defense Language Institute from the beautiful Presidio of Monterey, California. Additionally, I attended a local Arabic class with primarily third-world students, and I can still hear the teacher, a huge, tall and stocky Sudanese in white thobe and turban: "Taleboon jedeed!" (new student) for the students to repeat. It occurred to me that the military was short-sighted. I wondered how we could appear effective with a disparate way of communicating and living our lives in isolated American compounds. It is just common sense that you make more enemies than friends with a separate mindset. Incidentally, "Taliban" (the creeps in Afghanistan) means "student" in Arabic.

I returned to the area after the bombing to assist with relocation to a terrible place called Eskan Village. A funny thing happened on the way to that desert destination. On 5 January 1997, Sergeant Kelly informed me that my household goods were lost in transit—all my worldly goods vanished. They were me-thodically packed, loaded, and shipped from Florida and then disappeared. The lord giveth and the Saudis taketh away. I have advocated an uncluttered, minimal materialistic lifestyle for many years. My reason is not just an affinity for Zen Buddhism, but people have been uncluttering me from an early age, from mother to ex-wives. Back in the desert, a decision was made to move the U.S. military to Eskan Village, a city in the industrial sector that was built in 1983 for the Bedouin, who never took the bait, refusing to move there.

Eskan Village reminded me of Starrett City in Brooklyn, a huge place with high-rise buildings and one-storey housing units. It may seem funny, but for the renovation, the Saudis and U.S. each kicked-in $100 million—and the construction sign at the entrance, in big bold letters: BIN LADEN CONSTRUCTION COMPANY—the dad's company and not to be confused with the terrorist son, Osama Bin Laden.

I was allowed to move in with my new wife, Luchia, and the apartment was in need of work. The water faucets poured brown water, but there is another Arabic expression, *"al-hamdu lilah"* which means "thanks be to God." That was certainly how I felt about having Luchia there with me, when she was not working as a nanny for that crazy American family.

I used to buy all kinds of vitamins and supplements in those days—maybe 15 bottles. She opened the kitchen cabinet and thought, *Oh my, this guy must be very ill or something.* She had never seen healthy people take pills before. Now I realize that *most* supplements are bogus, but good for business. The futurists and *the Jetsons* pedaled the idea of meals in pills and it has caught on like cotton candy at the circus.

People who work around the world are by definition adventuresome and sometimes eccentric and I am no exception. I like to entertain people, and on my overseas assignments, I employed various jokes and pranks. One of my favorites has two versions—the fake, round poop for the floor, and a different but effective shape for the toilet seat. Luchia told me she jumped two feet when she saw this thing wiggle on the floor. A lot of people around the world have never seen these types of novelties. The marketplace also has available hidden safes that conceal your valuables in an ordinary household product with a screw-off bottom. These Can Diversion Safes are used as hiding places for valuables to keep prized possessions from being stolen by burglars and thieves. When we visited Eritrea (East Africa), I brought a (Diversion Safe) Jock-Itch can and put 30 hundred-dollar bills in the inside. When Luchia's father unwrapped his present, he didn't know what it was. I told my wife to translate that it was for jock-itch while I did a spraying motion with my hand toward his crotch. Well, those parents' jaws dropped in disbelief (that I would accuse the father of having an itchy groin) until they were told to unscrew the false bottom. Due to my contribution to the family, my wife's father built a toilet in an outhouse and a shower. Previously, I had a bath in a cut-off barrel and the toilet was the usual hole in the ground.

I can't help but bring novelties and bags of candy when I visit places like Africa. The children in the distance yell "*firangi!*" when I come into view, which means foreigner or white person. My favorite trick is a foot-tall flame from my hand that explodes, but since I am expert with it, the flame appears to be nearer the audience than it actually is. During a party in Qatar, a local Qatari gentleman was evidently upset by this trickery or sorcery and just couldn't imagine how it happened—of course I found this quite amusing! Pranks are a lot of fun and you don't know what you're missing unless you try it. It's also one way to express your inner child. I like to consider that Richard Feynman had a similar quality; the famous physicist was known to bang the bongos at the local strip clubs near Los Alamos and perform safe-cracking for amusement at the nuclear laboratory.

Getting back to Eskan Village, the Leaders or high-ranking military personnel were exempt from leaving their plush residences until new accommodations were constructed at Eskan Village—you know, leading from behind. Before these bombings, the U.S. military personnel had really swank accommodations in the expensive part of the capital; 3000 square-foot villas with all the extras. Wily Saudis—they got rid of their saviors and moved them to the desert dirt, close by the concrete plant and the poorest of the poor workers in the industrial zone. But, not to worry, I did remember to sign my ethics form.

The Rose Garden

Family life for the previous thousands of years was problematic and primitive but populations were humble in numbers and the global effects were nominal. Today's burgeoning population is placing an increasing demand on the earth's well-being. For example, global warming and pollution are endemic problems and getting worse. Just imagine the sewers of China with a population of 1.3 *billion* people. I'm not going to elaborate other than to say that is a lot of poop. People have a habit of eating but do not always think of the consequences and some customs seem unpalatable in comparison to the West. In some parts of China, for instance, eating cats and dogs is common practice going back thousands of years. But there are places with different extremes; a poignant illustration of a country out of control is wrapped in the phrase *it's raining cats and dogs* in America. There are 164 million of these pets in the United States, and Americans spend $41 billion annually on their critters, or more money than the GDP of numerous poor countries combined.

The populace has to wake up. A rampant family is a poor prescription for physical and mental health. If we do not grow well-balanced and educated youth, the current problems will increase and global lifestyles wither like a plant untended and forgotten.

It is ironic that progress and technology have provided an increased standard of living, but when misused can lead to the problems of pollution, nuclear weapons, and over population. One example is the misfortune at the Japanese (Fukushima) nuclear facility due to an earthquake in March 2011, the biggest industrial catastrophe in the history of mankind. The disaster may surpass the 1986 Chernobyl meltdown but was shelved from public scrutiny in order to avoid panic. In Michio Kaku's book, *Physics of the Future*, Michio mentions that the problems of nuclear power include meltdowns, explosions, and nuclear waste. The 2011 book must have gone to print just before the Fukushima disaster since it is not cited. However, the media showed us the obligatory coverage until some celebrity scandal took center stage as the lead story. Two thoughts come to mind for residents of Japan—be wary of any sushi that glows in the dark, and "isotopes are for dopes." Unfortunately, as a consequence of Fukushima, Canada detected large spikes in radioactive material in their air during March and April which may lead to higher rates of cancer. North America will receive millions of tons of radioactive flotsam and jetsam as well as chemical waste from Fukushima.

The proverbial double edge sword of "progress" is a blessing and a curse. Life was hard but simple in the good old days as opposed to our current hard-pressed and complex existence. There is no turning back unless a natural or, more likely, man-made catastrophe reduces the globe to its former barren and humble state. Therefore it is imperative that humans find a way to use our limited brain power to successfully steer a sensible course towards a future that ensures the integrity of the planet and its population.

It is assumed that warfare is a modern invention of the past 10,000 years, since previous ages lacked the reasons and populations for this type of activity. As humans progressed to a settled existence with steady food supplies and structured elites and hierarchies, warfare became an inevitable outcome for reasons of periodic depletion of resources and encroachment of competing populations. Although one would think that moderns should eliminate this self-destructive activity, warfare continues unabated around the globe with devastating effects such as the nuclear attack on Japan during World War II and the various genocides perpetrated against civilian populations in Africa. Common warfare is not a general threat to global stability and the resulting culling of various populations does not affect the geometric increases in numbers of humans berthed on the planet.

As of the year 2013, there are seven billion people on planet Earth. It is estimated that the world population will reach nine billion by the year 2042. Even deadly diseases such as AIDS, or other viruses in waiting, are unlikely to suspend the human propensity to increase their numbers. And it is no surprise that China poses the greatest threat to global stability due to the negative effects of their projected size of population. It seems hypocritical though for the United States to lecture China in view of our own fraud and corruption. Two words come to mind for U.S. politicians in regards to China: Keep Out!

Population concerns cannot be overstated as bringing

dire consequences, but the major cause for alarm must be the potential use of a rogue nuclear attack by extremist groups notably from the Islamic pile of militants. Neither biological nor chemical weapons pose this kind of danger since their dispersal mechanisms are not as effective nor are they of extreme psychological impact. But a nuclear explosion in New York or London is likely to cause wholesale panic. It would unleash not only radioactivity, but also anarchy that could result in collapse of the world economies and a total distrust of government's role as our protector. This scenario would be like the stereotype of the old American Wild West where lawlessness is the order of the day and individuals take the law into their own hands in a dog-eat-dog town without a Marshal. This is so frightening a prospect that the average person is unwilling to perceive the possibility of our prosperous lifestyle disintegrating in this pathetic way.

The Best of All Possible Worlds

In Steven Pinker's 2011 book, *The Better Angels of Our Nature*, the author contends that, believe it or not, (and he states most will not believe it) violence has declined over long stretches of time, and today we may be living in the most peaceable era in our species' existence. For this, the reader must endure 700 pages of excruciating detail that includes statistics, statisticians, logarithmic tables, studies, with 114 charts and graphs. There are 1,955 notes at book's end, and 1,127 references. Not to be outdone, the author favors the reader with anything but the kitchen sink and everything you wanted to know about violence but were too bored to ask. I have been reading books for well over 50 years, but this was more than I could take and the compilation should have been more like a compendium. Most schooled readers are somewhat familiar with the medieval rack, torture, murder, spanking and the rest of it, or man's inhumanity to man. It is advisable to refrain from beating the horse to death as in *Gone with the Wind* and concise this is not, but the Harvard psychologist, Steven Pinker, will probably receive another *pugilistic prize* (or is it Pulitzer) since the publishing business is a world unto itself. Celebrities and the intelligentsia are automatically treated with genuflection, homage, and front of the line honorifics. The voluminous nature of this work compares favorably with Stephen Jay Gould's last book, *The Structure of Evolutionary Theory*, which is a whopping 1,464 pages. Pinker states that contrarians will note that wars still take place in the developing world, so perhaps violence has only been displaced, not reduced. But violence is not just bloodletting. Indeed violence has been displaced with a new world order that shovels up alienation, anxiety, and angst. No one refutes the comparison of the dark ages to the space age, i.e., the downside that characterized most of human history and the affluence of modern civilization. But, although economists like to associate monetary levels with standard of living, we must consider the effects of the following compendium of issues that reflect quality of life:

☐ **Deteriorating mental and physical health**: The U.S. health system is the most expensive in the world, but comparative analyses consistently show the United States underperforms relative to other countries on most dimensions of performance in the practice of medicine. Pundits will declare that modern medicine has extended life spans, but they fail to offer advice on the sustainability of seven billion people. Ironically, after 700 pages of his book, Pinker's last sentence presages the yin and yang of this *best of all possible worlds*: "For all the tribulations in our lives, for all the troubles that remain in the world…cherish the forces of civilization…"[15] Fortunately, it doesn't require a Harvard academic to know that these benefits of civilization include an extreme decline in overall mental health throughout the world. Moreover, there seems to be a dark and ominous cloud over our individual psyche that is felt as a prevalent reminder of our changed and vulnerable circumstances.

☐ **Toxic air**: Cities in Iran, Mongolia, India, and Pakistan are among the worst for air pollution and the problem is getting worse over time. People are buying face masks in heavily polluted cities such as Beijing due to hazardous air quality. Back home in America, approximately 60% of us live in areas where air pollution has reached unhealthy levels that can make people sick.

☐ **Polluted water:** Water is essential for our lives but it is also the most threatened resource. Industrial pollution is contaminating the most vulnerable water resources. Across the United States, mercury pollution has contaminated 18 million acres of lakes, estuaries, and wetlands (43 percent of the total), and 1.4 million river miles. There are warning labels on cans of tuna fish, and the Inuit people in very remote locales have some of the highest blood levels of mercury and other toxic chemicals.

☐ **Toxic water:** A major source of pollution is caused by runoff during rains and flooding that deposits chemicals into lakes, rivers, wetlands, coastal waters, and ground waters. In 2011, already polluted rivers and chemical lagoons at Superfund sites were breached by hurricane floodwaters, the U.S. EPA reported. The lagoons had been seeping carcinogenic benzene 20,000 times regulatory levels all year into the Raritan River in New Jersey, according to the agency. Imagine the irrigation of the cropland in the Garden State with these toxic cocktails and the harvest to come. This gives a new meaning to the label *organic* for the Farmer's Markets in New York City. The energy craze called fracking is now being used to extract natural gas from shale deposits especially in the United States. This drilling technique bores horizontally through the bedrock, blasts it with explosives, and forces water into the cracks with a proprietary mix of poisonous chemicals that further fracture the rock. Some of this water will resurface along with benzene, brine, radioactivity, and heavy metals that for the past 400 million years had been safely locked up a mile below the surface.[16] It seems the energy companies are not content with being polluters but are devilish or vile to put it mildly. On the other hand are the mining companies that have been enterprises of environmental disasters. For example, the residues from metal mining in Montana (copper, gold and silver, etc.) have left a legacy of toxic wastes to include cyanide, acids, and other dangerous compounds. For the future, miners are setting their sights on asteroids as a potential source of profits from these commodities—*May the Force be with you!*

☐ **Adulterated food:** Prior to the 20th century, many food additives were toxic and poisonous. Of all forms of adulteration the most reprehensible was the use of poisonous coloring substances in the manufacture of sweets. The bright colors used to attract children often contained lead, copper or mercury salts.[17] Far more additives are present in foods than ever before, but their use is supposedly monitored and controlled. Thanks to free trade and market forces, we are inundated with foreign imports. But a string of food-safety scandals has given consumers cause to be very suspicious of the benefits of foreign shipments—from tainted milk from China to products from South America which often contain filth, adulteration, and the presence of dangerous food-borne pathogens. In recent times, China's news media have reported sales of pork adulterated with the drug clenbuterol, which can cause heart palpitations; pork sold as beef after it was soaked in borax, a detergent additive; rice contaminated with cadmium, a heavy metal discharged by smelters; arsenic-laced soy sauce; popcorn and mushrooms treated with fluorescent bleach; and bean sprouts tainted with an animal antibiotic. Even eggs have turned out not to be eggs at all but man-made concoctions of chemicals, gelatin, and paraffin. In 2012, Chinese police seized more than $182 million worth of counterfeit pharmaceuticals in the latest attempt to clean up a food and drug market that has been flooded with fakes. You have to wonder why anyone would ingest a food item from China. In 2012, four men in Mumbai

India were arrested for selling milk mixed with sewage water in plastic packets scavenged from garbage bins. More than two-thirds of milk in the country was contaminated with substances to include detergent. The sale of fake products in branded packaging collected from rubbish dumps is believed to be widespread in India. The latest bit of progress in the agribusiness world is Genetically-modified foods (GM foods) whereby plants can be modified in the laboratory to enhance certain desired traits such as increased resistance to herbicides. Although it sounds plausible and logical, Mother Nature has been tinkering with plants for millions of years—much longer than Dr. Frankenstein and his cohorts on the corporate payrolls. Humans can never leave well enough alone. They have to construct gift shops on parkland and metaphorically piss on fire hydrants. It gives you a belly ache to think about it all.

☐ **Widespread use of toxic chemicals in the home and environment:** In North America today, there are more than 85,000 chemicals in regular use and the number is growing every day. Yet just ten percent of them have been fully tested for their health and environmental effects. Among the chemicals that have been tested, many have already been shown to have toxic effects on both human health and the environment. Numerous health conditions, ranging from certain kinds of cancer to early puberty in girls, have been linked to chemical exposure.[18]

☐ **Destruction of the environment and other species:** The current threat to the world's oceans indicates a high risk of entering a phase of extinction of marine species unprecedented in human history. The manmade stressors include climate change, overexploitation, pollution and habitat loss. For instance, the Great Pacific Garbage Patch in the Pacific Ocean, which is mostly plastics, is estimated to be twice the size of Texas and is considered to be the biggest dump site in the world. And trash isn't limited solely to Terra Firma. Humans are trashing space with many thousands of pieces of junk. Due to their high velocities, fragments can have an impact equal to a truck bomb hitting a satellite or space station.[19] Although some of the world's most widespread coral reefs are found in places like the Philippines, they are under assault by fishing with dynamite and cyanide that cause ecological disaster. These destructive fishing practices are spreading to many other parts of the world. As E.O. Wilson mentions in *The Future of Life*: "It should come as no surprise that large numbers of species are crossing the thin zone from the critically endangered to the living dead and thence into oblivion." In the 1960s, Jacques Cousteau became a worldwide figure in the campaign to stop marine pollution and therefore the world has been on notice for over 35 years. This situation is similar to the burning of oil and coal. We have known for as long as 50 years the need to develop alternative energy but the cartel of fossil fuel companies has resisted any change. They have a lot invested in the dirty business and can't charge exorbitant fees if the sun were a major energy source.

☐ **My Ocean Dumping Grounds as a Child:** New York City's ocean dumping practices went on for decades in the Atlantic coastal waters off New Jersey and Long Island. Four city-owned barges traveled from municipal wastewater treatment plants every day and dumped their cargo in our ocean water, consisting of New York City-generated sewage sludge, from the 12 city wastewater treatment plants. The sludge contained solids and various chemicals used in the wastewater treatment process, including large quantities of heavy metals. The barges discharged five million wet metric tons of sewage sludge, one million tons of industrial acid wastes, 100 million tons of dredged material and one quarter of a million tons of cellar dirt. Furthermore, substantial additional potentially toxic contaminants came from the discharge of the Hudson-Raritan estuary and from atmospheric fallout. It had become one of the largest underwater dumping grounds in the world.

The bottom line is: Don't think that the Mafia alone conducts this kind of dreadful behavior; the government is complicit like any Capo of Cosa Nostra.

☐ **Global warming (believe it or not):** Regardless of the controversy, a majority of world climate scientists believe that human activity contributes to global warming. The consequences of rising sea levels would dwarf the evil deeds committed by Genghis Khan and his clan.

☐ **Over population with seven billion people and counting:** The ticking time bomb of the Haves and the Have-Nots could turn out quite unstable and explosive. The typical person in the bottom five percent of the American income stream is still richer than *68 percent* of the world's inhabitants. More low income people are reproducing who cannot afford the obligation of raising children properly. Unfortunately, the ones who can afford the costs of childrearing are delaying or remaining childless. This is a prescription for further dumbing down of the population.

☐ **Urban crowding:** Many lives are spent in bumper to bumper traffic. For example, in August 2010, a line of cars and trucks 60 miles long had snarled the road along the Beijing-Tibet 110 Expressway for nine days.

☐ **Widening poverty:** The rich are getting richer while everyone else is in a *wait and see* mode. The master has displaced the whip of slavery with economic servitude. It's simply violence of a different kind. As far as violence is concerned, a burglary takes place in the U.S. every 14.6 seconds. One of every 39 Americans will be the victim of a violent crime; one of every six women will be raped in their life time (80 percent are unreported). One in every three Australians is a victim of crime. Pinker doesn't offer any advice about defending yourself in the face of violence, but since I had some connection to the military, ladies should consider the following: Be aware of predators and trust your instincts. If confronted with trouble, anything can be used as a defensive weapon; a pen, a hair pin, or any sharp object. Without thinking, you must jab the perpetrator in the head or other sensitive area as hard as you can and then run away like hell. Don't think about being a victim and the bad guy will not expect this kind of ferocity on your part.

☐ **Missing children:** In the year 2011, approximately eight million children were expected to go missing throughout the world.

☐ **Nuclear weapons proliferation and probable use:** The Doomsday Clock, which is only five minutes to the figurative midnight in 2013, conveys how close humanity is to catastrophic destruction, and monitors the means humankind could use to obliterate itself. As a result of the spread of civilian nuclear power technology, substantial quantities of highly enriched uranium, one of the materials necessary for a bomb, remain in more than 40 non-weapon states, according to the International Panel on Fissile Materials.

☐ **Nuclear leaks, nuclear accidents, waste and containment:** The terrible consequences of Chernobyl and Fukushima may be few and far between but they are everlasting. One of the most contaminated waste sites in America is leaking nuclear waste according to US officials in 2013. The Hanford Nuclear Reservation stores material from the production of atomic weapons, in tanks which have outlived their 20-year lifespan.

☐ **Lethality of advanced conventional weapons:** The new world order is getting more dangerous by an increase in the sophistication of weapons. Due to the corruption of the military/industrial complex, the nations of the world are armed to the teeth.

☐ **Light weapons:** On average, small arms and light weapons kill 300,000 people worldwide every year, and many more are injured, abused, bereaved, and displaced.[21] Currently, there are more than 100 million landmines located in 70 countries around the world, according to One World International. Since 1975, landmines have killed or maimed more than one million people.

☐ **Global financial crises and theft:** Globalization is one of the current popular buzzwords but so are bailout and the phrase "too big to lose." Capitalism is out of control and rampant materialism is the order of the day. Some other uncommon terms used in the criminal world include derivatives and credit default swaps. And the preferred form of government: Kleptocracy.

☐ **Cyber war:** China is waging a potentially devastating cyber war against the United States, aimed at stealing its most sensitive military and economic secrets and obtaining the ability to sabotage vital infrastructure. This represents a massive vulnerability since developed countries are extremely dependent on computer networks.

☐ **Pop culture:** The tentacles of the information age have a grip on popular culture. Pop culture is the appetizer of the meal called dumbing-down of the population. The main course is the stomach-churning educational system.

☐ **Eroding family values:** Marriage is on the skids. Divorce is as common as table salt, out-of-wedlock births are soaring, and single parent families are the new norm. It seems that society has lost integrity or its moral compass.

The bottom line is the notion that there are probably many more wealthy optimists than poor ones. Although we may consider ourselves optimists, we should think and act as realists.

There is no good reason to be placated to believe all is well when our senses and gut feelings indicate otherwise. You often hear comments about how nice some millionaire seems to be, as if it is a revelation. If I were wealthy, you would be surprised by the author's congeniality as well. My wealthy aunt was able to pull up in an ordinary Volkswagen, wearing last year's winter coat but she could easily have done the same in fur and Mercedes. The true benefit of wealth is the comfort of knowing that you are financially secure and free from worry about the status of the next meal.

Optimism—believing that all is good and everything will turn out fine provides the important benefits of encouraging us to persist toward our goals and overcome obstacles. However, unchecked optimism can detach us from the cold harsh truths of reality. A pessimist, on the other hand, holds negative views on a subject, when there is actually evidence to the contrary. Our minds are wired to select and interpret evidence supporting the hypothesis "I'm OK." A variety of mechanisms: conscious, unconscious, and social, direct our attention to ignore the bad and highlight the good to increase our hope and reduce our anxiety. We work hard to retain the belief that we're OK even when faced with significant losses. Self-justification is deeply ingrained in each of us. And mental schema makes it easier for us to perceive information that supports what we already know or believe. Unfortunately we often get it wrong. Our brain distorts reality to increase our self-esteem through self-justification. However, people perceive themselves readily as the origins of good effects and reluctantly as the origins of ill effects. We present a one-sided argument to ourselves.[22] In Pinker's case, the devil is in the details. I would advocate that, although overt violence has decreased, this is not shaping up to be the best of all possible worlds. In view of the fight or flight propensity of humans which is the body's response to perceived threat or danger—circle the wagons!

CHAPTER 4

The Rat Race
Lose the News

"No news is good news" indicates tidings are generally not good, which brings to mind the notion ignorance is bliss. The idea behind these sayings is that news or information has been revolutionized in comparison to snail mail, horseback, or wooden ships. In the past, news of any kind was a happening. It had previously trickled in like the slow drip of a faucet but now we're bombarded with information, and of course like radio static, a lot of it is pesky noise; the explosion of news and information is not conducive to serenity and mental health.

A 1000-piece puzzle makes no sense until the pieces are correctly placed together to form a picture—just the facts madam. All the information we now receive is difficult to keep hold of. In a related item, the rare personality with a photographic memory can seem a genius and access millions of bits of information with perfect recall. For example, the Welsh actor, Richard Burton, was thought to have a near photographic memory. Burton kept listeners spellbound by reciting Shakespeare at great length. But such talent may not necessarily equate with an ability to integrate all stored information and be deemed wise. Some eidetics, as they are called, may be able to memorize the local telephone book but might also be thoughtless personalities. They say wisdom comes with age. More likely, age comes with age, and the associated problems of any dilapidated or rundown system. Evolution's survival of the fittest does not automatically require a strong measure of wisdom; but perhaps with a bit of luck, beneficial genes, and a smidgen of cunning, you could be a survivor. So maturity finds it terribly hard to fit in these days because there is a lot of news or noise, and much of it sells only if it is bad news and therefore, to a more placid or older generation, no news is indeed good news. It's funny that in the good old days, your mailbox was a receptacle for letters from friends and relatives. Now the postal service is bankrupt but delivering bills and junk mail.

It is almost impossible to avoid the bombardment of noise unless you live in an igloo at the frozen arctic. It is the challenge of modern man to handle this overflow of information in such a way that living in this sea of noise can still make sense. But without a proper filtering or integrating mechanism, the average intellect will be battered among the waves like plankton, without much more meaning.

Although the human brain has an innate processing, storage, and filtering capability (such as hiding the bad old memories), it seems imperative that we raise a helping hand to foster wisdom in order to help individuals cope with the schizophrenic pace of life. We can lead a calmer life, take simple joys, and coexist peacefully rather than perpetuating the brutal past or the struggle to win at all costs. The tools can surely pay off by an investment in the capital expenditure for education with an enlightened agenda. To continue feeding billions of hungry humans, who in turn procreate more empty minds and stomachs, is not a practical course of action. That is not enlightenment, no matter what the do-good religious zealots contend. It is defilement or more simply put, dense. If all the craziness and seeming insanity makes you think of running for the hills, you're not alone. It's a comforting thought to imagine a placid seaside bungalow or cabin in the outback but it's not for everybody. But one can still enjoy sitting on the back porch and watch the fireflies as the summer evening turns to dark while the leaves on the trees wink in the breeze.

Life is Short

I recall my dad driving us into New York City and how really alien it looked, that tremendous skyline of concrete and imposing buildings. Like a stranger in a strange land. We cruised up the New Jersey Turnpike (North) in a 1964 Ford (Country Squire) station wagon with the windows down, our dad smoking a five-cent Dutch Masters cigar. Ah that's living! If we passed a vehicle, it would more than likely be a garbage truck, with the kids cheering along. One of the only negatives of the drive was the rank smell near Linden, New Jersey, from the refineries with their belching orange flames and associated industrial machinations.

But New York City was a fanciful place, despite all the crazy crowds and imposed anonymity. The cliché fits aptly, a nice place to visit, but I wouldn't want to live there. Some of our favorites included going to Yankee Stadium to see Mickey Mantle and Roger Maris or visiting the old neighborhoods with the elevated train (EL) screeching overhead. We would visit our grandmother in a nursing home near Riverside Drive in Manhattan. At the tender age of eight, I learned the notion that life is short by walking the hallways filled with wheelchairs, white hair, and the void—all in a state of rundown and ramshackle helplessness, the aged and sunken eyes of the inmates drinking in our youth, and feebly remembering days and decades gone by. The whole place seemed a bloomin' wreck. I swore this would never happen to me. If that is the golden years they could have it. It's not the quantity of time, it's the quality.

Luckily my dad's wealthy brother, Uncle Robbie, paid for the nursing home. My dad went in for the government job (with seven children) while his brother went into Standard Oil and had only three kids. Robbie's wife was wealthy on her own account through her parents' connection with the garment business in the city. And although residing in the affluent New Canaan, Connecticut, you would never otherwise know of their wealth—the same socks, the same car, and the same coat.

Uncle Robbie was a wonderful man who was esteemed by our family as our dad was in their clan. Both gentlemen enjoyed singing Spanish songs, even a parody on their knees, especially of Carlos Gardel, the famous (Argentine) tango singer who died in 1935.

My parents were able to walk across the Harlem River Bridge

at night which was torn down in 1955. In the 1970s, my dad would drive through their old neighborhood in the Bronx but we would instinctively roll up the car windows and lock the doors.

New York gives the impression of total chaos but somehow it works (particularly if you have lots of money). But unfortunately for others, much of the world's population live in shacks of a slum and would trade places with us in an instant—if only the genie in the bottle would fall out of the sky. The disparity of living standards throughout the world is astounding. I compare my wife's place of birth in Eritrea with that of Europe. One country has Rembrandts (Netherlands) and the other has restraint and hunger; one has coupons and lines for flour and sugar, and another has a feast. On 22 March 1998, more than 16,000 people ate lunch in the Portuguese capital, Lisbon, sitting along the longest dining table in the world. The table was five kilometers long and covered almost a third of Europe's longest bridge, the *Vasco da Gama,* with almost ten tons of a traditional Portuguese dish made with pork and beans. Until about the year 2000, when their president turned into a tyrant, the people in Eritrea seemed quite content and enjoyed simple pleasures, even with their hardships. For example, my wife's childhood was devoid of candy, cake or ice cream, but they have excellent teeth and a lower rate of obesity with associated illness. Alas, comfort and paradise are only available for a price that is becoming dear indeed and we don't take it for granted anymore.

Many people struggle to accumulate wealth at the expense of enjoying a simple and contented life, while billions simply struggle for the next meal. Rich and poor alike can be found lamenting their condition. The rich want to be richer and the poor look on in envy. A gourmet meal at Le Cirque in New York would be inconceivable to the masses, and yet a simple hot dog can seem a feast when one is hungry. My father liked to comment that people love to eat. It seems obvious and I suppose, as a cosmopolitan New Yorker, he ran the gamut from Horn and Hardart automats to a simple bagel.

We usually had a good laugh when my dad's brother visited.

Our rich aunt would chirp like a bird at the dinner table, alternately talking and pushing her food around the plate with her fork. I was mesmerized by this etiquette because we poor vultures wouldn't dream of playing with food. At our table of nine, you either dived in and dined or were done. Naturally we had to hide our Halloween candy from one another, and until this day, I still hide food in the refrigerator and believe me you won't find it.

Our view of the world or experience is dependent on perception; as my mother would say "Life is not fair," which seems an obvious view when things are not going our way. The idealism of youth wants everything for everyone, although the tenets of Marxism (from each according to his ability and to each according to his need), has fewer followers these days. Unfortunately many people fall into the trap of existence. Through no fault of their own, they not so much live but rather exist from day to day, allowing circumstances to dictate instead of directing their own course. Free will is a concept that often seems in short supply. The dictatorial religions preach that the gods are orchestrating the scene and the actors are their puppets. It's easy then if everything is predestined. There's nothing to think about when the Earth is on autopilot.

This is fine for the mindless crowds and good for the hucksters, rulers, and despots who wouldn't have it any other way. Free will comes with a price because it is not easy to be a free thinker and be open to life's possibilities. It is much easier to be a group thinker, partaking in the tribal mentality. I found an excellent example in my military Boot Camp with the Coast Guard. Here in the time-tested groupthink environment, recruits are broken down like an untamed horse in a corral, and built back up in a cohesive formation of indoctrinated troops, ready to take orders and fit into the pecking order of the military hierarchy. Anyone who attended a military Boot Camp can never forget the cadence of marching: "Left, your left, your left 2, 3, 4, your left (silence 2, 3, 4), Left..." To my mind, the Company Commanders were petty tyrants (don't get me wrong, that's their job) and could call out any gibberish and we would march just the same: "Lepp, your lepp, your lepp hee, haw, heh, your lepp." We had a crazy Vietnam veteran as the Company Commander who, instead of drilling with discipline, left his Echo Company on their own to sort things out, using the hands-off or laissez faire style which was painful. In Boot Camp each company of recruits is scrutinized for potential. Cooperative "leaders" are picked to rule the group and squash independent or imaginative individuals in order to advance a disciplined corps. It kind of reminded me of the book *Lord of the Flies*, the story of children stranded on a tropical island, competing for leadership and command. The Marines are known for extreme discipline and group identification—once a Marine, always a Marine—*Semper Fi* (always faithful). This is optimal for military affairs. The objective of killing involves a tightly knit group of individuals who can subjugate individual interests in order to promote the goal of the unit. Societies, however, cannot and should not operate like military units and that is why military juntas in charge of civilian populations are a drawback for successful nation building. Militaries have been the backbone of nations but not the brain of the apparatus. I didn't fit in so well in Boot Camp since I was somewhat older at 25 than the typical recruit of 18. My independent and free thinking mentality did not fit the regimentation that is the modus operandi of the military mindset. Then again it was another notch in my gun of life's experiences.

Discipline is well placed in a military organization, and the same applies to other institutions such as schools as well as the family. I can't say that my Catholic schooling was akin to the Boot Camp experience although the prevalent joke makes an analogy to the Nazi regimens of World War II. The nun teachers were the camp commanders, sometimes sadistic and otherwise, stroking the ruler-dominated pupils into God-fearing and, more often, rebellious subjects of academia. The difference is that disciplined Catholic schools forced the inmates to learn at a young and impressionable age; that is not totally bad because in the spoiled Western world, where anything goes (like wearing pants with half the backside hanging out), the clients are going to learn or receive a boot in the backside for lack of trying. Not to say this commandant type learning is optimal but is better than the free-for-all education experienced in the unenlightened school systems of the world. The point to be made is there must be a balanced approach to living and learning. We try to learn from our mistakes. This is the meaning of enlightenment. The phrase 'history repeats itself' seems to indicate the same old mistakes will go on. This presupposes a lack of enlightenment from generation to generation, and will certainly be true if we allow the same dilapidated norms to be perpetuated time and again, i.e., keeping the people ignorant and gullible.

Recently we had a door-bell visitation from the ubiquitous bible proselytizers whether Jehovah salesman or what not. I opened the door to observe an old man about 75 with a 20-year-old, pretty Filipina (nice work if you can get it) and I politely told him to hit the road. You might wonder why these salesmen don't sell their wares in poor neighborhoods that need salvation rather than affluent ones. They fortuitously avoid the ghettoes where the reception might become a crime scene. Similarly, religious missionaries regularly ply the waters of foreign countries that are easy prey for western indoctrination such as south-east Asia, rather than helping the great unwashed in Newark or Detroit who can benefit just as well.

There is another type of Boot Camp called the job interview. As a young pup, I was interviewed by a financial company in New Jersey for a broker's position in their small investment firm. He looked down at my resume, looked up at me, and repeated this procedure several times, increasing my nerves and moving me to the edge of my seat. Then, he proceeded to tear me down like a raw recruit, before building me back up and swearing I was just the man for the job. Of course the recruit went AWOL. Upon a suggestion, my brother Michael took an interview *and* the job, but due to certain shenanigans, part of the remuneration turned out to be financial ruin. The company supported the 16-year search by treasure hunter Mel Fisher of Key West, Florida. His Treasure Salvors, Incorporated, finally located the Spanish wreck

Atocha that went down in the Gulf of Mexico during a hurricane in the year 1622. My brother literally had some of the booty, a pocketful of rare gold coins, but lost it all—argh, mateys!

The enormous struggle for existence is amazing because it is a product of millions of years of evolution from single cell organisms to the somewhat complex life forms now available in your neighborhood. Today you make of it as you can or as you wish, to a certain extent. True, if you are serving tea in Bombay (now called Mumbai to confuse), choices are few and far between and a good deal of work or luck is required for escape to better digs. (Dreams will get you nowhere but a good kick in the pants will take you a long way, Baltasar Gracian).

For the well off, choices abound and the sky is really the limit. If you think your neighborhood is bad, take a look at Bangladesh but don't eat the fish or drink the water. One of our large seafood restaurant chains is the chief customer for Bangladesh shrimp. The farming of shrimp ruins the field for productive crops, so as you munch on the shrimpy critters, you are sucking the blood of the poor in that impoverished country.

It's too bad that many of us do not recognize life's potential or accomplish the things we dream of. Most people are on autopilot and coasting along to the tune of what others imagine them to be.

You want to do *what*?

You want to *be* what?

No way!

People need the tools to get the job done but these are plainly missing from the average child's upbringing. Even the parents are not aware of what is required to steer a proper course. The lucky ones have the resources available, such as money, and a keen awareness of how to focus their attention. With the needed resources, a focused guide can provide a sober and serious assessment of choices and alternatives. That was lacking in my Catholic High School since the guidance councilors were first and foremost the jock coaches for 'ball playing.'

The current prospects appear dim; in the good old days you

had a job for life, but now you have a life of looking for jobs. Youthful aspirations assert I want to be a fireman, a doctor, or an astronaut. At this early stage, it is all they know; they see and imitate. "Life is what happens to you while you're busy making other plans" (John Lennon). Obviously a king's son will be a king but what of the Bombay tea boy? The middle-class lad will "fall into something" as Mr. Macabre would say in the Charles Dickens book (*David Copperfield*). Something will turn up.

For the majority it all comes down to happenstance. I wanted to be a Harvard biologist but I got a job on Wall Street peddling blondes or bonds. I'm stuck in the rat race and I can't get out. No, you can get out, but it takes work and imagination. How do you teach or encourage imagination? It's not on the average curriculum in school or evidenced at home. Not everyone needs to be imaginative, at least not on the job. Yes we need bricklayers, electricians, and manual laborers, but those employments should be filled with those who naturally gravitate there and are content with that. But to aspire to rocket science and end up somewhere else is a sad affair. So the role of education is to make sure that the hopeful rocket scientist gets to the lab, and to guide students to their respective places in life. To give purpose to people's lives is to make a better place for all. That's the true mark of a great educator—to inspire. We can move up in the world with this idea, or we can continue to watch the malefactors spread havoc due to the ignorance and corruption of a failed system of education.

My parents raised seven characters but Dad if truth be told hated his life and/or government job towards the end of his career. He was lost in a rat race that he joined but wanted out of. Dad had the world on a string, but I suppose he regretted moving from New York City, with simply the memories of stickball, Yankees baseball, and the culture of city life. My father was an intelligent fellow and I can't recall him ever doling out physical punishment although his five boys tried his patience a bit. He could devastate with words such as "uncouth" in response to the snickering blare of farting. He also had a wonderful way of twisting his facial muscles such that the nose and lips quickly jerked to the right and just as quickly released; this was a sign of disapproval or disapprobation that I have adopted for similar reasons. It is a unique gesture that requires no words and is similar to the Filipino use of the lips for pointing or the lifted eyebrows to indicate approval or affirmation. Retribution, on the other hand, was left for my mother (wait till your father comes home!) who could instill the fear of God, but more likely the fear from a fiery Irish temper when riled. And a bar of the popular white soap is no less palatable in the mouth as it feels on the outside of the skin.

Mayhem takes its toll. For example, when my two older brothers and I were bathing in the tub at seven, six, and four, a huge commotion was abruptly responded to by our dad. Evidently, I spontaneously unleashed a submarine of a bowel movement to the whoops and howls of my siblings (when you have to go, you've gotta go). Our dad, who had the tendency to instill either fear or laughter by removing his trousers belt, doubling the leather, and snapping it with an inward/outward two-handed motion, was quite beside himself with snapping then.

During his formative years, he might have had the world on a string, but later on in life, he undoubtedly found the world had *him* on a string like a puppet, or in the ring like a rope-a-dope fighter. Bless him, but perhaps he could have changed his life with some tough choices; he might have changed course and made not only himself contented, but the rest of the family by association. That unhappy life did not translate to peaches and cream for the others around him.

It's a matter of saying, "Listen family, I have to make some changes and it might not be easy, but it will be better for all of us over the long haul." You can change your life or turn it around if necessary when circumstances warrant such action. And it's never too late, especially if you have the guts and determination to see the benefits. My dad was from the old school, the era of the depression, and was not predisposed to turn any corner if it meant taking a big risk. He hid the bottle in the cellar like any loyal partisan would in times of trouble. However, since I consider that a character flaw, bottles in our house are always out in the open for inspection or consumption.

Morality and Ethics

If there is not a clear-cut purpose in life, there are at least some decent targets to aim for, such as helping someone else. This might be one of the primary driving forces of life, but in his book, *The Selfish Gene*, Richard Dawkins advises: "Let us try to teach generosity and altruism, because we are born selfish."[1] The phrase "nice guys finish last" concisely describes his belief that we are machines created by our genes, and a predominant quality to be expected in a successful gene is ruthless selfishness. On the other hand, the primatologist Frans De Wall, in *The Age of Empathy*, describes that we are preprogrammed through evolution to reach out to others, and that empathy is an automated response over which we have limited control. Humans and some other animals are very sensitive to fairness. Human fairness goes hand in hand with communal survival.[2] Frans De Wall indicates that the main reason humans seek fairness is to avoid negative consequences of perceived inequity. Even chimpanzees can go ballistic when they feel snubbed. In one instance, a perceived slight during a food incident resulted in two chimpanzees chewing off a man's nose, face, and buttocks; they tore off his foot and bit off both testicles. We are all sensitive creatures; if you don't think so, try this experiment which I call, *what's in a name?* Start calling someone you know by a different name, and watch the reaction.

We find it easier to identify with those like us, with the same cultural background, ethnic features, age, gender, job—and even more so with those close to us, such as spouses, children, and friends.[3] Hence the saying "blood is thicker than water." The cited book is terrific but I disagree with the monkey man on page 200 that "Robin Hood had it right. Humanity's deepest wish is to spread the wealth." I see this as a left-leaning propensity to give the farm away.

Besides Dawkins and De Wall, there are innumerable men of science who have followed in the footsteps of one of the most brilliant of all. Darwin's *Theory of Evolution* was based on natural selection (survival of the fittest).[4] Although the title contains the word "theory," it is actually considered a fact that there is a gradual process by which the living world has developed following the origin of life. Darwinism includes a set of concepts to include the theory of common descent and natural selection, whereby individuals strive for success to pass on their genes while the species as a whole benefits.

Natural selection is a process involving chance or randomness, particularly in the production of genetic variation. And it is the randomness of variation that is responsible for the tremendous diversity of living creatures. It is not viewed by many biologists as the necessary progress or progression as some see it. Rather it is a process without significant direction and therefore life has no ultimate meaning or goal directed position.

The famous quote from Charles Darwin in *The Origin of Species* reads, "I am inclined to look at everything as resulting from designed laws, with the details, whether good or bad, left to the working out of what we may call chance."[5] Darwin did not mean chance in the vernacular senses of random, without meaning, or incapable of explanation. By stating the proviso, "what we may call chance," he implicated a view of life for which he had no word, but which historians now call contingency. Nature's facts (the details) exist for immediate and definite reasons subject to scientific explanation. But these facts are not integrated into any controlling fabric of a planned and deterministic universe, with intended meaning in the fall of each petal and every raindrop.[6]

The fact that mammals and later humans were able to evolve with the extinction of the dinosaurs is a matter of circumstance or chance contingency as expressed by Stephen Jay Gould. Our lucky break was caused by a meteor slamming earth 65 million years ago that spelled doom for King Kong and T-Rex. Consciousness evolved by chance in our animal relatives and is not a necessary and predictable step on the way of evolution. If time were rolled back 4.5 billion years to the earth's formation, the chance is slim to none that beings with consciousness would evolve again, according to scientists such as Gould. It wasn't a directed or voluntary process by the gods. Just as erosion by water for millions of years is the cause and effect for many of the earth's dramatic geological features, such as the Grand Canyon, it is a mechanical and elemental process without emotion or intent. It is only the conscious but simple humans who read intent and structure from clouds in the sky.

It took Darwin many years before he published *The Origin of Species* in 1859. He wrote a friend in 1856: "What a book a devil's chaplain might write on the clumsy, wasteful, blundering, low, and horribly cruel works of nature." It's really not a good news/bad news story, but the good news is that we must admire Darwin for his tremendous insights, but on the other hand, we came to understand and cope with the cosmic indifference to us.

From caveman to spaceman is a story of how to control fire, how to manipulate tools, how to control food and water shortages and perhaps most importantly: how to control other humans! As in Hollywood or Bollywood, there have always been the good guys and bad guys with the evolved brain as the arbiter of cultural issues. Morality goes far back in human history and is a consequence of human evolution. Physiologically our ancestors knew to put a hand on the fire was wrong and to eat tasty fruit that didn't kill you was right. And therefore it is easy to imagine the extrapolation to more abstract concepts: is it right or wrong to club thy neighbor? It depends of course if he is on the same team; naturally if he looks different—the club. Is it right or wrong to womanize? It depends of course if one gets caught—no different from the current crop of priests, reverends, and politicians.

There have been stacks of books written on the subject of ethics. Paul Ehrlich explains in *Human Natures*: "Human nature is clearly the result of biological and cultural evolution, and in some sense the ethical feelings and behaviors that are part of our nature must have arisen through these same processes. There is no sign that ethics are transcendental, that they exist without empirical explanation by human minds or human history."[7] Ethics indicates that only humans with the faculty of language have formulated a set of standards of right and wrong behavior that prescribe what they *ought* to do. You often hear that, without the presence of a heavenly superintendent, humans would have no reason for good or moral behavior. But there is no evidence that doubters are less law-abiding than believers or consider themselves exempt from the Golden Rule "Do unto others as you would have them do unto you." So ethics are a construct of cultural evolution that gave us a moral code of conduct to include empathy, altruism, and justice. These ancient sentiments contributed to survival and reproductive success through time. Ethical systems and indoctrination were formalized with the acquisition of language and writing. By the dawn of civilization, one had no question as to who was in charge, i.e., the director or boss.

Society has experienced a string of atrocious ethical offenses such as the following list:

- [ ] Bernie Madoff was jailed in 2009 for defrauding investors of $50 billion.
- [ ] Catholic Priest sex abuse scandals continue for decades and are worldwide.
- [ ] The Enron Corporation bilked investors of nearly $11 billion in 2001.
- [ ] The U.S. invaded Iraq in 2003 on faulty grounds at a cost in excess of $750B.
- [ ] Mortgage-backed securities and housing scandals started in 2007.
- [ ] The Federal Reserve committed nearly $8 trillion in previously undisclosed loans to the nation's banking system.
- [ ] The Solyndra Company (solar energy) was given a $535 million loan guarantee in 2009 and filed for bankruptcy in 2011.

- MF Global, a major global financial derivatives broker in 2011, headed by a former New Jersey governor, represents the 8th largest bankruptcy in American history with a $1.2 billion theft of investor's funds. How was this possible? Crony capitalism.

- In March 2012, U.S. authorities charged 29 people with smuggling $325 million in counterfeit consumer goods from China, including phony sneakers and handbags, through Port Newark-Elizabeth Marine Terminal. The bust was one of the largest counterfeiting probes in U.S. history.

- In February 2012, federal authorities made arrests in the most expansive case of Medicare fraud to date. The case involved a Dallas doctor and dozens of home-health providers accused of bilking taxpayers for more than $375 million in bogus claims. A few months later, more than 100 people were charged with an estimated $450 million of false billings to defraud various federal health programs.

- In December 2012, American authorities stated that the British bank HSBC had helped Mexican drug traffickers, Iran, Libya and others under U.S. suspicion or sanction to move money around the world. HSBC agreed to pay $1.9 billion, the largest penalty ever imposed on a bank. Not one person went to jail, alluding to the idea of "too big to prosecute."

- Imagine the grand thefts that we don't know about!

The top guns are stealing millions while the poor are jailed for pilfering pennies. Whether in the outback or the city, humans seek justice. And during these days, they get it alright. I was summoned in 2011 for the first time on jury duty and upon arriving at the designated one of two courthouses in downtown Dallas, looked up at the steps of that imposing 14-storey building like it was the Parthenon. I muttered to myself, "Yeah, this is justice." I was lucky to get there amidst the crazy construction on dirty, one-way streets, and arrived with the added benefit of paying for parking. Meanwhile, the minions are subjected to annual sessions on Ethics Training and must sign forms to certify they will not pilfer the treasury as their superiors are lining their tailored and deep pockets. You would need more than an abacus to count the politicians who are routinely caught with their hands in the federal till—but who's counting? I ask why they are not in Hollywood instead of the Capitol since the acts of proclaimed innocence are worthy of academy awards. While they snicker behind mouth-covered hand, government officials convene conferences and committees to "study the problem" and their corporate brethren print ethics manuals by the gross for distribution to the humble pie in their employ. In the good old days of the American Wild West, Jesse James was known as a legendary outlaw who robbed banks and trains of some thousands of greenbacks. Jesse seems quaint and whimsical compared to the current band of banditos who are stealing tens of billions of dollars.

Pundits love to debate conflict and wars. I must say that the Iraq war that started on 19 March 2003 (Operation Iraqi Freedom) did not make sense to me. The guy at the top made a monumental error. You do not stir up the hornet's nest if you are in the exterminating business. Many more Islamic converts to terror and violence were recruited by his cowboy mentality and gun slinging. Even very moderate Muslims in the Middle East were incensed enough to join the team of Bin Laden and Company.

But one thing is certain; the American people fancy a good shock and awe, especially if the Command allows the footage to be televised for our viewing pleasure. Indeed the previous Iraq war in 1990 (Operation Desert Storm) involved an enormous load of weapons and bombing. During that first Iraq war, approximately 227,000 bombs and missiles were expended by U.S. fixed-wing aircraft. For the 2003 Iraq war, they used 29,900 munitions but they were more advanced.[8]

While we were in Qatar during the 2003 Iraq War, someone sent me one of the video clips of an American F-15 airstrike in

Afghanistan. The mission involved three components to include the F-15 aircraft, a forward observer, and command and control operator. The video starts with approximately 15 bearded cockroaches (Taliban) exiting a concrete building and running down a dirt road:

Forward Observer: I have the target in sight, do you copy?

Aircraft F-15 pilot: Roger that.

Command and Control: What is their position, over?

Forward Observer: The group has left the building and they're running away, over.

Aircraft F-15 Pilot: Should I take them out?

Command and Control: Take them out.

Next you see the upshot of a M61A1 Gatling gun which has a variable rate of fire of between 4,000 and 7,200 rounds of 20 mm cannon shells per minute. One might imagine the remains are indistinguishable from the dirt road.

The video ends with a statement by the **Forward Observer:** Whoa! Dude!!

There is no doubt that we have the greatest military on Earth. I have had some part in it and was able to work on Coast Guard boats, ships, and aircraft as well as obtain flights with the Army on the Black Hawk helicopter in Honduras and Korea, the C-130 Hercules aircraft in Panama, and the KC-135 Stratotanker from Saudi to Dakota. I believe we need a competent military force but they have been inappropriately used on a continual basis. U.S. troops are stationed at hundreds of installations in scores of nations around the globe. Although the country is running on financial fumes, we continue to maintain commitments that do not make sense in the Teddy Roosevelt approach of, "Speak softly and carry a big stick." We are all familiar with the oxymoron "Military Intelligence" just as we hear of the "Noble Savage."

Whether it is the U.S. military or the United Nations, large institutions with world-wide locations, are rife with waste and fraud. For example, government lawyers are occupied full time with the numerous cases of disappearing dollars from the wars and reconstruction expenditures. What a business; you destroy a country and then rebuild it afterward! Then you import boatloads of the people who will not assimilate, but work for less, and alienate and frustrate the rest of the American inhabitants.

In many countries, transactions involve *"baksheesh"* or bribes as a normal business practice. Here is one example of how it's done. In overseas procurement offices, they are supposed to solicit competitive bids to obtain fair and reasonable prices. But some foreign contractors have multiple sister companies that submit collusive bids with noncompetitive prices. Now if the procuring official is dishonest, he can leak the price of honest bidders to allow the undercutting of the bidding process. And by rotating the awards to the sister companies there is less exposure of collusion with only a single foreign contractor. There is a lot of scratch-my-back larceny that is endemic in the academic and professional world. For instance, think of the thousands of *conferences* held every day throughout the world. Here's how it works for some: you invite me to your conference for a $15,000 speaker's fee, and I will return the favor and invite you for a similar fee at *my* next conference. The practice goes unnoticed because most conferences involve esoteric topics and are generally not open to the public. This is an interesting notion. Oh how I would like total information access to the Swiss Bank accounts. You could imagine what a fantastic read that book would be with all the dirty and black money stashed away by the various characters. However, the Swiss recently came under pressure to ease banking rules with certain countries, granting assistance in cases of tax fraud; but Switzerland is not abandoning its banking secrecy laws.

Frankly, I can't stand the military (Army) mindset in that every young cub or seasoned old hand refers to himself as a Commander and they constantly proclaim the words Command, Commander, and worst of all *Leader*. We were in Qatar for three years, before 9/11 through the Iraq war 2001-2004. At the time of our arrival, Qatar was a sleepy but rich country, due mainly to natural gas. Qatar is a thumb-size country jutting from the Arabian Peninsula and slightly smaller than the state of

Connecticut. The leaders at the Camp paid a local company for a Headstart Training Class for American personnel to include Arab history, language, and customs. We couldn't believe it, but they invited a Qatari Imam (religious leader) to speak to the class audience that included these young, impressionable troops. He told them that they should reflect on their actions and check their conscience before killing Muslims. Why not invite the fox to the henhouse? And you won't believe where this black Imam was originally from—Brooklyn, New York! Holy Cow! (As Phil Rizzuto of the Yankees used to exclaim). The Iraq War ended in December 2011, and here is a good laugh, academics and bona fide writers will be occupied for many years, researching the many benefits of the crusade.

The word security was once upon a time, a wholesome and appreciated term. But after the tragedy of 9/11 and the ensuing wars in Iraq, Afghanistan, ad nauseum, it is now a dreaded word and sounds akin to fingernails on a blackboard. If I hear the term Military Intelligence, it's time to run for the hills.

Working in Qatar during the Iraq war was tedious enough with the overwhelming precautions and security measures. Upon entering the Army's Camp As-Saliyah, vehicles were subject to inspection by the combination of U.S. DynCorp contractor employees and guards from Nepal. They used undercarriage mirrors, electronic explosive detectors, a physical inspection of interiors and trunks, *and* the dogs. One fine morning, I had to drop some report at the nearby U.S. Air Base, Al-Udeid. Both locations are outside the capital of Doha in the dusty desert or in other words, it's not Palm Springs. One of my co-workers came along, and we delivered the report, with the usual vehicle searches before returning to the camp. Unfortunately, during our return vehicle inspection, the frisky dog sat down which indicated a bomb or other nasty item to the security personnel. Mama Mia! All hell broke loose and both of us were immediately separated and interrogated some 100 yards away. They swore and claimed there was C-4 explosive in the rear interior of my spanking new, government-provided Chevy Tahoe! They did most everything except repel out of helicopters. One of the

EOD (Explosive Ordnance Disposal) sergeants even had some scrapings of the supposed material. Security tried to sell the idea some terrorists or perpetrators entered my locked vehicle for their nefarious intrigues. But since my vehicle is driven by a master organizer, and ever so clean, it would seem an impossible scenario. I mumbled something to the affect that, come-on this is some kind of exercise or drill, right?

The circus went on for several weeks as if we were suspected of "bin-doing something." *Where did you go and did you make any other stops? Now, let's go over this one more time, and we need to get this recorded and on paper; raise your right hand and can you describe your whereabouts one more time? At 7PM, "hello this is the security sergeant calling, and can we go over that morning's events again for the record?"*

Luckily, both of us stuck to the story of driving to the Air Base, and not leaving our vehicle otherwise. However, we performed some extra driving for the purpose of "area orientation." I was *not* about to say something stupid such as stopping to buy a case of beer and depositing the beverages at our apartments. It should be noted that in Qatar, one can buy a drink in the swanky hotels such as the superb Ritz Carlton, but there is only one place to buy beer or booze for home consumption; the QDC (Qatar Distribution Center) requires a stamped permit from the employer, a $275 refundable deposit, application form, copy of your passport and residence permit, plus certification of religion (no problem). The foregoing was only a tidbit for the potential tourists among the readers. In the grand scheme of things, we wouldn't admit to such a schlep, especially on company time—no, sir.

In the final analysis, I was informed after several weeks that my Chevy Tahoe was available for pickup; it was sitting all by its lonesome in the desert dirt at a considerable distance near the perimeter fence.

During my time in government, I had three passports: the Black (Diplomatic), the Red (Official U.S. Government), and the Blue (Civilian). Even with the diplomatic passport, my bags were searched at London's Heathrow Airport because my passport included a stamp from Jordan. With the Official passport, I was questioned in the Schiphol Amsterdam airport, and coffee notwithstanding, they inquired as to why I seemed nervous.

During a visit to the UK from Saudi, I proposed that my two brothers in New Jersey fly to Heathrow and meet our wealthy, distant cousin from London. When I cleared customs, a silver-haired gentleman approached me with an identification card and stated, "Mr. Kingsley, I am from Interpol and need to question you." Being circumspect and suspicious by nature and experience, I asked to look at his identification more closely, and stated, "Hey, this shows Prudential Finance!" It was the wily cousin (of Irish descent) who was trying to pull my leg. Nothing would surprise me about "security measures" and the associated personnel. Many of them pretend to be a CIA spook, James Bond, Rambo, or Jack Bauer. I know, it's all for our own good. Tell that to the 90-year-old grandmother as Airport Security drags her out the wheelchair for a pat down. That's why the Italians have an expression, "*Cavone!*"

Before the Iraq war, I was exercising at the Intercontinental Hotel in Qatar when a fire alarm drill sounded. I went outside and it seemed all the employees were there and just me. After the war started, all the premium hotels were constantly booked. So war is good for business.

The fall of Saddam Hussein led to a thriving business of currency speculation. The new Iraqi dinars were purchased by outside investors who hoped to profit from the country's new currency when the economy improved. The 2013 exchange rate, as specified by the IMF, is 1170 dinars per U.S. dollar at the Central Bank of Iraq. But there is still no set exchange rate and so international banks do not yet exchange Iraqi dinars. Small fortunes were spent on this currency mania and even my wife bought 600,000 dinars in Qatar which converts to about $512 (not the best of investments). As a side note, I was fairly surprised at the amount of hanky-panky that was going on in the military in Qatar between both sexes, married or otherwise. Supposedly it is not quite a state secret but they try to keep it hush-hush, and remember, sign that ethics form *tra-la.*

The Leaders in our Army camp used warehouses to accommodate the troops, and shipping containers were outfitted as living space for two people, to include beds, TV, and storage space. The containers were stacked-up, maybe four containers high with metal stairs constructed for access. We spent a short time in one of these containers. The warehouse's restroom facility was quite large with dozens of showers, sinks, and toilets. It sort of shocked me in the morning, that with all those guys doing their business, not one word was spoken, just silence, no jokes or kibitzing. It appeared sad and "shit, shower and shave" will never be the same (Hoo-ah!). You can forget about making any intelligent suggestions relative to the wasted expenditures by the military.

In 2013, the federal government employed about two million civilian employees and 1.4 million military personnel. But most people don't realize the armed forces employ over 750,000 contractor personnel at a staggering cost. They learned from past missteps, and now have the general public in an unquestioning, flag-flying form. The country went bi-polar from the questioning days of Vietnam to (hush-up!) suppressing information or access of the media to the battlefield. They conditioned and bamboozled the public to accept as taboo, any dissent relating to the military, its troops and veterans. For example, no one would argue the need for disability benefits for *bona fide* injuries, but it is scandalous that questionable claims for partial disability are paid like many of the union police and fire departments. After all, it is impossible to refute an assertion of back pain or other similar anomalies.

The government and media use the term "boots on the ground" in lieu of a term for real, live people. That seems odd doesn't it? What do we need troops on the ground for anyway these days? Isn't aerial bombardment sufficient and why don't they subcontract the cleanup to some other country that makes boots.

The federal government has a baffling array of procurement laws and regulations that makes it virtually impossible to properly purchase the annual $500 billion of products and services. For example, I defy anyone to makes sense and explain the Buy American Act and the Trade Agreements Act (see Federal Acquisition Regulation, Part 25) (Good luck since the laws and regulations are written by *law-yas*). Over a period of many decades, the various congressional laws have carved-up the federal carcass, at taxpayer expense, to feed the various jackals in the military-industrial complex as well as the corporate and other societal leeches. To the uninitiated, the military-industrial system is a revolving door of government functionaries who scratch backs as their "open sez me" onto the corporate carpets (shades of Ali Baba and the Forty Thieves). It is part of the scene called crony capitalism. Although the big boys get the best of the kill, the government in 2013 doles out some portions and crumbs as follows:

- 23% of all prime contracts are to be set aside for small businesses.

- 5% of all prime and subcontracts is to be set aside for small disadvantaged businesses.

- 5% of all prime and subcontracts is to be set aside for woman-owned businesses.

- 3% of all prime contracts are to be set aside for HUB Zone small businesses.

- 3% of all the same is to be set aside for to Service Disabled Vet-Owned Small businesses.

The government tries to legislate its way towards moral issues and income distribution, which is perfect for front companies who pretend to be one of the above minority-owned or other selected enterprises. Most people are aware that the government is a poster child for waste and corruption and a few funny examples will demonstrate this proposition. During the Iraq war, the Army required bottled water at one particular installation, but they requested sodium-free water for the troops since they believed it was more healthful. When the supply sergeant was questioned about the requisition, and the fact that personnel were loaded with salt in the mess hall that served everything from burgers with French fries, steak and lobster, they wanted the expensive sodium-free water regardless. The procurement office used a credit card to purchase $50,000 (not a kosher transaction and quite inappropriate) of this water from Germany to be delivered by ship, and they followed that up with another $50,000 credit card purchase. When the shipments were finally delivered, no one really had a handle on who took possession of the numerous pallets or whether they were all accounted for. I *do* know that one of the fair-haired, civilian ladies at the installation used the sodium-free water to wash her hair because the gossip suggested you could experience hair loss from the local faucets. Imagine spending $100,000 for sodium-free water bottles and the installation was in a peaceful, non-combat country of Qatar in the Middle East! In another instance, the same office purchased a large shredder or disintegrator from a U.S. company for $13,000 but spent $23,000 to ship the machine by Federal Express. The bottom line is we are broke but continue to pour money down the drain. Although the General Accountability Office (GAO), the congressional watchdog, has uncovered hundreds of billions in wasteful spending, the beat goes on.

There was a news report on the internet dated 31 August 2011: "*Widespread waste and fraud in war spending.*" That same article could run any day of any month in any year. FAR Part 3 contains everything you wanted to know about standards of conduct and violations. There is a lot of money involved here, and remember, sign your ethics form (*Hee Hee!*).

Today ethics is out the window—it's a free for all now. The news of the day is the have-nots are still here and salivating, but there are more of them around and there will be many more tomorrow.

It is advocated that capitalism is the best economic system. In The Wealth of Nations, Adam Smith demonstrated that, in a free market, an individual pursuing his own self-interest tends to promote the good of his community through a principle that he called "the invisible hand." He argued that each individual, who goes after revenue for himself, maximizes the total revenue of society as a whole. The world is struggling with this concept in view of the hungry faces outside our window. Something must be done to prevent or mitigate the possibility of anarchy and chaos and we need to start with discipline and education right away.

Pirate best describes the character of commerce today. Pirates were, once upon a time, a sacred part of the imagination with the likes of Blackbeard and Captain Kidd, but the notion has been made sacrilegious by mass marketing. The fascination is no longer fancied from the stories of *Treasure Island*, one of my all-time favorites, where the young Jim Hawkins meets the mysterious and ragged old seaman, Billy Bones and the peg-legged Long John Silver. Robert Louis Stevenson once said the seed for the novel and *"Dead Man's Chest"* came from a list of island names in a book by Charles Kingsley (no relation to the author) in reference to Dead Chest Island in the British Virgin Islands.

- *Fifteen men on a dead man's chest* **Yo ho ho and a bottle of rum.**

- *Drink and the devil had done for the rest* **Yo ho ho and a bottle of rum.**

In Robert Louis Stevenson's *Kidnapped*, David Balfour is shanghaied by the murderous Captain Hoseason of the Covenant, but is set free with the help of Allan Breck who gives his companion a silver button from his uniform as a calling card to the Scottish highlands.

One of the best venues for the pirate experience is the water ride, *Pirates of the Caribbean* in the Disney theme parks, "Yo Ho, Yo Ho, A Pirate's Life for Me." It's a wonderful attraction for young and old alike, but upon exiting, customers are obliged to navigate through the pirate shop and drown in a sea of mass merchandizing (to rob the booty in your pockets). It has become big business so the corporate interests have beaten the idea to death with the following sales:

Hoist the Jolly Roger! Conformity rules like tattoos and earring Skull & crossbones with red bandana and eye patch—I don't get that one, but there's no accounting for taste:

Movies
Toys for toddlers
Video games
Cartoons with clownish pirate and pirate-playing imps
Broadway and London plays such as the *Pirates of Penzance*
Pirate Soul Museum in Key West, Florida
Taverns and restaurants
Festivals, pirate walks, and pirate talks
Rummy Rums

I'm not particularly interested in the distinction between pirates, buccaneers, or privateers. Basically pirates were seafarers who were known to steal the gold, but mostly silver, from the thieves who plundered the inhabitants of South America. Some were freelance and others such as Francis Drake, whose name struck fear in the Spanish colonies, and who had a hand in the English defeat of the 1588 Spanish Armada, operated with the nod of the Queen.

In the 1790s, President Thomas Jefferson was fed-up with the policy of paying tribute to the Muslim pirates of North Africa who used their Koran and judged the infidel Americans ripe for plunder. A series of American engagements led to the birth of the U.S. Navy and Marine Corps ("From the Halls of Montezuma, to the Shores of Tripoli") such that by 1815, pirate attacks on American commercial ships in North Africa were effectively ended. Today there are many more pirates than roamed the ports of the Caribbean, but they now wear suits and their Jolly Roger is a tie around the neck.

Dreams and Dreamers

Dreams are part of our reality but seem the red-headed stepchild of our mind. Dreams elude scientific understanding and are thought to cover either psychological duties such as problem solving, or physiological functions that include *day residue* and *cleaning the software*. People generally know that the body's senses interact with the brain, especially while we are awake and conscious. The body reacts to the environment and receives signals to deal with hunger, danger, and other survival aspects. Various brain structures orchestrate conscious thought. For example, the prefrontal cortex is regarded as the seat of humanity since it affects empathy, foresight, and personality. Freud contended that dreams are a connection to the unconscious mind for wish fulfillment. He emphasized the interpretation of symbols found in dreams and related them to repressed sexual desires. Therefore, a dream of driving through a tunnel really translates to the idea of sexual intercourse—such imagination! But he did note that, sometimes a cigar is just a cigar. We are not pretending to be Daniel Dennett or looking for a Nobel Prize here, so the following ideas are speculative in nature. Before the triumph of language, there was some form of thinking on a primitive level. Wakeful ancestors managed life by instinct and cunning to include determining prey/predator, tool making, and day dreaming about the girl next door—you know; the nine-to-five drag. It seems that even animals dream such that you see a dog twitch and yelp in the sleeping state. Animals also think on some level so they can memorize where objects are located, and they can read your intentions to a certain extent. For example, dogs feel guilt when they do some behavior that the pet owner dislikes.

We differentiate between the brain and mind and some liken these to the hardware and software of the body respectively. The human brain gives us a mind to reason with. The organ has dozens of structures and various neural circuits that work in tandem. There are circuits for short and long-term memory, decision making, and many other purposes. It's strange that some people can recall breakfast from 20 years back, but others cannot remember what they had for lunch yesterday. Actually we have a load of bric-a-brac constantly on our minds, but there is a need for some forgetfulness because humans need a clear mind to navigate the pitfalls of existence. We must not hold on to every sight and sound in order to avoid appearing as zombies walking in a fog.

On a simple level, dreams are like a projector or projection of scenarios. Dogs do not dream with any language involved, and probably dream of a dog's life. They were bred for various traits like loyalty and hunting. Similarly, our early ancestors probably dreamed of animals, the new girl on the block, and symbols such as snake-shaped objects.

Some scientists contend that the early ones did not differentiate between being wakeful or dreaming. That reminds me of a Filipina who believed there were ghosts in the trees; this struck me as an odd cultural idea that almost resembles a dreaming state. We wonder if infants dream and they probably do so at a very early age.

In another off-hand remark, there are these crazy adults who actually market books about teaching philosophy to your toddlers. I was lost at university in the midst of Immanuel Kant, but it seems lunatic to peddle it to little tots!

The typical adult dream is like the one I had recently. I am in a car in my old hometown, and after backing up, I see the police behind me with lights flashing. The policeman walks to my driver's side window, which I lower, but it is actually a nun and she starts whispering to me (sorry Sigmund, not sweet nothings) but I can't understand what she is saying. At least I awoke before getting a ticket but this is the usual nonsense that constitutes most people's dreams.

The old saying that a picture is worth a thousand words connotes something about dreams. Ancestors painted images on cave walls—it speaks to us, art and music. Why do musical notes hit us in the gut? Dreams are a projection of events and the moderns look to interpretations of dreams as having some relevance with monetary value.

Do dreams represent some remnant of the primitive brain that serve no modern purpose as some believe? Why do we dream of relatives not seen for many years who appear to us during sleep like we never left them? When I nod-off for a few seconds while reading a Dickens's novel, the brain switches tracks to a different projector; I was consciously reading *David Copperfield*, but immediately an amorphous scene is projected that is totally foreign to the book on my dozing lap. We don't dream only in the REM (Rapid Eye Movement) cycle of sleep. Neurologists have documented certain brain dysfunctions that affect thinking such as schizophrenia which points to the gray line between dreaming and the conscious state. There is also drug induced perception with the use of hallucinogens such as peyote and LSD that seem to cause dream states. The person using the drug might see monkeys walking past them rather than other people, and this indicates that brain activity can be deceiving. For instance, there is no credible evidence for ESP (extra sensory perception) and self-proclaimed psychics are as fraudulent as astrology. Some people advocate that there are extra-ordinary senses, like being able to discern when others are looking at you. The extreme notion of this is Carlos Castaneda whose books advocated a reality of beings just beyond your peripheral vision. All of us have experience with Coo-Coo birds and most of them are relatives unfortunately.

Dreams give the impression of meshing or tangling everyday experience in a jumble of crazy associations. Is there some evolutionary advantage to this staged forgery or are dreams meaningless? Most people have had the experience of passing a stranger on the sidewalk. But in some instances, for no apparent reason, we instantly feel an extreme dislike and the blood boils. Was it the body language, because we certainly did not speak to each other? The experience finally passes like a shadow and we later scratch our head and wonder what *that* was all about? Perhaps the brain will shelve that experience and jumble the perpetrators and scenery for a future dream, but this is still unknown.

Cultural activities of the ancients might have had an impact on dreams. The unusual behavior of shamans included magical talents, healing, trance states, divination and rainmaking. Such characters could drive people to a state of physical arousal that bordered on frenzy. They were the original middlemen of the spirit world, and have been influenced by fakery, hallucinogens, as well as mental disorders. These can be scary people and even my wife witnessed trance states in her native (African) country of Eritrea. I can imagine the impression made by animal-skin-clad ancients on the tribesmen, with the accompaniment of drumming and dancing rituals. Life was precarious whether awake or sleeping and dreams would have been exacerbated by the rituals of the tribe. Psychologists will tell you, for instance, that people attend to, and remember, things that are unfamiliar and strange, but not so strange as to be impossible to assimilate.

Children have an innate fear of the dark that derives from our ancestors' foraging lifestyle. To be left alone without protection in the night would have lessened the chance of survival. Contemporary children inherited a fear of the dark, and are not generally subject to hungry animal predators, but cultural experiences such as Frankenstein and Jack's beanstalk would appear to be ready made for dreams, and quite memorable. Some memorable trends become forgettable such as the recurring zombie fad when thousands of our youth don fake blood and guts to dream and sleepwalk like zombies. They seem to be acting out a dreamlike state. The zombie capital of the world is apparently Asbury Park, NJ, where an estimated 13,000 zombies paraded along the boardwalk in October 2011. There is no doubt the Asbury Park record will be exceeded because there are plenty more zombies around. As a youngster, I used to sleepwalk and would find myself downstairs in the living room. My father had the idea of making me sit with him and watch several innings of the New York Yankees at 11:00 PM, which was a sure cure.

Unlike an inorganic item such as a computer that shuts down by a switch, the brain does not shut down, ever. Just as the heart must continue pumping regardless of the state of wakefulness, the brain is continually working. In fact, the brain is the locomotive of the body and uses more energy, ATP (adenosine triphosphate), than any other organ. Yet the brain requires an occasional time-out and therefore a person will nod off for an instant or actually sleep for an extended period. The brain's apparatus switches tracks so to speak and consciousness is not evident. You let go. The brain is thereby empowered to perform housekeeping duties and to recharge various circuits of neurons. But the brain has to work all shifts. By analogy, the brain does not go on vacation but it gets to power-down and is relieved from the sense of being on-duty. It can relax at a lower energy level and switch the thinking apparatus to the more primitive stance and therefore is available on-call. The conscious conductor is not punching tickets but the train rolls on—Rahway! Linden! Elizabeth! Next stop Newark! Who or what is in charge when we nod off or sleep? Could it be the "third string" or more primitive part of the mind? If I nod off for one second, the thoughts immediately switch tracks so that the conscious "I" has no control of the story, and the nun is whispering to me as the car window is cranked down. It might be that dreams are a remnant of a primitive stage of the brain, and the advanced evolution of the human brain, to include the cerebral cortex, has given us conscious thinking.

Dreams are the unconscious relatives of religious belief. In *The Descent of Man* Charles Darwin wrote that a belief in all-pervading spiritual agencies seems to be universal.[9] Scott Atran, the author of *In Gods We Trust*, notes that religious belief is an outgrowth of brain architecture that evolved during early human history.[10] What scientists disagree about is why a tendency to believe evolved, whether it was because belief itself was adaptive or because it was just an evolutionary byproduct, a mere consequence of some other adaptation in the evolution of the human brain. Is religion at its core a vestigial artifact of a primitive mind? Gould and Lewontin introduced the idea of spandrels as any biological feature of an organism that arises as a necessary side consequence of other features, which is not directly selected by natural selection. Since organisms are complex and highly integrated entities, any adaptive change must automatically throw off a series of structural byproducts, like the mold marks on an old bottle or, in the case of an architectural spandrel itself, the triangular space left over between a rounded arch and the rectangular frame of wall and ceiling. Such byproducts may later be co-opted for useful purposes, but they didn't arise as adaptations. Reading and writing are now highly adaptive for humans, but the mental machinery for these crucial capacities must have originated as spandrels that were co-opted later, for the brain reached its current size and conformation tens of thousands of years before any human invented reading or writing. Similarly, it may be possible that conscious thinking and dreaming are related to spandrels of the brain, a side-effect or by-product of some other function.

Matter and Materialism

One of the most exciting topics in the physics community of 2012 was the discovery of the Higgs particle at CERN (The European Organization for Nuclear Research) in Geneva, Switzerland. An international team of scientists work at the Large Hadron Collider, a 17 mile tubular track buried a few hundred meters under Geneva that winds its way across the Swiss-French border and back again. The announcement of the Higgs particle was made nearly 50 years after Peter Higgs published the theoretical groundwork for the elusive particle in 1964. The particle has foolishly been dubbed the *God particle* which sparks media attention and creates unnecessary controversy. The finding correlates to a theory about the nature of reality. The darkness of empty space, with all matter removed, would still be permeated by a Higgs field, redefining the idea of nothingness, and filling otherwise empty space with a substance capable of conferring mass to particles. This field is supposed to act like molasses, exerting a drag force as particles try to accelerate through it. The stickier a particle is, the more the molasses-like Higgs field affects it, and the more massive the particle appears.

Both science and science fiction spawn imaginative ideas. For example, there is some notion of the possibility that either our universe has been manufactured by beings in another universe or we are living in a computer simulation like that of the *Matrix* movies. These insights are interesting to contemplate, but most of us shuffle in the here and now and we require everyday routine in our lives in order to feel normal. If you perceive the glass as half empty, measures should be taken to be more optimistic— not necessarily of the world or society in general, but of your own story-book adventure. I previously referred to myself as a half pint, but what I mean is that my pint glass is half full and not half empty. One suggestion is to reverse personal clutter, both physical and mental. For example, the typical American home and garage are overloaded with cheap possessions of the useful or useless sort. And the extremes of hoarding behavior are probably more common than one would suppose. We should be aware of a general knowledge of psychology such as various defense mechanisms which we employ unconsciously. For example, overcompensation can lead people to keep buying material possessions whether they need them or not. Those who grew up in a poor country and succeeded in emigrating to an affluent one will fill their residence from stem to stern as overcompensation for their meager childhood.

When I was five, our neighbor had every imaginable contraption in his yard, collected from roadside refuse. This included a large, rusting water tank, and during the good old days, when youngsters could ramble, he told me it was a rocket ship that could take me to the moon. I ran back to mom and we returned with a brown-paper bag with the ubiquitous peanut-butter & jelly sandwich for my trip to the moon. (Now my wife wistfully wishes that I *had* gone to the moon, bang-zoom!) But that burly and wonderful Mr. Phillips, jack of all trades, also had a two-car garage filled from stem-to-stern, top to bottom, with roadside junk that he claimed would come in handy one day.

Look at your own residence and determine if clutter is extensive, and take action to maintain a simple lifestyle. It's easy for me to say since I am an organizer. Perhaps most students should attend a course on Organization-101 due to the obvious muddled and jumbled state of their affairs.

I learned a lesson from my mother. What do you call a good-looking Irish girl? Answer: Lucky. Well, my mother was lucky alright, and also had something else I can only describe as elegance that might remind you of Maureen O'Hara. I cannot recall anyone denying any request from my mother. It was unheard of—butter during World War II rationing, no problem. You name it, she could get it. My mother could charm the devil for a cold block for her ice box. But was she organized?—no. She had an interesting cleaning style in that anything and everything went indiscriminately into any drawer. So every bureau and drawer was packed with a hodgepodge of items and it was impossible to find anything.

The old man would ask, "Where's my pen?"

Here Dad, use mine."

Scissors? Forget about it. I know you're going to shake your head with a tsk-tsk, but to this day, I have a scissors in every room of our house and maybe more than one.

Look to the Japanese for some wonderful insights. There's a new notion floating around. Perhaps you've heard of it—*Danshari*. Three kanji characters signify, respectively, refusal, disposal and separation. Prosaically it means cleaning or tidying up, but there are psychological and religious dimensions, deriving in part from yoga, which suggest the disposal of mental, along with physical, junk. One should practice self-reflection and consider consumption patterns and number of possessions.

Hideko Yamashita, a popular writer and speaker on *danshari*, boils it down for us. "Why can't I ditch the possessions—all that stuff accumulated over years and still accumulating? What binds me to them? Is it that things have the upper hand over life? Pack rats are clinging to the past, escaping the present, or frightened of the future. Few of us are none of the above. Most of us, therefore, are probably pack rats. It's a form of madness, as is its relative, compulsive shopping."

You may have heard of the philosophy of Zen—listening to the pattering of a gentle spring rainfall. Zen means waking up to the present moment. That is, perceiving this moment exactly as it is, rather than through the filter of our ideas and living in the now. Each moment, whatever you're doing, just do it. When you're sitting, just sit; when you're eating, just eat; and so on. According to Zen, existence is found in the silence of the mind (no-mind), beyond the chatter of our internal dialog. Existence, from the Zen perspective is something that is only happening spontaneously, and it is not just our thoughts. All of life that we perceive is constantly in a state of change. Every atom in the universe is somewhere different every millionth of a second. Alright, let's move on.

Ghosts, Goblins and Other Illusions

We cannot actually read minds, see ghosts, or verify other metaphysical phenomenon. But the supernatural is very big business indeed—and why not since it is fun? Do you believe in ghosts? It seems there is standing room only for apparitions, as tourists will discover, in countless English castles, halls, hotels, houses and inns. They have been watched, photographed, and interviewed but somehow the film always turns out defective.

Ghosts are contagious and because we are social beings with empathy, it is easy to spook each other. You may recall the Abbott and Costello 1941 comedy, *Hold That Ghost*, where a small group of people frighten each other in the abandoned house of Moose Matson. I have an abiding interest in the unusual, not to say *the dark side*, a phrase that has become stale in recent times. Leave it to the imagination is my motto because it becomes monotonous to gain experience vicariously through movies and television alone. Perhaps I should have been an archeologist with a sign in the shop window "Gone Exploring-Be Back Soon" digging up the past and disturbing the ghostly layabouts of history. Yes, there is a tinge of envy for that profession because it seems an easy sort of life. It's like taking a cruise ship vacation; although we have never taken that opportunity, I'm sure they are just fine, especially if you like the soup-to-nuts treatment without lifting a finger. But when you're younger, or (hem) young at heart, certainly you can explore the world without "Alright darlings let's all get back on the bus!"

Come along with me to the Emerald Island for a minute. We have been to Ireland five times and always fly and rent a car. I inherited a penchant for planning and know precisely where to go but there is always flexibility for side excursions. I don't travel on a lark and try to avoid what the Filipinos called *pee-pee* (poor planning). It only takes about 10 minutes to navigate on the opposite side of the road and off you go on your adventure. It's the out of the way or unusual spots that are of real interest and you generally want to avoid the cruise ships on wheels (the bus) since they are unsightly and do not dress well with the scenery, e.g., charter busses do not routinely pull up to the (five-star) Sheen Falls Hotel in Killarney. Additionally, I try to avoid some obvious dodgy traps like *kissing the Blarney Stone* because I don't bend over backwards generally speaking, and, in my opinion that is baloney. Anyway, not to boast, but I can out-talk and out-sing the Irish. Sometimes roads turn into or become pasture trails and we don't realize it until we see the livestock. We stop and talk to a farmer as he shears his sheep. It's unfortunate that many visitors want to see the whole country in a marathon sort of style; if it's Tuesday then this must be the Ring of Kerry. But I try to visit a location as if we live there, i.e., in a leisurely and timeless frame of mind. I have yet to experience such an excellent place as Ireland, and the only ghosts about were in the mist of my mother's eyes.

Who likes the reverie of John Wayne and Maureen O'Hara in the movie *The Quiet Man?* I have been to Ireland many times, and in 1998, we were scheduled to fly for an Irish vacation. But during that time, my wife's country of Eritrea was fighting a war with the larger neighbor, Ethiopia and thousands marched to their death, just senseless. Ideally, I felt compelled to do something or make a difference and constructed an eight-foot letter, addressed to the famous television icon, Oprah Winfrey, to enlist her support for this tragic state of affairs. The project was sent by Federal Express at a total cost of $1,000, but we had to fly the next morning. I had a notion of contacting the television media to broadcast the project but that was not meant to be. In any event, the celebrity's staff did not respond to my appeal, and so it goes. Perhaps they were more interested in championing off-beat and vacuous authors for her book club. As of 2013, the country of Eritrea is suffering under President Isaias Afewerki because of very restrictive policies and his go-it-alone attitude about outside assistance. My wife's aging parents can no longer find help with their fields of barley and other crops since the children are not available and the older ones are attending to their own interests. Young people are forced to work national service for an extensive period of time. There are no jobs to speak of and many of the young men and women are illegally sneaking to other countries for a decent life. However, the refugees are subject to capture or kidnapping in certain areas such as Sudan and Egypt; tragic stories abound of kidneys and other organs being cut out of their bodies for sale. Most Americans are unaware that there are places around the world with communities of refugees waiting to get into the United States and paying bribes, rents, and other expenditures in order to survive. For example in 2013, in order to obtain a (legal) visa to the United States, my wife's parents had to traverse Eritrea, Uganda, and still wait over four months in Kenya. The Eritrean people are some of the nicest people in the world—very honest and hard working. In the capital of Asmara, there are no steel bars or other security measures in the small currency exchange shops on the street. On a down note, I noticed they use leaded gas in their vehicles which is detrimental to pedestrians especially the children. The outside world is generally unaware of conditions and the members of the media are silent or complacent. Some western banks are too big to fail, but some minor countries are too small to succeed.

During one of my flights from the Middle East to Ireland, I once upon a time called Kathleen O'Driscoll, whose telephone number was given me by Uncle Bill from New York. He had travelled the old sod three decades before, and they remembered him as if it were yesterday. I landed at Heathrow London at 7AM and called Kathleen, although we didn't know each other. I phoned and said I was in England and would land in Cork in one hour.

She asked "Now, just who are you?"

I replied, "I'm your relative and I'll be there in an hour."

She said, "Yes, but who are you?"

I repeated "I'm your relative from America, and I will land in an hour."

When I arrived at Cork airport, Kathleen showed up with some family backup for security and generously brought me to their home. I explained that our maternal great grandmother had 13 children and my mother was in that family tree. The Irish took me in and showed their hospitality. Those were the days when my testosterone levels were somewhat higher than might be accounted for now. I suppose those were days of an outgoing nature; Nowadays I am more like Howard Hughes but without the money.

Next we will continue to explore some more oddities.

Some More Odd Tidbits

My preoccupation with the odd or unusual includes some additional tidbits for a humorous break in the narrative:

I get a thrill from reading the opening of *Our Mutual Friend* with Gaffer Hexam and his daughter Lizzy sculling the Thames for broken and drowned bodies in search of pocket change.

For years I had a fantasy about publishing a book and entertained the idea for a coffee-table edition that would be called the *Bums of New York City*. If that volume were successful, I would have follow-on projects such as *Bums of India and Pakistan*. The idea was sparked from the sidewalks of New York during the 1970s where all kinds of street people lived their unconventional lives. For instance, some individuals trolling through garbage cans were indistinguishable from the containers since their attire was black plastic bags. As of 2011, more than 110,000 homeless New Yorkers, including more than 40,000 children, slept in the municipal shelter system. But back then, many of the clients, who would later be housed at taxpayer expense, were conspicuously on the streets. This was not a sight for the tourist trade, and as a consequence of aggressive litigation on their behalf, the largest shelter system in the country was built. You might think of me as rude and tasteless, but we *all* traverse this vale of tears in our own ways, and rich or poor, we share the same road with a sign that reads "Dead End."

Some years ago, I entertained the idea of selling a *Certificate to Heaven* by mail. The document was designed on my computer and some nominal classified advertising was attempted in one of the National tabloids, but little or rather nothing came of it. Well, I thought it was better than selling the shtick of naming heavenly stars for customers and dreamers in a star registry, which is equally dubious; celestial nomenclature is regulated by the Astronomical Union, which never sells naming rights. If I were a rich man, bubba bubba deedle deedle dum. (Russian based *Fiddler on the Roof*).

When I was working in Saudi Arabia, I had a fantastic idea but it never got off the ground. The brainstormed scheme was to obtain pictures of various mosques throughout the Muslim world and include them, like baseball playing cards, in bubble-gum packages. Instead of Mickey Mantle and Roger Maris, the youngsters could shuffle the following as a proposed sample:
Masjid an-Nabawi (Saudi Arabia)—the Mosque of the Prophet is one of the holiest sites in Islam and is the final burial site for Prophet Muhammad.
Al-Aqsa Mosque, Jerusalem, Israel—the mosque stood on a site regarded as the holiest site in Judaism.
Great Mosque of Djenné, Mali—this mosque is the largest mud brick building in the world.
There would be a picture of the mosque on the front and the name with description on the reverse. Additionally, a contest would be held to identify a mystery mosque from which there are many to choose. The contest prize could be a special prayer rug or a trip to Disney in Orlando.

Just as rich Christians had private chapels on their estate grounds, many Muslims have mosques in their home compounds or living quarters. They pray five times per day and what better path than to toddle across the lawn, and by the same token, to keep an eye on the resident females. Incidentally, the stores close five times per day and the times change daily by the lunar calendar. I often forgot about the prayer times and wasted considerable time at the local supermarkets. There is no accounting for the number of mosques in the world but it might be over two million. I am awfully excited about this idea because there are about 1.5 billion Muslims in the world and that represents a lot of customers. If I were a biddy-biddy-rich, yidle-diddle-didle-didle man.

The old pubs in England and Ireland are some of my favorite experiences. Some people call me eccentric, but I can't drink the beer from just any old glass; it has to have my approval as to shape and weight; it's no laughing matter. I still have a handful of authentic pint glasses that were donated by an English pub with the official crown seal etched onto the glass. You can tip a glass in Las Vegas, but I just can't stand the noise of the place. They want the customers up and able to gamble, so music is pumped into every square inch with no respite for the weary. It's much richer in the English countryside and to think that you're standing at the same bar as did clergy and highwaymen of the past and you just know there are ghosts there. Vegas can keep their Rat Pack look-alikes.

For those who must smoke cigarettes, I would suggest "rolling your own" like Bogart did in the 1941 film, *The Maltese Falcon*. When I visit Cocoa Beach, one of my nightly stops is at the Beach Shack, a blues joint overlooking the Atlantic Ocean. There I invariably spot a character who I think of as "Tex." He mentioned hailing from that state originally and you'd never know it except for the cowboy hat and boots, the same faded blue jeans, matching style of shirt with double pockets for his cigarette-rolling stuff. He's a knockoff for Willie Nelson but much thinner, like a toothpick. You might say he's wiry with a beard and droopy mustache and he drinks one or two cans of cheap American beer and then exits. Tex rolls his own cigarettes, and from the looks of things, it's a sight cheaper and besides, you can't chain smoke 'em.

I often play a game, of observing older people and trying to guess which ones might have been a real SOB or jerk in their younger years, but now seem doddering, placid old fools. One can imagine that the old rube being helped to cross a street might have been a real humdinger some years ago. Just as dog owners often resemble their pets, I like to imagine what occupations people might have based on their looks. For example, by the looks of things, Tony Blair, the former UK Prime Minister, would seem to make a good hair stylist. George W. Bush might have been better off as a bus driver (and the rest of us would be better off if he had been too). Another pastime is to look at young faces and ponder which will turn out to be monstrous. Even monsters have mothers.

People-watching is a popular pastime and it's free. As bodies pass each other, there can be episodes of smiling which might be as brief as a passing breeze. The smile can go on and off like a light switch and that is telling.

Unfortunately, we were sent to an old dentist in our youth. And although I didn't see any wagon wheels on the property, Dr. Mulholland did not use any sort of anesthetic before drilling our teeth. The only distraction from the pain was a bird feeder just outside the window. Due to my dental history and self-consciousness, I am more of a smirker than a smiler.

I had a dream the other night about visiting Einstein where I opened the conversation with a knock-knock joke.
Kingsley: Knock-Knock.
Einstein: Who's there?
Kingsley: God.

Einstein: God who?
Kingsley: (Silence and blank stare).

Very few people are familiar with the Black Market for currency in foreign countries. It's mysterious and tinged with danger. This almighty greenback, the U.S. dollar, is revered and viewed as a relatively stable store of value especially throughout the Third World. At the present time, $340 billion dollars, roughly 37 percent of all U.S. currency is believed to be circulating abroad. I have exchanged dollars for African and other currency on the black market and was generally unaware of the consequences of these transactions. Basically holders of hard currency are able to use the black market to buy the local currency at better exchange rates than they can get through official channels. One of the reasons for this is the inability of local residents to profitably invest in their own country.

The black market is a way of getting around government controls of local and foreign currency holding. Therefore citizens exchange the local currency for U.S. dollars and transfer the money abroad for investment. For example, relatives in the United States or Canada can open shops and other businesses from the dollars provided by couriers who will carry the loot on overseas flights. By the same token, the expatriates earning dollars abroad send remittances back home that will be exchanged on the black market at a higher rate than the official pegged value. Although foreign direct investment (FDI) is an important form of private external financing for developing countries, some sovereigns such as Eritrea, prefer to limit the influence of wealthy outsiders which is understandable. But fear of inflation, low interest rates, and economic and political instability promote the demand for foreign currency in the black market.

Interestingly, India, China, and Mexico are the top three remittance *recipient* countries while the U.S., Saudi Arabia, and Switzerland are the top remittance *senders* in the world. The moral argument against using the black market is that you are robbing the third world government of valuable hard currency in order to make your cheap holiday even cheaper. You must be discreet when attempting to use the black market because the money changer might be an undercover government agent. Therefore, typically relatives or known individuals are the safe option to complete a transaction of this type. Countries with active black markets often experience runaway inflation for goods and services. As a reminder of inflation and misfortune, my wallet contains a few $100 *Trillion* Dollar bills from Zimbabwe. These bills are occasionally included as a tip for my meals in instances of exceptionally good service.

One of my ruminations on rituals...concerns the seasons and the holidays. Why is it that the holidays seem to come around so swiftly—like Ground Hog Day? I suppose it's due to the number of them; there are actually 89 holidays and observances. Once again, we have a cultural problem. There is New Year's and then there is the Chinese New Year on 31 January 2014; the Islamic New Year is 24 October 2014 which on their calendar is the year 1436 since they are in a world of their own. Then the Eastern Orthodox New Year (my wife's Eritrean family uses) is 14 January 2014. There is Mother's Day and Father's Day and if you happen to be neither of these, you keep busy on those occasions or go to a dark movie theatre. All of these observances have one thing in common and it is not bell chiming—it is cash registers ringing up the sales. People are so lazy that they have to buy sappy greeting cards all year long instead of using crayons on paper for free. One wonders why friends and lovers need a middleman to express their emotions. When Thanksgiving rolls around, the turkey goes in the oven—Easter (ham and cut-rate candy), St. Pat's (corned beef), Ramadan (sheep). Actually Ramadan is interesting in that for 30 days they flip night/day time. Muslims should refrain from drinking, eating, or smoking from about dawn to dusk. But when the sun goes down its party time all night long! Besides all the holidays we have to keep track of, there are the Daylight Savings Time changes to observe such as "spring forward and fall back."

Various countries have to put up with whole months of observances such as the popular Black History Month in February which is the butt of sarcastic and sniggering comments because the embrace of diversity is self-serving and mainly lip service. The month of May is dedicated to Asian Pacific American Month. This encompasses the entire Asian continent, and the Pacific islands of Melanesia, Micronesia, and Polynesia. Why not an Extinct Animal Species Month? The PC (politically correct) crowd knows no bounds.

We also keep busy with ceremonies and religious rituals such as weddings, birthdays, baptism, communion, confirmation, and bar mitzvah which all require gifts and expenditure of funds. You might be on the short end of the stick for lack of children and so the contributions would be a one-way street which seems unfair. The birthday cake is an illuminating example of a ritual in that a silent wish is made as the birthday boy or girl blows out the candles on the cake to the dirge-like singing of "Happy Birthday to You." And the icing on the cake is the fact that the sugary confection will be dragged out, each and every year.

We are creatures of habit on a timetable so many people prefer the customary holiday routine but it becomes tiresome and too predictable. Weddings are problematic these days since, after your contributions are cashed and banked, there is about a 50 percent chance that divorce is in the cards. Of interest is the Islamic marriage that includes a prenuptial agreement which specifies a sum to be paid to the wife upon divorce. The sum is specified but cleverly cannot be renegotiated after the marriage; if the husband prospers significantly in the future, the woman is SOOL (shit out of luck) as far as benefiting in the increased wealth. What about wedding anniversaries? The retailers have to persuade the spouses to buy Pearls on the 10th year, Silver for the 25th, Gold for the 50th, and a 10-carat Diamond on the 100th anniversary. Are they crazy or do they just think the rubes are that stupid! The average consumer might need a 50-year layaway plan for that one. Times changed and the older *traditional* suggestions advocated buying Tin for the 10th year and Ivory for the 14th year (poor elephants) but the current list is much more expensive and can best be appreciated by the rich and/or conformists. I can imagine that the millionaire executives have a curvy secretary who takes care of all his mundane purchases for the holidays and other obligations.

During the Christmas season, Americans are preoccupied with exchanging junk most of which is made in suspect Chinese factories. This rampant consumerism is the engine of economic activity for a Gross National Product (GNP) of the country. Worse yet, the mobs continued to rampage through the malls in 2012 and fight over $220 footwear endorsed by the basketball "hoop man" (Michael Jordan) who had been retired for the previous nine years.

Most observances are arbitrary unlike the calendar dates such as harvest occurring near the end of summer with Halloween, and Easter representing spring renewal. Since dates are no longer relevant to the holiday, there may be no reason to keep them sacrosanct. Consider the analogy that music used to be played with a defined set of songs on vinyl albums, cassettes, and compact disks, but today we can load and play tunes randomly so that there is less boredom in knowing what will come next. Similarly, why should observances be different? I realize that this idea is eccentric, but imagine if holidays became randomly observed. Try to visualize shuffling the dates such that New Year's could be changed to the start of summer and Labor Day might be at the winter time. Also, since Jesus was born near 4BC and not four years later, and December is also problematic, Christmas could be moved to the hottest days of summer with a resultant reduction in shoppers' frenzy and the maddening crowds. Or perhaps we would miss the entertainment of the mobs rampaging through the stores and fighting each other for hoop-man footwear.

When we go to New York City, I want a borough tour of *the hood*, where I might see one of their famous drive-by shootings. Instead I take my eldest brother on a walking tour of the Lower

East Side with a local tour guide. It includes a stop at the 1887 Eldridge Street Synagogue where we might hear a Talmudic reading while admiring the architecture. I like to talk to strangers because I can say anything I want without worry of running into them again. My favorite trivia question for New Yorkers is, "How many bridges go out of Manhattan and what are their names?" The answer is 20:

Brooklyn Bridge
Manhattan Bridge
Williamsburg Bridge
Queensboro 59th St. Bridge
Ward's Island Footbridge
Triborough RFK Bridge
Willis Ave Bridge
3rd Ave Bridge
Park Ave (Railroad) Bridge
Madison Ave Bridge
145th St. Bridge
Macombs Dam Bridge
High Bridge Footbridge
Alexander Hamilton Bridge
Washington (Heights) Bridge
University Heights Bridge
Broadway Bridge
Spuyten-Duyvil Bridge
Henry Hudson Bridge
George Washington Bridge

In *The Great Bridge*, David McCullough's phenomenal story about building the Brooklyn Bridge, we learn that 20 men were killed during construction, according to the chief engineer and the contractor. The local tour guide provides a ghost tour but has never actually seen a walking spirit. That will not stop the commercial sale of ghosts and their stories since it is marketable with the right advertising campaign. Speaking of which, the next chapter is all about that hideous and hair-raising topic.

CHAPTER 5

The Never-Ending
Advertising Campaign
Drowning in a Sea of Advertising

Scientific discoveries are closely followed by the business community because their job is to separate you from your money. For example, the terms "memes" and "mirror neurons" have implications for sales and profits. The Marketing 101 course in university was a persuasive sales pitch that the terms 'need' and 'want' are one and the same. For example, a consumer definitely needs food, but the gas-guzzling SUV, of a size to mirror the buyer's arrogant attitude and aggression, is just as important. The marketers ran a television commercial for toilet paper that featured an effeminate supermarket manager from 1964 to 1985. The actor worked only 12 days per year, while earning an annual salary of $300,000. (Nice work if you can get it!). Advertising is big business, very big business. I have some experience from working at the Zenia Gazette in Ohio, the Yellow Pages Company, and our college Student Directory. One of our roommates, a shyster from New York, dreamed up the ad project for the Student Directory. Between beer and bullshit sessions, we collected quite a bit of money from the local shopkeepers, but we could have been the municipal dog catchers for all they knew. A dog-eared directory did make it into print, but I don't think it weighed heavily on our respective resumes. It did verify that people are more than willing to part with their money.

You can imagine the money connected with the advertising business. I'm certain it is well over $500 billion annually. The media include television commercials, radio, newspapers, internet, phone books, and an endless, pathetic parade of hucksters for cereals to snake oil. Instead of calling it poppycock, the producers of computer spam, pop-up ads, and junk mail refer to free-speech or free-enterprise. There is advertising on church bulletins, variety playbills, restaurant placemats, and personal business cards. You might be thinking that advertising is ubiquitous, but there is no escape from this free market cavalcade of business as usual. The Yellow Pages advertizing is in a unique position because their joint venture with the telephone companies ensures the cost for the ad is invoiced on the customer's phone bill; no payment, no phone. They have advertising for shopping channels on cable television.

Even the Government is in the despicable act of advertising the lottery to life's losers. You have a much better chance of being struck by lightning than winning the lottery, and yet it is a fantastic source of fantasy for millions. Speaking of fantasy, if you became filthy rich, where would want to live? Answer: anywhere is fine with enough wealth, even Bombay or Baghdad, since you can always get away on your private jet. The lottery sales increase every time there's a bigger jackpot because the dim-witted consumers are clueless about probability and they have big eyes. Put it this way: It's a great ploy to tax the poor. My eldest brother has the best rejoinder: you have to be in it to win it. Even the military departments advertise for recruits since it is an all volunteer force. They have a lame group of government (affirmative action) cadre who dream up the following pathetic slogans and Trade Marks:

- U.S. Coast Guard: "Born Ready" (*Hello?*).
- U.S. Army: "Army of One" (*Right, Sure*).
- U.S. Army: "Army Strong" (*You Betcha*).
- U.S. Army: "Be all you can be" (*Allright*).
- U.S. Air Force: "Aim High" (*Why Not?*)
- U.S. Marines: "The Few, The Proud, The Marines" (*OK, not bad*).

Companies have slogans ad naseum; some are burned into memory and some are forgettable:

- Got Milk? (*Milk mustache on celebrities, great!*)
- What Are You Drinkin'?™ (*Coffee dunking*)(*Yeah, I added 3 fingers of Bourbon*)
- I'm lovin' it. (*Hamburger joint*)
- Just do it. (*Just do what?*)
- Does She or Doesn't She? (*Don't ask me!*)
- You've Come a Long Way, Baby (*Cigarette; cough, hack, wheeze*)
- Finger-lickin' good. (*"Deep fried, honey!"*)
- Plop, plop, fizz, fizz. (*Doesn't sound like a seltzer movement*)
- M'm! M'm! Good! (*Soup–But read the ingredient label below!*)

Ingredients for Broccoli Cheese soup (get your reading glasses and Sherlock Holmes magnifying glass):

Water, broccoli, vegetable oil (corn, cottonseed, canola and/or soybean), wheat flour, modified food starch, onions, contains less than 2% of: salt, cream, cheddar cheese (cultured milk, salt, enzymes) dehydrated whey, sugar, soy protein concentrate whey, enzyme modified cheese and butter (cheddar cheese [milk cultures, salt, enzymes], butter, cultures, dehydrated enzymes, parmesan cheese flavor base (granular and parmesan cheese [milk, cultures, salt, enzymes], water, salt, lactic acid, citric acid), potassium chloride, dehydrated buttermilk, beta carotene for color, lactic acid, cheddar cheese (milk, cultures, salt, enzymes), flavoring, disodium phosphate, sodium phosphate, zinc chloride (to maintain color) granular cheese (milk, cultures, salt, enzymes), semisoft cheese (milk, cultures, salt, enzymes), blue cheese (milk, cultures, salt, enzymes), vinegar.

Phew! I need to rest after typing that. It's quite a list and the above ingredients are word-for-word from the can's label. By the way, the label also shows that the can contains 820 mg of sodium per serving; no wonder it's "M'm! M'm!" But, hold on, dear reader! In more small print on the can, it shows there are 2 ½ servings in each can, so that's 2,050 mg of sodium per can! (If my math is correct). Note: Add another "M'm M'm" into the formula. When I leisurely meander past the soup aisle of any supermarket, it is noticeable that a certain brand seems to "occupy" more than a third of the shelf space; that elicits a pondering murmur, *not* a "M'm M'm" but a "Hmm."

Advertising and politicians are cozy bedfellows. Candidates, party committees, and outside groups combined spent as much as $2.5 billion on television advertising in the 2012 election in the United States. Television is still the preferred way to reach passive, couch potato voters. Losers of election races are all too familiar with the effectiveness of attack ads, lies, and distortion that are the modus operandi of well financed campaigners. Even the supposedly objective mass media are advertisers for the various candidates of different political parties and it is blatant favoritism. And where do you suppose they get the treasure chests for such spending on this dirty business?

You can run but you can't hide from advertising. If you relax at the seashore, there is a banner-toting plane droning back and forth overhead. When I was a toddler at Takanassee Beach, this was considered quaint until I learned the meaning of ubiquitous.

Companies have a line on their balance sheets called an advertising budget. This is from a random Google search of *advertising budget* on the internet:

"Buy enough frequency. We are constantly bombarded with advertisements and images, and in order to penetrate the conscious-ness, it is important to be seen with some frequency."

The corporate world admits that we are bombarded with their drivel and they advise that advertisers should pile on with even more nonsense. The corporate CEOs are a wily group and want to get the biggest bang for the buck. How do they undertake this objective? Think of rituals again. They invest in dumbbell sports celebrities and actors, strutting mannequins, and other overpaid role models, but remember to have them sign the ethics form with a morals clause in the contract. Advertising is splattered at sport stadiums and entertainment amphitheatres, and municipalities sell the arena naming rights to corporations. And starting in 2012, American universities started selling naming rights for their toilets; so, if you have lots of spare cash to flush down, have at it. They closed down Yankee Stadium and sent the Brooklyn Dodgers packing. The Garden State Arts Center was changed to *PNC Bank Arts Center* in 1996. Everything is for sale in America, hence the term sell-out in a soulless society. The corporate masters know it's not survival of the fittest; it is survival at any cost. And the cost is a lower standard of living for the cotton-picking customers who watch jobs melt and slither overseas. You're out of a job. After all, these advertising budgets must be justified. It has become a crass and no-class society of buck chasers and sycophants.

On Sale for Only $99.99

We all notice how advertisers display prices such as $3.98, or $99.99. *Who* do they think they're fooling? So their marketing research shows that consumers can be duped to accept an odd dollar value as if that is somehow more palatable. Is $99.99 actually 100 dollars? Yes, and of course more with the tax. Question: then why do the Americans still use pennies when these copper tokens are worthless and cost more to make than they are worth? There may be several reasons (1) Businesses can fool customers with the $99.99 gimmick; (2) Americans are so skeptical that they fear eliminating pennies would round prices up to the five cent (nickel) value—and then what's next? Eliminating the ten cent (dime) coin and you can see where that is going. There is a hot metal simmering in the marketplace called Gold. When we were living in Saudi in 1996, the price was $400 per ounce and in the year 2011, the price skyrocketed to $1,900. Based upon the frenzy of soaring prices, the advertisers of gold purveyors came out of the woodwork to hawk their wares on a 24/7 basis. As the price went through the roof, they advised consumers to get in on a good deal as if the metal would climb forever with the contention that the sky's the limit. Good luck. I have an analogous inkling that gold will be as beneficial to the average portfolio as Yoko Ono was to John Lennon's career.

In the good old days, advertisers were more respectful, with some anomalies such as the *Lucky Strike Radio Show* starring Frank Sinatra. But consider, most men wore hats and also smoked during World War II, but they didn't know the effects—not of wearing a hat, but of smoking. Back then men smoked everything, constantly and everywhere including on the throne or on the toilet. You could puff into your child's face, with windows open or closed, ad nauseam. My dad alternately smoked unfiltered Camel cigarettes, cigars, and a pipe. The eminent physicist and father of the atomic bomb, J. Robert Oppenheimer, smoked a pipe (a stress reliever). This Jewish genius headed the secret Los Alamos Laboratory while being hunted by J. Edgar Hoover at the FBI for alleged communist associations (would one do more than smoke?) Starting in 1954, Robert spent several months of the year living on the island of St. John in the U.S. Virgin Islands and I highly recommend a visit. If you are well heeled, you can stay at the former Rockefeller estate. And don't forget to order a "Bushwacker" cocktail that is made with Rum, Vodka, Amaretto, Kahlua, Baileys Irish Cream, cream of coconut, then blended with ice, *al hamdu lilah!* (Thanks be to God, in Arabic). You might consider skipping the boat ride to nearby St. Thomas for the junk-collecting shopping spree—the Newark of the Caribbean. Back to smokes, after being spanked with over $200 billion of settlement costs, the tobacco companies still lace the cigarettes with addicting nicotine, and face declining use in this country. In spite of this, business is brisk in overseas markets because China alone has 1.3 billion people. We export our manufacturing pollution there, due to the insatiable demand for cheap Chinese products, and from the looks of it, smoking is the least of their problems.

Smoking Old Movies

The classic movies are remarkable, but we just have to mind that everybody smoked—Bogart and Bacall, Frank, Sammy, Deano, and just about everyone except Tarzan (Johnny Weissmuller). One thing classic movie producers didn't do was to accept advertising fees from cigarette sponsors to put a smoke in the star's hand. There is quite a bit of advertising in the contemporary movies and television; corporate sponsors are paying for the various products to appear in the show (product placement), and you name it, from cars to colas. Digital advertising goes one step further than product placement by using computer technology to add products to scenes that were never there to begin with. This practice is common in sporting events coverage, where ads are digitally inserted onto the billboards, sideboards and playing surfaces in arenas and stadiums.[1]

Marlboro is the largest selling cigarette brand in the world. The advertising pitch includes the "Marlboro Man," a rugged cowboy puffing away. But interestingly, the Marlboro brand was launched in 1924 as a woman's cigarette, based on the slogan "Mild As May." In the 1920s, advertising for the cigarette was primarily based around how ladylike the cigarette was. I personally do not have a problem with smoking as I try not to be a hypocrite. Recent research reveals that the typical sedentary job today, which involves sitting on your tail all day, is just as bad as smoking. And watching the boob tube is also known to shorten the viewer's lifetime.

The corporate sponsors reeled-in the ideas of memes and rituals as a way to occupy the minds of consumers. They tirelessly pull out all the stops to change perceptions in order to induce more sales. The product may be loaded with sugar, sodium, and chemicals, but they will persuade consumers that it is actually good for you. The corporate heads have succeeded to a great extent; consumers now believe that they may safely live their lives as prescribed by the advertising industry, rather than living by basic human necessities and common sense.

Pharmaceutical drugs are now routinely and incessantly advertised on television as if viewers have *any* clue or understanding about these potentially dangerous substances. The direct-to-consumer advertising has bloomed since the 1990s with a resulting huge increase in sales. Advertisers pay large sums to sports celebrities and other shills in order to convince viewers that they need a prescription or an over-the-counter purchase of their drugs. Generic brands are much cheaper in price, but the advertisements are produced to counteract the logical tendency of consumers to save their money. It smells of unethical practices. Patients are now taking a different pill for every ill and what a witch's brew of chemicals is bubbling in their stomachs. Shakespeare's *Macbeth* comes to mind: "Double, double toil and trouble;fire burn, and cauldron bubble

For example, one of the competitors for a male erectile dysfunction drug, which promotes a woody salute by the man's member, has a commercial which shows a couple laying side-by-side in separate bath tubs in some romantic, outdoor setting; so as not to seem uncouth, I will just refer to those advertisers as 'banana heads.' The drug companies follow-up the boob tube advertisement with a two and a half page ad in golf magazines and other vacuous periodicals. The advertisement tries to hook men (like fish) with a 30-day free supply of the drug. And one of the comical "side effects" listed in the ad is: "An erection that won't go away" (Hello?). You wonder who reads all the sophomoric magazines on the store shelves since a major portion of the content is mindless advertisements, never mind the two and a half pages of a woody extender drug.

Would you be surprised to know that there are over 7,000 magazines available to the choosy public? And guess what follows the drug ads on television? Naturally, the advertisements of attorneys, who like vultures, are ready to sue on behalf of the victims of negative side-effects such as disability and death. They bring to mind the image of the glib talking Walter Matthau with drooping jowls. The funny thing about the male woody ads is that none of them are humorous like the palaver that is the majority of commercial advertising; apparently, watching the male flag-pole salute at less than half-mast is no laughing matter, and the drug companies recommend that the male consumer ingest their pills 24/7—just to be sure they are ready all day and every day (pray for their women). But do you wonder how many of the partner-less guys are prescribed the drug for (sorry to say it) masturbation or choking the chicken? Moreover, we do *not* want to enquire if the drug contributes to their fascinating wet dreams or virtual reality tours. It is a sick society and everything short of the propensity to self-medicate as cadres of drug salesmen bribe their way into doctors' offices.

Advertisers' Goal: How to Annoy

Armed with the tools of memes, ritual, and perceptions, television advertising was changed to be maximally annoying and obnoxious, attributable to the counter-intuitive notion that negative sensory input will catch the mind's attention. The advertising (pitch men) want maximum eyeballs to view their commercials and strive to prevent commercial avoidance or so-called zapping the ad by ignoring them. Therefore, they use a variety of gimmicks and deceptive strategies to promote their products and maximize viewer interest such as pulsing, in which the brand is inserted briefly and intermittently throughout the commercial and fast-pace scene changes. You may be aware of the strategy of daily soap operas with constant scene changes and interruption of concentration which is a form of manipulation similar to Rock & Roll music videos where the camera angle is constantly shifting from player to player so that the producers determine what and for how long the audience will be allowed to focus. And remember, the TV trade is not in the business of selling programs to audiences; it is in the business of selling viewers to advertisers.

These commercial short-term memories are converted to long-term by repetition and burned onto different circuits in the brain. The corporate jungle has short-term goals (maximum revenue) and a long-term "strategery." The CEOs covet high pay, bonuses, stock options, and a golden parachute on their exit. They are not overly obsessive with the long term, since millions can be amassed in a short period of time. Institutions such as the military actually have long-term strategies because someone else is paying for it—the taxpayers! NASA has a long-term strategy but funding constraints have put them on the back burner. Forget about the Moon or Mars, humans are barely able to keep the lights on in a near-earth orbit Space Station. I am not an astronomer, but even an amateur can judge and need not read "space travel for dummies," to understand that only machines should rocket to the stars.

In recent memory, the advertising on television has hit an all time low. It was low enough several decades ago when they started to put a nautical, preppy-dressed guy in the toilet bowl during the 1970s to sell their products. But earlier advertising was different. They've gone from Mr. Clean starting in 1958 as a muscular, tanned, bald man with an earring. Today men are portrayed in commercials as fat, dumb, and lazy or poor examples of a role model. The majority of this type of advertising is an insult to the intelligence, assuming the viewer has any cognitive force, topside. The car insurance companies come to mind with their advertising; they compete all day long with each other as to who is the superior blockhead.

We often mute the boob tube, with the remote control, during commercials. I have a suspicion that the sense of hearing is more significant rather than the sight of the advertising. It is counterintuitive to think the ears take precedence over the eyes, but sight can be turned off (such as averting the eyes) but sound cannot.

About 90 percent of all commercials have music or jingles because humans will listen even when they are not paying close attention, and music has an enormous affect on the mind.

There seems to be some discrimination between seeing a rascal and listening to one. Consider the W.C. Fields movie *It's a Gift*, in which the nagging wife drives hen-pecked Fields outdoors where he tries to get some sleep on a porch swing. The moral is that husbands who can zone-out the sound of a nagging wife get on much better, but who can?

You may test this idea of sight versus sound. The next time you are involved in a road rage incident, roll down your window and pretend to be deaf with some hand signals; the perpetrator will melt back to his car. I have noticed that some radio personalities introduce a commercial as if it is a continuation of the commentary—an obvious attempt to fool the listeners. They begin telling a story but then you realize it's a scripted advertisement for some product or service. The point here is that advertisers are exploiting the viewing consumer who simply wants to see the show. Granted that the content has to be paid for, but how is it justified that an actor for toilet paper only had to work 12 days per year?

On a recent flight, the lady next to me discussed one of her duties as an advertising administrator. Part of her job was to attend various golf tournaments to confirm that the sponsored celebrity golfer was adequately showing the can of soft drink that he was paid millions to promote.

Advertisers have now switched tactics and you might have noticed that the majority of commercials are now funny. The ad men swivel about their New York office towers and crank out whatever nonsense they imagine the swarm will swallow. They are out of touch with the average consumers who are wading through pits instead of the cherries. There seems to be a dark cloud over the economic landscape, but the ad men are oblivious to the barometer of discontented feelings. Not every experience of reality is funny unless you have a mental disorder.

Naturally, with all the money involved, there is an Ad Council that acts as a coordinator and distributor of advertizing campaigns. Some of their memorable public service ads include "Friends don't let friends drive drunk" and "A mind is a terrible thing to waste." One can easily imagine that, like the fox in the hen house, the Ad Council has nothing to do with tackling deceptive and harmful advertising. Don't get me wrong.

Believe it or not, the Catholic Church has been airing TV

advertisements in recent years even in light of the towering, clergy homosexual-abuse scandal that has traumatized countless young boys. Let's see: what does the bible say about shame and disgrace? "We lie down in our shame, and our confusion covereth us" (Jeremiah 3:25). I believe we can go one better with "I never wonder to see men wicked, but I often wonder to see them not ashamed" (Jonathan Swift 1667-1745).

If you agree with these ideas on the subject of advertising, some action can be effectively taken by each of us. For example, I recently informed my car insurance company that I was canceling their policy and switching to another, less funny insurer. That really gets their attention because, for all they know, your action might be a trend. Many corporations have a toll-free telephone number as well as an email address. Please take the time, once in awhile, to let your opinion be known to the merchants of Madison Avenue. An excellent way to avoid commercials is to subscribe to noncommercial radio syndicators or download your favorite radio shows as a podcast on a portable electronic device; a three hour program is thereby reduced to about an hour and a half, sans commercial annoyance and interruption. I regret that this was unavailable for previous icons of the AM radio dial such as Jean Shepherd and Barry Farber.

Besides annoyance, viewers are manipulated by advertising at the subconscious level. Gerald Zaltman, a professor at Harvard Business School, contends that 95 percent of what we do every minute of every day is performed beyond our conscious awareness. That explains how we can drive and negotiate the bends in the road without consciously calculating angles and centrifugal force. Consumers may remember how the Coca-Cola Company made a huge mistake in using data from a blind taste test between Coke and Pepsi, in which Pepsi was definitely preferred by most participants, and disastrously changed the recipe for a New Coke in 1985. The company failed to understand the subconscious images that the Coke brand invokes in their customers. Ironically the cola wars had a casualty during the prior year of 1984 when Pepsi signed a record-breaking commercial shoot with Michael Jackson that resulted in the tragic accident of Michael's head catching on fire.

Advertisers are in the business of finding out what motivates us and how those snap decisions of the unconscious can be exploited. They often use a symbol, such as a check-mark, and associate it with a product. For example, a company will pay millions of dollars for a celebrity endorsement and hope that naïve consumers will form a personal bond with the symbol and buy their products. Even though the symbol and celebrity are meaningless, people strive to form an identity of their own with the aid of golfers or a basketball hoop man. Symbols seem to confer identity; Christians wear cross jewelry which symbolizes spirituality. Vehicles are overt symbols of ourselves that are dressed up with bumper stickers and window decals such as the NRA (National Rifle Association) or military decals. Conversely, the fad sign Baby on Board has faded from Mini-Vans and other utility vehicles, and was the butt of many jokes because most drivers saw the sign as too self-serving.

The overload of advertising is a cause for parental concern in that children can be exploited more easily if they do not understand the differences between television programming and commercials, and if they do not know the selling intent of commercials. Consumers are exposed to hundreds of commercial messages per day in one form or another or tens of thousands each year! And the viewers incredulously submit to this propaganda voluntarily.

The most incredible and brainless story with reference to advertizing is about a company that wants to place advertisements or logos on the Moon's surface, which according to them could be watched from Earth. Never underestimate a defective mind. Now for an obnoxious employment of advertising: NASCAR racetracks and the drivers' torsos. Car racing is the junkyard dog of advertising. Logos and ads are splattered on the arena, hats, uniforms, and vehicles. It's a circus of colors and monotony that attracts the herd of mediocrity; it used to be America's second most popular sport but is now a has-been. I never understood the draw of watching pieces of metal circling round and round but I suppose the crowds are actually there to catch the sporadic crash scene. I also never understood the tendency of consumers to buy clothing adorned with advertising logos. These idyllic customers are walking billboards and they pay for the privilege which must have the corporate boards howling in cigar-chomping good cheer. And if the apparel has a sports team logo, they can expect to pay triple. Also in the clothes department, advertising has been showing up on the rear of ladies pants that signifies low-rent fashion models.

Advertisers and marketers will become much more intrusive as time goes by. One of the newest tools in the trade is Facial Recognition Technology, even though privacy concerns have been aroused. As people roam through the commercial district, they might be unaware that digital displays, incorporating camera and facial recognition software, can tailor advertising pitches based on the viewer's gender, age, and race. For example, a bar can track male to female ratios, average age, and the number of customers at a particular venue. There are plans on the drawing board for internet-connected eyeglasses. The eyewear frames will employ tiny cameras and on-lens displays that will provide the wearer with a plethora of information ranging from things that tease to sleaze and of course the endless advertisements.

Right now in the United States, there is a company with more than 23,000 computer servers collecting, collating and analyzing consumer data in a multibillion-dollar industry known as database marketing. The servers process more than 50 trillion data transactions a year and the database contains information for about 500 million active consumers worldwide, with about 1,500 data points per person. That includes a majority of adults in the United States. In the year 2013, Advertising Age ranked Epsilon Data Management, as the biggest advertising agency in the United States, with Acxiom Corporation second. Some corporate systems are designed to recognize consumers, remember their actions, classify their behaviors and influence them with tailored marketing. Still, there is a fine line between customization and stalking. While many people welcome the convenience of personalized offers, others may see the surveillance engines behind them as intrusive or even manipulative.[2]

Let's not bypass another eyesore, the advertising billboards that are plastered on our American scenic roads. You don't see this extent of crass commercialism in more natural countries like Ireland or the English countryside. In the year 2000, rooftops in Athens had grown so thick with billboards that it was difficult to see its famous architecture (although you might want to skip it since the place has become a disaster area of the Euro Zone). Many cities have high densities of billboards, especially in places where there is a lot of pedestrian traffic such as Times Square in New York City. Because of the lack of space in cities, these billboards are painted or hung on the sides of buildings and seem to be part of the architecture. It's not meant to feel relaxing. I wonder when we will see advertising tattooed on the foreheads of our impressionable youth as an income stream. God loves the proletariat.

I'm left wondering if Tarzan and Jane have a spare room in the tree house. The next short chapter contains sundry but not uncouth snippets of close encounters of the sexual kind with some humorous stories.

You Call This Living?

CHAPTER 6

Sexcapades

The following bits and pieces are offered as an amusing break from more thought-provoking affairs. It's not hard to guess which of the following three items of interest are the oldest in terms of human history: Love, Money, or Sex.

Both salesmen and consumers know that sex sells. I still have a newspaper clipping from 28 January 1989 (well over 20 years ago). The Doonesbury comic strip by Gary Trudeau shows a busty woman in a bikini and her dialogue purports, "Sex sells! It doesn't matter what it is, magazines, books, movies, TV shows. It's all about hyping sales and ratings!" (Budding entrepreneurs take note). It takes genius to state the obvious like George Carlin: "Tonight's forecast: DARK! Continued mostly dark tonight, turning to widely scattered LIGHT in the morning, man!" The idea that sex sells is self evident. The most popular internet search topic is (snare drum, cymbal) sex. You probably didn't think it was quantum physics.

An internet search on Goggle reveals 3,820,000,000 results for "sex" as opposed to 722,000,000 for "religion."

In recent times, the marketers argue that sex does *not* sell; they claim that men ogle the commercials but can't seem to remember the content. This is the conundrum of our present time. For every truism, there must be a crowd that asserts the opposite. All issues are painted in battleship gray and open to debate, rhetoric, and semantics, e.g., "It depends on what the meaning of the word '*is*' is." There is too much dichotomy or contradiction in our discourse. It's annoying when media commentators pretend to be fair and balanced, covering both angles of a controversy in a news whiplash fashion. For example, the news reportage see-saws back and forth as to whether things are good or bad for you—coffee, red wine, red meat and red food dye. For the generation of baby boomers, clowns were the opposite of sexy; rather they were viewed as funny, such as Bozo, Red Skelton, and circus clowns, but certainly not scary. Even the famous hamburger chain has a clown for a mascot to act as a counterweight to their penny-pinching fast food. They may have to can the clown, however, if he is perceived as a mask or diversion from the flawed nutritional value of the food on the menu.

Popular culture and Hollywood have perverted innocent entertainment and created phobias by portraying clowns as demons. My first-hand experience is telling; I occasionally wear a clown's nose in unusual places such as vacation spots like the Caribbean where the residents and tourists are not expecting eccentric visitors. I like to walk into an establishment, such as a restaurant or bar, and stand silent to see the reaction of the crowd, and they love it, usually. Unfortunately, my clown's nose didn't go over well at the elegant rooftop bar at 350 Fifth Avenue in New York; the young, serving diva said she was afraid of clowns. My brother-in-law, who is a wanabe musician and ham like me, once asked: "Why do you *do* all this stuff?" to which I replied "Thaaat's Entertainment!" The bottom line is that it's all about perception. Sex does sell and if you still don't believe it check with the people that sell chicken wings and beer.

You may have heard the story of Calvin Coolidge and his wife touring a government farm. Mrs. Coolidge was in the lead and saw a rooster busily engaged with a hen. "How many times a day does he do that?" she asked. "Dozens of times," the farmer replied. "Tell that to the president," she said. When the story was told to Coolidge, he asked "Same hen each time?" When told it was a different hen each time, Coolidge easily replied, "Tell that to Mrs. Coolidge."

In the good old days, 42nd Street in New York City was famous or infamous for its seamy businesses and clientele. As a young lad, I entered one of those bars but couldn't just drink a beer in peace. One after another blonde or brunette would sidle up and ask, "Will you buy a girl a drink?" I had to leave after realizing that the supposed gifted cocktails would be poured ginger ale and at an extravagant cost. I am not the Lord Mayor of London. You live and learn.

Even the swanky Plaza Hotel has its movers and shakers. Some years back, my two brothers and I were sitting in the hotel bar and noticed the occasional visits by street walkers who needed to take a load off their feet. The two elders finally went up to our room and I became the object of the street traffic. My only contribution, however, was to politely buy a Coca-Cola for a few of them although *that* hardly took the edge off their sales pitch. There are times when I feel like Henry Higgins but don't know what to impart to the pupils. The ladies even wanted to visit the two sleeping brothers in the room above. Can't blame them for trying I suppose.

My parents were a product of the depression. And since my mother was Irish Catholic, they did not practice contraception, and thus had seven children, which was characteristic of many other similar families in the suburbs. With this experience under his belt, my father would impart some sage advice to his five sons such as, "Keep your pecker in your pocket." I suppose this suggestion was embraced, to a point. And to that I will add: average men think and talk with their organ and so my advice is to zip it!

Infidelity and evolution for some people, any old excuse will do for fooling around. It is supposed that monogamy evolved in situations where the offspring have a better chance of surviving if both parents work to raise them. This explains why humans *tend* to be monogamous, since children take many years to mature. Sexual fidelity does not come naturally, however, and the majority of animals on the planet, including humans, are not monogamous, and we will not engage in some preposterous number such as 99.44 percent like some sudsy, caustic claim. Although biology predisposes us to seek multiple sex partners, monogamy is a *choice* that requires commitment and continual effort. Of course, no mention of this topic will exclude the anecdote of Wilt Chamberlain, the life-long bachelor and hoop-man who slept with thousands of women during his busy schedule. Speaking of reprehensible fellows, as a consequence of her husband's philandering and the divorce settlement, Tiger Woods' ex-wife bought a $12 million mansion in Florida in 2012 and bulldozed the whole thing to build a new home. It appears that some men have a distorted idea in their mind of curvy versus scurvy. Infidelity may be excusable in lower animals, but for humans it hurts and is unworthy. Sexuality is just one of life's dichotomies as expressed by the following.

Variety is the spice of life.

Absence makes the heart grow fonder.

The grass is always greener on the other side.

Till death do us part (or some other _____ [*fill in the blank*] reason).

Regardless of the comparisons of humans to birds, rats, or snakes, people have a conscience and awareness. There was good reason that humans stuck together through the ages and it doesn't necessarily need to change overnight. Some other things *do* change rather quickly such as the incidence of filthy, sexually transmitted diseases. Chinese poem: "Look at a passing beauty as you would a passing cloud." Advice: Just make an effort, gentlemen, for Pete's sake, that your eye is the only wandering organ.

Hello ladies and germs. Beauty is a source of fascination for most people and especially female beauty since they are so much better at it. The phrase, beauty is in the eye of the beholder, suggests it's a matter of one's predilection. But actually, there are universal standards of beauty that are innate or encoded by evolution.

Just as we are programmed to enjoy the pleasure of sweet fruits, or prefer a savannah-like landscape, beauty is also part of our genetic heritage. Bilateral symmetry of the face or similarity, so that left and right sides mirror each other along a vertical axis, is an attribute of beauty. Another feature is average distribution of facial features, rather than extremes of facial structure. After all, there is a difference between beauty and sexiness or a thong and a bikini, if you will. Facial features are indications of health, the absence of parasites, and thus reproductive potential. "It also happens that symmetry and intelligence tend to run together, because both go with developmental stability. We may find symmetrical faces attractive because they imply the steadiness of genetic development, which creates valuable assets for choosing a mate, like better general fitness and a relative lack of stupidity."[1] Even tiny babies recognize a beautiful face and will stare at one for a longer time than otherwise. I know this, because many babies and young children want to go to my wife, even though she is a stranger to them. They are simply and naturally attracted. Now if men want to consider a potential mate, they have only to observe the mother in many cases; just as my wife's mother is 70 but has flawless looks and skin. You get the picture.

Now consider the following snippet from David Bohm, the long-winded physicist, who was quoted at the beginning of this book. Can you believe this?

"Beauty is not simply a matter of personal opinion, dependent primarily upon the eye of the beholder. It is the result of dynamic, evolving processes that consist in order, structure, and harmonious totalities."

Beautiful women spend more time in front of the mirror. I suppose they have more to lose or have too much face time invested. They purchase a myriad of lotions and potions, at enormous cost with problematic outcome, and the purveyors of beauty products are very big businesses. For example, my wife covers most surfaces of our bedroom and bathroom like toy soldiers in a child's play set. As an aside, my grandmother had very nice skin but only used the economical brand of lotion. With a blitzkrieg of modern advertising, women will pay dearly for various expensive formulas of crème ala *Ponce de Leon* and the fountain of youth. I suppose many women are not comfortable in their skin, but I earned my wrinkles and "Let it be."

Unfortunately for the average woman, they try to imitate the fake hair, nails, and makeup of the celebrities they see plastered on the frivolous fashion magazines. It should be evident that many of these supposed beauties have a Jekyll and Hyde appearance when the makeup comes off. Without the makeup and perm, many of them look as attractive as any run-of-the-mill lady. Women of beauty also buy more shoes and pocketbooks than the average, although this is also a function of wealth. For example, Imelda Marcos of the Philippines owned about 3,000 pairs of shoes. If you don't agree she was a "pooch" in view of all the poor women in that island nation, then at least consider yourself lucky not to be a college graduate there selling shoes. Imelda only represents the average women's propensity to gather about thirty pairs of shoes and she just took it to a higher level of magnitude.

Woman of beauty are often well-off such that you don't usually see one standing at a municipal bus stop. Women often wear clothes of vibrant colors, although Western men are now dressing with the same flair at the gym and other venues. But shouldn't only Santa Claus be seen in fire-engine red?

In my wife's country of Eritrea, the men are very conservative dressers and the traditional colors for their clothing are gray or black. They would never wear pumpkin orange, lime green or cherry red.

Women have been wearing jewelry for a quite a long time and there is evidence of shell necklaces being worn 100,000 years ago. An interest in lighter skin is noted around the world. This may be more of a cultural preference rather than a universal concept. Examples include skin bleaching by Asian women and Michael Jackson. Smooth skin is a feature of beauty. Humans lost most of their hair as a skin cooling advantage. Consequently, a shaggy-coated female would not be preferred and modern females resort to creams and laser treatments to reduce unwanted hair. The naked skin allows sexual signaling changes such as blushing and the sex flush; it is an attractive feature in that the prominent protuberances are more easily viewed. I've expressed quite a few controversial opinions in this volume, but after much soul searching, decided to forego any slight or stronger remarks on the following three subjects:

1. **Vladimir Putin:** If you're reading this Vladimir, let me just say that you are the John Wayne of Russia and I don't aim to piss you off.

2. **Tattoos on women's bodies:** I'll be honest; cowards tend to avoid excoriation and running the gauntlet (Mama didn't raise no fool). My mother-in-law from Africa is an exception; she has a tattoo of a cross on her forehead.

3. **No fat jokes.**

There are some interesting and odd cultural pageants of beauty in far out places. The women of Papua New Guinea do not consider hair to be of great importance. Their heads are usually covered with a feathery headdress that often matches their brightly colored face paint. Women of the Kayan tribe near Thailand start wearing brass rings around their necks from as young as five. As they grow older, more rings are added, and eventually, their necks start to look stretched out, giving them a giraffe-like appearance. For these women, the shiny brass rings are the typical sign of feminine beauty. And some neck pieces can weigh up to 20 pounds. Many cultures are equally sick with their female slavery. The Chinese subjected women to foot binding in the 10th century and for the next thousand years. To bind them, feet were first soaked in a warm bowl of herbs and animal blood, which caused the dead flesh to fall off. Toenails were cut back as far as possible to prevent ingrown toenails and infection. Silk and cotton bandages were dipped in the solution and were wrapped tightly around the feet after the toes were broken. Four toes on each foot were broken and folded under.

The big toe was left intact. Feet were often bound so tightly that women couldn't even walk short distances. You don't have to be a rocket scientist to understand that woman could not run far from the boys in the hood. Lastly, a fashionable issue relates to whether blondes have more fun. The question was supposed to be a rhetorical gimmick for a hair color advertising campaign. Of course, Marilyn Monroe was untouchable as the ideal model and (sex) symbol of beauty. It's probable that many viewers would insist that *Cleopatra* or Elizabeth Taylor was their ideal. But if I were Don Quixote, I would be on the lookout for the famous strawberry blonde from the past, Rita Hayworth.

It might seem amusing that, when I found my first honest to goodness girlfriend at university, I purchased a condom but didn't know how to use it. I supposed that it should be unfurled but had a Dickens of a time trying to get it on. As O.J. Simpson's liars said, "If the glove doesn't fit, you must acquit." I didn't seem to realize that you must unfurl the thing on your thingy. This girlfriend was of German stock which was typical of the population there. So, when I brought her to New Jersey to visit the parents, my mother mentioned something about "krauts" but little did I know my dad was originally a Katzman with their memories and bias of Germans in World War II. When I went home for a Thanksgiving vacation, I went to Tiffany's in Manhattan and bought her a Christmas present that was affordable. At that time, Tiffany's was not splattered in malls across America. During Christmas we drove to her parent's house in the Ohio farm country, Mercer County, and the girlfriend and her mother watched in awe as I brought forth this small, Tiffany box; they naturally assumed it was an engagement ring. But no, it was a $25, silver peanut-shaped pill container, in vogue during President Jimmy Carter's reign. The romance didn't last much longer. But that's alright; there were no carpet burns to commit to memory.

When I worked in Riyadh, Saudi Arabia, my girlfriend and another couple drove 13 hours, southwest toward the Red Sea to the unusual area of Abha, which is 7,200 feet above sea level and therefore cooler and wet compared to the rest of the country. You see sleepy towns along the way where foreigners are rarely expected. It is a mountainous area and can be quite frightening, with mist and fog covering the roads. It reminded me of Eritrea (East Africa) right across the Red Sea where I had to turn around after attempting to drive from the mountains of Segeneiti down 7,500 feet to Massawa which is at sea level on the Red Sea. I have always had a fear of heights and had plenty of dreams about the GWB (George Washington Bridge) in Manhattan, although I enjoyed dinner at the *Windows on the World* restaurant in the now destroyed World Trade Center North on the 107th floor.

When we arrived at Abha, we stopped at a mountain view and observed a troop of baboons fearlessly perched at the edge of the precipice and they quickly surrounded us with threatening gestures. It's hard to believe but they knew which of our group of four were females and made no pretense of their aspirations, playing with their pencil-thin dicks. Human males are possibly outdone in that department *only* by bonobos. We had to retreat and head for the hills of our hotel. No wonder these creatures are lower on the evolutionary bush!

Some years ago I had the opportunity to visit Korea as an employee of the U.S. Army. Still a young pup, I was escorted around Seoul by the old hands and they definitely knew a lot of the nooks and crannies of the place. At some of the bars we visited, there was a handful of girls who would pour your beer after every sip, light your cigarette if smoking, and as the obvious green horn, that's all the attention I received.

I couldn't help notice that in Germany, the spas are routinely co-ed and naked. This can be disconcerting to foreigners who are not aware of the relaxed attitude. For the uninitiated, *one* of next best things to nirvana is the spa experience. Only the premier hotels have a world-class spa such as the Ritz Carlton in Doha,

Qatar, or the Fairmont Sonoma Mission Inn & Spa, California. If you can afford the treatments which are countless and expensive, welcome to the cluster of the wealthy—and it is a different world indeed. They have facials that include exfoliation, steam, moisturizers, masks, and peels; body treatments of aqua therapy, body polishes, and salt scrubs followed by body wrap in mud or seaweed, and Vichy showers.

I had the opportunity to float in the Dead Sea in Jordan and carted away 10 kilos of the mud and some of the salt water. My Jordanian friends, the Shanqiti family, must have had a good laugh. Just one speck of water in the eye will make you tearful for some time and factories convert the mud into beauty products that are sold around the world.

I don't have to mention the ubiquitous massage since it is the common denominator of spa treatments. Obviously it all adds up for those living in the lap of luxury but is prohibitive to the average weary body. I focus on the facilities such as the exercise equipment that precedes the reward of the spa. After a workout, you may have a range of sophisticated amenities to include the sauna and steam rooms, cold plunge pool, hot Jacuzzi bath, swimming pool, waterfall pool, lounge chairs with towels, special lighting with candles, complementary bottled water, and fresh juice and fruits. It takes a few timeless hours to complete the circuit and afterwards, you are rejuvenated and feel like a new person. As for the amount of dress or undress, I can take it or leave it. Most Americans on the other hand are too puritanical for that type of exposure at spas.

President Reagan sent the 82nd Airborne to Honduras in 1986... and I was there to pick up the paratroopers with contracted buses. After our three month tour, my co-workers in the contract shop planned a final night out for some beer. The chosen bar, El Presidente, turned out to be their joke, a house of prostitution. But not one of us played with the hostesses, other than to buy beer and dance all night. I suppose the girls couldn't believe it. And only our translator, a Mexican-American sergeant, could speak Spanish.

Soul music of the old school is...still enjoyed by many listeners. I find it amusing though, that every other song was written with the intention of getting the booty.

- ☐ "Get down on it"— (Kool and the Gang).
- ☐ "Let's get it on"— (Marvin Gaye).
- ☐ "Sex machine"— (James Brown).
- ☐ "Ecstasy when you lay down next to me"—(Barry White).
- ☐ "Turn off the lights"—(Teddy Pedergrass).

And there are scores of similar songs in the same vein.

And speaking of sex and songs, why is it that Black Americans revere their mother as a saint, but the girls next door are called bitches and ho's?

After returning to New Jersey from the (Catholic) University of Dayton in 1977, I had the inspiration of writing a book on aphrodisiacs. This was another project that did not get off the ground but was a terrific idea. On a lark, I took the train to the main branch of the New York Public Library at Fifth Avenue and 42nd Street and gleefully discovered a paucity of references in the card catalog. Instead of the strong follow-through on my pitch, I was somewhat dissuaded by my eldest brother, Howard Kingsley, who mumbled something to the affect of, "not a good idea."

It's a fascinating topic, that is, the lengths men will go, to make their "rod of divination" salute in an upstanding direction. As to the comparison of customers who use pharmaceuticals like Viagra versus the natural animal parts and plants, that's a no brainer. The crazy Chinese will ingest *anything* if they think it will make their ding-dong hard. Traditional Chinese medicine shops sell deer antlers, seahorses, deer penises, sea cucumbers, dried lizards, monkey brains, sparrow tongues, deer tails, rabbit hair, tiger penises and the fungus that grows on bat moth larvae as aphrodisiacs. Chinese men also consume bull and deer penises soaked in herbal wine, bull's penis cooked with Chinese yam, fertilized duck eggs and snake bile to boost their sex life. That's enough for now; this is another financial scheme that has eluded the author. Perhaps I need to consider bank robbery as a viable path to wealth and meanwhile cry over the spilt milk.

Candles have always held a fascination with me starting with the mysterious flickering votive lights in the church alcoves for the purpose of intoning the hierarchal powers for some prayer or favor. Then there were the Dickensian eerie scenes that required waxed sticks for illumination and spooky shadows. But I used candles in my sparkling youth for romantic assignation and consider them head and shoulders above a dimmer switch. They mirror life, flickering like an anticipatory thought in the breeze, that they might go out and leave us in the dark. On the other hand, the Hollywood trade picked up on the idea some years ago and, not to be outdone, created scenes with fifty or one hundred candles whether in a bath or boudoir; they have the money to be ridiculous and trite.

I've heard that jokes are now passé; who knows since I don't get around much these days, but for decades, any gathering of two or more guys would spark any number of amusing stories. That reminds me of the three anthropologists working in the jungle of the New Guinea highlands. The trio runs into a ferocious tribe of cannibals who are incensed at this intrusion. The chief shouts, "Your punishment is death or bunga-bunga!" He asks the first scientist, "Shall it be death or bunga-bunga?"

- The tortoise shell glasses replies, "Well, I want to live, so I'll take bunga-bunga."
- The savages quickly pile on and have their way with him.
- The chief asks the second scientist, "Shall it be death or bunga-bunga?"
- The wispy hair replies, "I don't want to die, so bunga-bunga."
- The savages surround him and have their way with him.
- Then the chief asks the third man—the Clark Gable type, Will it be death or bunga-bunga?"

- The moustache man says, "I saw what happened to those other guys, so I'll take death!

- The chief screams out, "He'll take death! Death! Death by bunga-bunga!"

This question occurs to me: for the sake of posterity, do you have a naked photo of your girlfriend, wife, mother, or grandmother when they were young? Why not? This might be a grand addition to the photo album of the family tree or bush. Note: men need not apply. Did I tell you the story of my mother in the bathroom? When I was three years old, I toddled into the privy where my mother was naked and doing her business. She didn't think anything of it at the time, and I didn't either, at the time.

According to one of the most recognized intellects on the planet in 2013, Steven Hawking advocated that, "The biggest mystery in the universe is women." Hawking, the famous English theoretical physicist and cosmologist turned 70 on 8 January 2012.

Once upon a time I fell asleep on the sands of historic Takanassee Beach and woke up to what I supposed was sunrise but it turned out to be a massive, phenomenal full moon just rising at the eastern horizon. I was stunned and so was my girlfriend.

If you're considering spinning "In the Mood" tonight from Glen Miller by candlelight, try this out for size. Obtain a double cassette player and place Frank Sinatra on the left side ("All My Tomorrows" or similar tune) and the haunting Sade ("Is It a Crime" or similar song) on the right. Push the play button on both sides so the two songs play together—and watch the sparks fly!

Unfortunately I am stuck in a dead end zone not really of my choosing. This supposedly metropolitan area is a low class, no class locale. For instance, they have various retail stores such as "Condoms to Go" and I wondered what *that* is all about since one can buy these rubbers for lovers in a pharmacy or any dingy bar toilet. Due to my curiosity, I recently visited one of these stores and inquired about the name, Condoms to Go. Why the name? I don't see a drive-up window, and is the alternative Condoms to Stay? After one look, I could figure it out; the store is like a hardware store of sexual devices hanging on the walls like a Radio Shack of degeneracy. Obviously they are getting around the visceral nomenclature of seedy establishments called Adult Sex Toys Shop.

Urban areas also have free publications available in street-side boxes such as the Dallas Observer which is part of the many free types of newsprint under the umbrella of Village Voice Media. These inky papers ostensibly cover hard-edged investigative stories about government, politics and business, as well as provocative coverage of sports, music and the arts. But actually, they are a boring waste of time for an urban readership. One aspect they do have is a conduit for sex advertisements. In a typical edition, there are approximately 135 advertisements for the sex trade to include 90 ads with a small female photo and 45 classified text-only advertisements. The take-away seems to advocate a sexy photo as a sure lure to the hungry and lurid consumers. No wonder it's free newsprint, only useful for wrapping up fish or lining the bottom of the bird cage.

After the first Gulf War in 1992 I flew from Saudi Arabia and met up with my two brothers from the U.S. to meet our wealthy English cousin (of Irish descent) in London. Pat picked us up at Heathrow, and the first attraction he drove to was, not the Tower of London or Hyde Park, but a cheap London strip joint. My jaw dropped on seeing third-rate tricks who danced as a hat was passed around for a few quid as a gratuity. If this is your kind of entertainment, there is no comparison to the Baby Dolls franchise in Florida and the other states where the girls are knock-outs. But you have to consider, the English are very thrifty and well—you know what I mean. By the same token, I visited a third brother in Tampa, Florida, prior to another tour in Saudi in

1995. He took me around the local dive bars including one seedy strip club. At one point, a young lady approached and informed me that Michael had paid $20 for my lap dance. For the naïve or uninitiated, you can imagine what a lap dance involves in the darkness at the back of the establishment. I politely declined the offer so my brother did the dirty rather than see his $20 go for nothing.

You have to wonder about the sex scene and old geezers... Supposedly for those over 80 years old, 29 percent of men and 25 percent of women still engage in sexual activity. They are gleefully supported by the drug companies that conjure a cornucopia of pharmaceuticals to boost the bottom line. Pills go hand-in-hand—more pills to extend your life and some to keep you busy in the meantime. The benevolent corporate executives want to help women with hormone replacement therapy and tinker with men's testosterone levels as well as erectile dysfunction; treat the causes of sexual difficulty due to diabetes, arteriosclerosis, dementia, and Alzheimer's (when you simply forget what you're doing or how to do it). All this leads to lower expectations and a revised mindset where the emphasis is changed from fireworks to fizzle, or striving for a bunt at the plate rather than the homerun or "grand slam."

In Saudi Arabia, old geezers in their 80s often marry teenagers as a third or fourth wife, so a penile prosthesis might be just what the doctor ordered and besides it's free in the government hospital. One word suffices—creepy.

Due to an aging population, the market for porn films with elderly actors has doubled over the past decade in Japan. That makes excellent business sense because a young knock-out can command $100,000 per film whereas the droopy old bird would be lucky to get $2,000.

This obsession with sex must come to an end; it's embarrassing. And let's face it: Imagine elderly sex during a rocket-launch countdown near Cape Canaveral, Florida...10, 9, 8...Ok dear, goodnight.

On one of my trips to the Philippines...I was supposed to kill time and so occupied myself at a bar in one of the provinces. It was interesting that all the bar maids were wearing a large necklace with a number attached. My female companion had dropped me at the bar for some reason or other, and that was curious enough because they were jealous females to the point of psychosis. I don't recall any spontaneous conversations but, now that I remember it, #23 was especially nice looking.

Before we move on...there is an attractive insight about sex apropos of nothing. In his book, *The Naked Ape*, Desmond Morris introduces the idea of sexual self-mimicry of our human ancestors. At some point in antiquity, we must have been using the rear approach for sex. If the female of our species was going to shift the interest of the male to the front, for social and face-to-face purposes, one might very well expect to find some sort of frontal self-mimicry. And this, it would seem, is precisely what has happened, with the female carrying a duplicate set of buttocks (breasts) and Labia (lips) on their chest and mouth respectively. Desmond mentions that the modern use of lipsticks and brassieres immediately springs to mind, and I would add the recent cosmetic procedure of boob jobs as well as lip augmentation or plumping the pucker.

CHAPTER 7

Dead End Kids
The Universe in a Nutshell

For some unknown reason, the universe came into existence about 14.7 billion years ago. Theories include the Big Bang Model that surmises the universe emerged near time zero from a very hot, dense state and has been expanding and cooling ever since. The initial mass was compressed to a size much smaller than a pin head—that is, the head of a pin.

The Inflationary Cosmology Model explains the possible existence of a Higgs Field that provided an outward blast of repulsive gravity, driving space to expand.

In the Cyclic Cosmology Theory, two universes collide and bounce away every trillion years to begin the process over again and again. With the emergence of the universe, galaxies formed out of the material that came into existence from the hot plasma, and most of the universe is made up of so-called dark matter and dark energy. Only about five percent of the universe is what we term ordinary matter that humans can see and touch. Although Einstein thought the universe was static or unchanging, in 1929 Edwin Hubble observed that all galaxies are rushing away from each other and the farther a galaxy is, the faster the recession or moving away. Creation is thus rushing away and space in the future may be mostly empty, although we will not be around to worry about it.

The human mind finds it difficult to grasp the vastness of the universe since it was formed to perceive local or parochial interests. For example, the eyes can only see so far or into certain dimensions. The experimental psychologist, Steven Pinker, views the mind as more like a Swiss Army knife: a large set of gadgets, language being one of them, shaped by natural selection to accomplish the kinds of tasks that our ancestors faced in ancient times. Our eyes did not evolve to see microwaves or gamma rays. Luckily we cannot see things on the microscopic level without instruments, for then we might be disturbed by the world of microbes, mites, and bacteria that make a living from our bodies and habiliments. Actually there are 100 trillion good bacteria that live in or on the human body and in some sense we are made mostly of microbes. Half of your stool is not leftover food. It is microbial biomass. But bacteria multiply so quickly that they replenish their numbers as fast as they are excreted.

When I would visit home from college, my mother would see to it that any such habiliments and suitcases were duly, "aired in the sun." Clever woman—and when my East African relatives come to visit, I can't help but wonder, "What the hell are they bringing along?" Sorry, that's my view, especially after getting dead-dog sick from *bugs* in their neck of the woods.

Evolution is a game that prepares organisms and beings for localized environments. The human ancestors left the forests of Africa for the Savannah. They initially had the advantages of bipedalism (Lucy can run like hell on two feet) and later, language, to successfully dominate competitors and subdue the environment. Evolution didn't prepare us for life on Mars or Venus where the atmosphere cannot sustain oxygen breathing beings. Many perceptions of scenes outside our neighborhood are considered alien or foreign, such as the uncivilized savages who look funny, speak a different language, and have weird customs—you know, the new neighbors next door. Since we are not really far removed from our savage brethren, we still think in primitive terms and from our own perspectives naturally. Mindsets however can be changed, rebooted, and reprogrammed. This is what is needed to continue to survive, if you call this living.

We are programmed to survive wars, concentration camps, and diseases like cancer. So it is a robust system which is a popular buzzword. Robust generally means able to work more than 40 hours per week for as little pay as possible. The planet will continue to spin and wobble, until we blow up the place, and leave bacteria as the most prolific life-form on Earth—as it is now. Either way, life will continue on other planets in other galaxies.

Philosophers have been contemplating the nature of reality for thousands of years. Just what is reality? A search of the internet would result in a headache inducing hodgepodge of articles and books on reality—mostly unintelligible. Most people think that a falling tree is real whether or not there is someone in the forest to hear it. To the average person, reality means everything that exists. It is what we can perceive in a common-sense way, although perception and thought are imperfect processes for most of us. Our notions of reality are shaped by our senses such as sight and hearing. We are built to see flowers and not the sub-atomic particles that comprise the thing. Many species, including bees, can see a broader spectrum of light than we can. Ultraviolet light, invisible to us, uncovers colors and patterns which draw bees to the source of pollen and nectar. Unlike people, bees can see distinct patterns that act as landing strips which guide the bees to the nectar on which they feed.

Some people perceive sensory input different than the norm. Due to a neurological disorder called synesthesia, there are those who taste colors, see sounds, or hear shapes. For example, they see the color blue when they hear a particular musical note. Perception is a slippery slope on the toll road of reality and things aren't always what they seem. For all the Freudian ego, personality, thinker, and dreamer selves, we are a captive audience of one person against the wave of the *others*. To swim against the tide implies wading through the flotsam and jetsam of contrary notions and opinions, but this is a noble course for the daring and adventuresome.

Mankind is making headway with the science of physics as we try to understand the incredibly small subatomic world and the cosmos at large. In an onion analogy, scientists work to peel back the layers of reality only to find more layers. This passion to know the nature of reality leads to full lifetimes of occupation.

For example, Einstein died at the age of 76 on 18 April 1955. By his bed they found 12 pages of equations. And the final thing he wrote, before he went to sleep for the last time, was one more line of symbols and numbers that he hoped might get him, and the rest of us, just a little step closer to the spirit manifest in the laws of the universe.[2]

According to the talented physicist, Brian Greene, penetrating analyses are leading us to what may be the next upheaval in understanding: the possibility that our universe is not the only universe.[3] His book, *The Hidden Reality*, startles one to think that the term "out there" may include multiple or parallel universes. And if space is infinite in expanse, there will be a number of universes where *you* are the President of the United States. The latest string theory of physics is exploring an ultimate theory of everything. There may be more than the (three) space and (one) time dimensions of our daily experience, but we cannot see them.

Scientists released the power in nuclear reactions just as the primitives released the energy stored in coal and other combustible commodities. It is certain that future scientists will discover strange and contradictory manifestations of nature such as dark matter and dark energy. It seems that science has become the new supernatural and it can be disconcerting to some observers. Already even simple-minded terrorists can, with the requisite resources, put together a dirty nuclear bomb. Humans have come a long way, from ancestral use of stone tools 2.5 million years ago followed by extensive periods of stagnant innovation. But in just a few seconds of geological time, humans attained the ability to blast us back into the past. Paradoxically the morons among us will cause the unwanted catastrophe. We allow the miscreants this power as we stand around to watch them and bemoan our fate.

I'm not sure who the morons are any more. But we know about the dupes or those that were duped in recent years. Many people seem to be among the walking wounded such as homeowners who are upside down on their mortgages, owing more than their home is worth. There was a time when young people couldn't afford to buy a house while an older generation made fortunes with their real estate holdings. The word bubble is a beautiful description of the boom and burst of the dot com crisis and the housing mania. The thefts are perpetrated right before our eyes, or is this really the free market like the mortgage-backed securities?

What I would like to point out, though, is the rise of capitalism has been a boon, but could turn into a bust, if unchecked development and progress are not managed carefully. A profit-driven society can lose focus when money accumulation becomes an end itself, rather than permitting the greatest good for the greatest number of people. That is why ecological husbandry and sustainment have become popular concepts today. But who will stand down for the greenhouse effects of global warming? It's not my job!

There are some simple common sense behaviors that ordinary individuals can follow. On the small scale, if you keep feeding the ducks, pigeons, and seagulls, you will gain minor self satisfaction but we'll also gain the accumulation of droppings onto our beaches and parks; wild animals are supposed to appropriate their own diet and resources. In addition, a recent study by Woods Hole Oceanographic Institution found sand can harbor up to 38 times more harmful bacteria than nearby swimming waters. On a larger scale, if human societies continue feeding at the trough like pigs, by overconsumption of fossil fuels, and spoiling nature's resources, their actions will be viewed as despicable to future generations.

Humans continue to funnel their genes into the mainstream in the search for eternity. Ironically, in a few generations, the average being will be remembered as vividly as an innocuous dream. But there's always immortality to strive for. You can buy into cryopreservation, the low-temperature preservation of the body, and hope that resuscitation becomes possible in the future. A cheaper idea, and more cost effective, is to immortalize a snippet of your hair which contains the DNA necessary to clone another you when the time is ripe. You might even send it into outer space in the hopes that aliens will pick up on it. You wouldn't mind if the aliens don't accomplish the pickup for a million years or so, right? This will only be a physical you without the memories or experiences but some of these could be placed on a microchip and kept with the DNA sample. The idea may strike you like an egotistical exercise for immortality but just do it for a lark. Imagine how long the relatives will keep your identity locket in the family safe or shoe box. It also helps to fund this expedition, but then again, can you trust future relatives to keep the covenant for your eventual but 'long in the tooth' comeback? Or will they throw a big party and go to Bermuda on your remittance? In fact, enlist close friends or relatives to join the venture as a kind of Noah's Ark (without the riff-raff). Hopefully any potential aliens won't consider you as repulsive as you might view them but that's the chance you take.

This idea is similar to the religious malarkey of living for life after death. It doesn't sound like a good bet because living after death is the quintessential mirage. It's analogous to working for retirement. We are normally supposed to work to live. The television evangelists and other hucksters love them for it. "Empty your pockets for the lord (and my new hot rod) and you will be saved, brother!" People have this crooked notion of living forever. That's why vampires are so prolific and you just can't seem to get rid of them; they hang around for a long time in movies and books. I would venture that most people have not really given proper consideration to immortality.

So much has been written on the subject, that you would definitely need to live forever to cover all of it. In the strange story of Oscar Wilde's *The Picture of Dorian Grey*, a handsome young man is able to keep his youthful appearance eternally while his portrait changes hideously as time goes by. Just how much pizza can one consume, an endless amount? And what is the difference between living, say 80 years as opposed to 90 years? Obviously the question has some relativity involved. For example, fans bemoan that Michael Jackson died young. Yet he had a tortured and talented life with a long-lasting legacy. In my opinion, his music will be played for perhaps hundreds of years, alongside Sinatra and Pavarotti, but I do not relish seeing the moonwalk for eternity. Even the terminator said, "I'll be back!"

Like the phenomenon of near death experiences, hospital patients have alluded to out-of-the body awareness and certain euphoric feelings related to catastrophic brain malfunctioning. We simply don't know where the relatives went when they left, but it has been a prolific source of curiosity throughout human history. This includes certain societies that practice ancestor worship like the Chinese. In their extreme beliefs, earthquakes are viewed as an ancestral sign for regime demotion, and the joke that "you can't take it with you" was not pleasing for the ancient Egyptians either. The greedy Pharaohs were mummified and fortified for a balmy afterlife and they packed gold and grub for their journey as well as unwitting spouses, concubines, and dutiful slaves to grease the funereal wheel of fortune. Speaking of near death, I can relate to one experience at the age of eight. We lived across the street from Franklin Lake that seemed frozen one winter's day. As the three of us stood at the far side of the lake, I offered my friend Frankie a nickel to cross the ice to the other side. Frankie proposed to split the five cents with my brother Michael to accompany him; so I ventured to tag along and took the rear for the heck of it.

At the middle of the lake, there was a pounding CRACK that reverberated down the lake (think Battle Star Galactica sound effect) and we were instantly surrounded by splintering, collapsing ice and plunged into the icy water. At that time, I was a little squirt; today I am a taller squirt or half pint. But it was every boy for himself, alternately pulling ourselves back onto the ice, and crashing back into the water, until we somehow managed the opposite shore. Although the lake was not so deep, it was probably over my head and years later I could hear the echoes of mother saying, "Good things come in small packages." Luckily, Frankie ran home and summoned his older sister Julie who ran down and carried me back home to my frantic mother who shouted to Jesus, Mary, Joseph, and the saints, as she filled the tub with warm water for my shivering, chattering body. In the final analysis, although there was a 25-cent coin in my pocket, and two bits was a fortune then, it was lost in the struggle. And to this day, if something is lost, I will look for it for quite some time like the ghost on Wuthering Heights.

Quiet! We're Talking Death Here

Christians have a ghastly custom of death burial. They employ a special class of workers called undertakers or funeral directors, who perform a high class type of mummification, the kind that's not quite everlasting. But for a princely fee, they will put you in a nice box and after some eulogiums, bury you six feet under or burn you in a furnace if you prefer. The cemeteries are reminders of man's propensity for ghoulish ruin of otherwise decent real estate. And it reminds me of the old joke while driving by one. Question: How many dead people are in there? Answer: All of them! They have mausoleums, garish statues, cement monuments, and as far as the eye can see; a sea of forgotten egos. For a ghoulish trivia item, the largest cemetery in North America is the 1400 acre Rose Hills in Whittier, California. They have properties to suit a variety of preferences, including many feng-shui properties, waterfront properties, and properties with sweeping, panoramic views. There are lawn spaces, monument wall spaces, semi-private estates, private estates, mausoleums, custom construction, and cremation properties.

For a funeral, people send arrangements of flowers, a desecration of nature's beauty; this stone-cold custom is another gruesome expenditure. Sinatra was remembered for a notable toast with a glass in hand: "May you live to be 100 and may the last voice you hear be mine." People tend to forget or simply don't understand that funerals are for the living, not the dead; the deceased are gone and only the dust remains. The mourners tiptoe around the box and marvel at the flowers. When you go to a wedding, one may delight in taking some flowers home; but at a funeral, we no more want takeaway flowers than we want cheap soap from a low budget hotel.

Death is a quiet and embarrassing time for some. It's the one given in life and yet we can't take it. People generally cry at funerals, and in China, you can pay for a professional crier. England sported paid mourners for hundreds of years. For some cultures, the burial place is a night out on the town with food and drink offered at the tomb for the deceased.

Death has always been celebrated and dreaded. The day of the dead on Halloween is an important occasion and now the second-biggest decorating holiday of the year in the U.S., right behind Christmas, and the 6th in sales.

Most people may not be familiar with Elizabeth Kubler Ross. Her extensive work with the dying led to the book *On Death and Dying* in 1969. In this work she proposed the now famous Five Stages of Grief as a pattern of adjustment. These five stages of grief are denial, anger, bargaining, depression, and acceptance. In general, individuals experience most of these stages, though in no defined sequence, after being faced with the reality of their impending death. The five stages have since been adopted by many as applying to the survivors of a loved one's death or other tragedies such as from tornadoes and hurricanes as well.

Many of us have heard about the late Dr. Kevorkian (Doctor Death), the medical pathologist who argued for the right of terminally ill patients to choose how they die. He challenged social taboos about disease and dying while defying prosecutors and the courts. Jack Kevorkian spent eight years in prison after being convicted of second-degree murder in the death of the last of about 130 ailing patients whose lives he had helped end.[4] Obviously, the good doctor had no qualms about "playing God." I have to include myself as one who shares a passion with the underdog.

There are some euphemisms about the business of death such as "he's passed" (passed where?) rather than he died. My wife's English employs the term "he's gone" whether someone died or if our grandson falls asleep, which makes me wince. We can joke about it but most people are afraid of dying especially if the grim reaper draws near during a medical or accident event.

People will stampede over each other's head, like bulls chasing Spaniards, to escape fire in a crowded hall. If there is a ghost of a chance of surviving a calamity, they will sell their soul to the devil and at the same time pray to the gods with some guaranteed bribe. Humans have an instinctual drive to cling to life because, if this were lacking in our ancient descendants, natural selection would have weeded them out. Alas, when it's time for lights out—"cried the raven nevermore"—it's notably sad if there are close relations who will be truly grieved and suffer emotional or financial consequences. Otherwise, who cares? Humans might have a deep seated capacity to deny the end, but risky behavior has no bearing on some natures. We have an obligation to live our lives as if there will be no regrets and to try our best to make some good choices in life.

Insurance companies profit from mortality with actuarial tables, calculus, and probability theory. In ancient Greece, for example, life expectancy at birth was 20. When the Declaration of Independence was signed, life expectancy was still just 23. Even as recently as 1900, most Americans died by age 47.[5] Today the life expectancy in the U.S. is about 78 and we rank 50th according to the CIA World Factbook. In view of longer life spans, you would suppose that the prosperous America should be working less but instead they are working more than ever. Many even work with their phones and other devices on weekends and holidays. Since the workers are living longer they naturally are expected to work longer. I can just imagine the future of the working class in wheel chairs and walkers. Forget the rocking chair; they don't make them anymore.

Speaking of the good old days, even the prehistoric humans put their dead in the ground with some ceremony, and ever since, various customs and taboos have arisen to bury the problem. Although it's as natural as passing gas, we shun it like the plague. Taboos are the cause for some strange behavior. Among the Maori, anyone who had handled a corpse or taken any part in its burial was considered unclean. He could not enter any house, touch food with his hands, or come into ordinary contact with other people. Arabs and Jews must be buried as soon as possible and they forego the elaborate or ghoulish preparations involved such as the Western custom of embalming and fancy casket selection. The Indian Hindus burn their dead on a funeral pyre. This open-air cremation tradition is certainly cost-effective and has the added benefit of forgoing valuable real estate as well as upkeep or maintenance. Makes some sense the way I see it. Some deceased bodies are laid out with a few trinkets of jewelry, and when the funeral home closes the box, do you ever wonder whether the jewels made it into the ground? And as the saying goes, "You can't take it with you."

A Smidgen of Ethical Issues

Unfortunately the human brain, although capable of complex reasoning, had a bumpy ride in its evolution, and can only get its hands around certain finite possibilities. The brain is indeed limited. Many of our unique mental traits seem to have evolved through the novel deployment of brain structures that originally evolved for other reasons. Feathers evolved from scales whose original role was insulation rather than flight. Evolution found ways to radically repurpose many functions of the ape brain to create entirely new functions.[6]

Humans have a short lifespan and are naturally predisposed to consider immediate concerns rather than think in terms of several hundred years in advance. Similar to pigs that wallow in the mire, humans are destroying their environment and choosing to live in and among filth. We will bequeath a mess to future generations if current trends continue. Just visit Bombay or Baghdad. And the continued proliferation of nuclear weapons-grade material poses a global risk of nightmarish proportions. If there are advanced alien civilizations in the universe, they would be more sophisticated life forms that have matured past the juvenile stage of existence. Perhaps they are able to survive and avert extinction due to the absence of self destructive traits or behavior. Life, if not humans, could potentially survive for millions of years because, even if we destroy ourselves, the DNA of humans and jackasses may be available via space craft for retrieval by the advanced beings. A slim probability—humans could be reconstituted like powdered milk. Actually serious first steps are being taken to revive and restore non-human species as discussed at the 2012 Aspen Environment Forum (Bringing Back the Dead). Stewart Brand, and his wife the geneticist Ryan Phelan, contend that we may be able to run extinction backward and propose a candidate, the Passenger Pigeon, a species that vanished a century ago. Advances in cloning and DNA sequencing have made recreating extinct species a real possibility. You might ask, what is the point to it? There is no doubt that humans will demand the return of certain majestic animal species that were allowed to slip away from existence. In a future time, humans could also be reconstituted and reengineered, as a new and improved model, and I don't have to wait for the commercial — available for a limited time only. These types of ideas have physical constraints that need to be overcome such as functional habitats and expected adaptation to the environment. There are also ethical ramifications that worry the conservative segment of society who do not want to leave their comfort zone. They wish to prevent the overload of psyche, and rather opt for baby steps, instead of plunging towards risky proposals and actions. For example, the crowd that agrees that we should not play God wants to be obeyed. But for our own well being to include future generations, we need to start playing the role of father to keep the human family going. For example, we require a universal or global ethic to prevent implosion of our human race from nuclear disaster, overpopulation, and other causes. Two affecting quotes come to mind "I won't think about that now, I'll think about that tomorrow" (Scarlett O'Hara) and "Frankly my dear, I don't give a damn" (Rhett Butler).

Many ethical issues are seen as gray areas with pros and cons that depend on a liberal or conservative viewpoint. Although the differences between liberals and conservatives run wide and deep, a new study suggests they may even be reflected in the very structure of their brains; liberals tend to have a larger anterior cingulate cortex and conservatives tend to have a larger right amygdala. This news is not very surprising since neurology seems to be the flavor of the month to explain behavior. I'm not sure these types of labels are really helpful in any event since there is a large continuum between liberal and conservative, and perhaps we need to focus on what is logical, reasonable, and intelligent. We can all chuckle at the cartoon character with the devil on the left shoulder (the idea of left is sinister) and the angel on the right shoulder. These little images are handy for describing our inner conflict of conscience versus temptation. However you look at it, we have to take a stand on the various ethical issues and not be afraid to reach reasoned solutions.

The following topics are some of the prominent *ethical* considerations:

Killing

Moral philosophers have long debated under what circumstances it is acceptable to kill. The sixth commandment states, "Thou shalt not kill." You can read numerous interpretations of this biblical directive until you are blue in the face. Although the King James Version of the bible translates into "Thou shalt not murder," the Old Testament is filled with many deaths attributable to God and his followers. For example, naughty behavior was punished in the Sodom and Gomorrah story.

In the following two scenarios, the moral difference is noted. For question #1, an out-of-control trolley is rushing towards five people on the track, who face certain death. You are nearby and, by turning a switch, could send the trolley onto a spur and save their lives. But one man is chained to the spur and would be killed if the trolley is diverted. Should you flick the switch?

For Question #2, the same trolley is about to kill five people. This time, you are on a footbridge overlooking the track, next to a fat man. If you were to push him off the bridge onto the track his bulk would stop the trolley and save the lives of those five people, but kill him. Do you push him? Study after study has shown that people will sacrifice the spur man but not the fat man. Yet in both cases, one person is killed to save five others. Evidently, people find some ethical distinction between the two scenarios, and perhaps they disclaim playing God. Is it ethical to invade a country such as Iraq and kill thousands of innocent civilians with the shock and awe?

Capital Punishment

One of our main problems is that society doesn't punish people because the justice system would rather annoy criminals than hand out punishment. Felons are given three "hots and a cot" at the taxpayer's expense and the accommodations for the thieves, rapists, and killers resemble a revolving-door clubhouse for psychopaths. Capital punishment is no longer recognized as a significant tool for societal management. The term seems to be somehow alloyed with the connotation of ethnic cleansing which is recognized as immoral. There is an ethical distinction between killing and murdering. Many forms of killing are justified, e.g., the slaughtering of animals for food. Murder is unjustified killing. If a society has justifiable reasons for using the death penalty then it cannot be considered as murder.[7] The paradox is that we cannot kill criminals, but with a push of a button on a fixed-wing aircraft, half of a village can be blasted to rubble; this is an absurdity.

Death row inmates in the United States typically spend over a decade awaiting execution. Some prisoners have been on death row for well over 20 years. Perhaps the term should be changed to "slow death row." And I don't accept the liberal proposition that we shouldn't assign the death penalty if there is a chance that one innocent will be killed by mistake. Nobody's perfect, and as they say in the cockpit "shit happens!" By the way, if you're at a party, how do you know if there is a pilot in the room? Answer: he will let you know. I'm not advocating a return to the gin-soaked mob of spectators who watched London hangings until 1783. But ethical issues like the death penalty are man-made, and should be discussed and resolved without reference to revelation or mysticism. Capital punishment deters crime. How capital punishment affects murder rates can be explained through general deterrence theory, which supposes that increasing the risk of apprehension and punishment for crime deters individuals from committing crime. Over the years, several studies have demonstrated a link between executions and decreases in murder rates. In fact, studies done in recent years consistently demonstrate a strong link between executions and reduced murder incidents. Americans overwhelmingly support capital punishment for two good reasons. First, there is little evidence to suggest that minorities are treated unfairly. Second, capital punishment produces a strong deterrent effect that saves lives.

Abortion

Abortion issues received much publicity in the 1960s and history recorded that there was public unrest about its morality. In the midst of all the controversy, the U.S. Supreme Court ruled in 1973, in the *Roe v. Wade* case, in favor of an elimination of all existing abortion laws. Therefore, women have rights to control their own bodies. The court decided that, in the first trimester, women have a right to seek an abortion and the unborn received no rights. In the second trimester, states have the right to legislate abortions to protect the unborn somewhat if it would not cause mental or physical harm to the mother. In the third trimester, states have the right to forbid abortions except to preserve the mother's life.

Since 1976, congressional action has barred the use of federal Medicaid funds to pay for abortions except in cases of rape, incest or danger to the woman's life. Some states, though, use state funds to pay for procedures in other cases for poor women. A substantial amount of political maneuvering has been organized, especially by the anti-abortion (pro-life) movement who maintain that the human embryo is a person and therefore has a right to life. The pro-choice supporters see abortion as an important facet of women's reproductive rights. Data indicates that about 85 percent of the people do not agree with the anti-abortion laws as promoted by the fundamentalist activists.

Abortion may be unpalatable to many of us on a personal level; we cannot conceive that *our* potential grandson would not be able to live and prosper, but considering the grand scheme of life, there is too much abuse of unwanted children that do not have access to the resources for a life worth living. Anti-abortion behavior has included violence, destruction of property, kidnapping, stalking, assault, murder, arson, and bombings. You know, just what you would expect from the Nazis of the religious right. Whether you personally agree with it or not, about 42 million abortions are performed worldwide, and the need is obvious. Approximately 205 million pregnancies occur annually. Over a third are unintended and about a fifth end in induced abortion. Most abortions result from unintended pregnancies. The anti-abortionists argue that life begins at conception and many contend the soul enters at that moment. But there is no organic awareness before 20 weeks. Only in the ninth month is the brain's neocortex developed beyond being a blob.[10] The religious right see themselves as pioneers, with their backs against the log cabin walls, on this issue of abortion. It is ironic that the religious fanatics will maim and kill to get their point across.

Genetic Engineering

Genetic Engineering is a revolutionary new technology for altering the traits of living organisms by inserting genetic material that has been manipulated by artificial means. This is the ultimate example that we are playing God in so far as human existence can be changed in either a beneficial or insidious manner. Without general awareness, already a substantial portion of crops have been genetically modified especially in the United States. Although the planet has billions of empty stomachs to fill, the do-gooders dream of increasing the food supplies to propagate the species further.

The new buzz words are Synthetic Biology. Mischievous

humans are a progressive lot; we start with changing mother's milk to powder or formula and work our way up to switching various genes to the on or off position. It all sounds good but many thoughtful individuals (corporate executives excluded) find technical and ethical reasons for concern. Among a host of potential problems are the selective benefits to the wealthy elite who can pay the cost and discrimination against those who cannot afford it. For example, the term mental retardation has been changed to intellectual disability. About 80 percent of boys with the *fragile X* syndrome, which is an anomaly at the end of the X chromosome, are mentally retarded. In addition, most children with *fragile X* syndrome have other characteristic traits including anxiety, hyperactivity, and a number of behaviors that are often seen in autism.[11]

The gene-splicers contend that this and similar faulty traits can be corrected by DNA testing and genetic engineering. But other characteristics can also be modified to include whatever is currently in or out of fashion—you name it: intelligence, height, eye color, or imagination (really?). Although we have roughly 22,000 genes, the three-billion-letter, human genetic code was previously thought to contain substantial junk but only about two percent of the genome is required to encode the whole range of human proteins. The portions of non-coding DNA or junk are now recognized to be critical regulatory elements which interact with genes and act like switches that control the conditions under which a gene will be on or off. And there may be a million or more of these switches. But what has all this to do with the average consumer and society as a whole? In addition to posing risks of harm that we can envision and attempt to assess, genetic engineering may also pose risks that we simply do not know enough to identify. The recognition of this possibility does not by itself justify stopping the technology, but it does put a substantial burden on those who wish to go forward to demonstrate benefits.[12] The risks must be carefully assessed to make sure that all effects of genetic engineering, both desired and *unintended*, are benign.

The corporate world sees obvious advantages here such as the example of baby formula; breast feeding is fine but powdered milk adds to corporate profits since it makes working females more productive. The obvious bottom line is to be aware of unintended consequences, and meanwhile, one should expect fights over patents and profits. Although the train has already left the station, some of us recall the story of Dr. Frankenstein, and I for one would drag my feet on the proliferation of genetic engineering. They can flail this beast all day long but it won't answer.

Guns

There are about 300 million privately owned firearms in the United States, but who's counting. The Second Amendment to the Constitution shows, "A well regulated Militia, being necessary to the security of a free state, the right of the people to keep and bear Arms, shall not be infringed." In 2010, the U.S. Supreme Court affirmed that the Second Amendment provides Americans a fundamental right to bear arms that cannot be violated by state and local governments. Generally, gun advocates say there are three main reasons for holding: (1) Protection against crime, (2) Target practice, and (3) Hunting. An underlying theme for gun ownership is to offset government tyranny as expressed by the American founding fathers. The opposing side is identified by two words—gun control. They claim that there is a correlation between rates of gun ownership and homicide and suicide rates. Gun opponents point to the daily coverage of drive-by shootings perpetrated by gangs, domestic violence, and mass shooting sprees. In 2013, many schools started to employ armed teachers and guards due to gun violence. Gun advocates counter that restrictive gun measures only help the criminals who will not abide by any law.

States with the largest increases in gun ownership also have the largest drops in violent crimes. I have known guys who possess 30 handguns and rifles, and that evidently is the American way, great collectors that they are. The majority are conscientious and safe handlers of their weapons. But the American government is targeting gun owners such that the Homeland Security Department has Indefinite Quantity Contracts to buy more than 1.6 *billion* rounds of ammunition in the next four or five years starting in 2013; this is an obvious underhanded action to affect the supply and punish the citizenry. Guns are endemic or common in this land, and the television and movies are rife with this preoccupation of bang-bang, shoot 'em up. But heaven forbid some *important* politician is shot. Then the wailing outcry will drown out all opinions other than gun control. Celebrities such as John Lennon can come and go, but targeting the ruling elite, from Lincoln to Reagan is out of bounds.

Now let's digress to the notion of guns and the military. I contend that we might agree that a sound military is crucial to our survival. Throughout history, nations had to keep in practice to defend their land and interests. Therefore they need to keep the killing machine well oiled and sharp. You may not like this, but an army and other armed forces must train and execute a death sentence to enemies or presumed ones. A country cannot skip a generation and forget the ability and aptitude to cut throats for the sake of sovereignty and endurance. But the past practice of extending multiple tours in Iraq and Afghanistan for year after year had nothing to do with ethics, but everything to do with common sense and an obvious drain on very expensive resources. These pathetic *leaders* and their pitiful civilian counterparts should be viewed by history as the sycophantic losers as they appeared. To be engaged in just wars is understandable, but to bankrupt us for these lost causes is treachery. The leaders have driven us to insolvency in order to replace one group of bandits for another in Iraq; the Afghans are producing more poppy for heroin production than ever. And when it comes to war, be advised: the gloves come off!

I don't understand the recent fodder of "speak softly and carry a big stick" shtick. Some of our supposed allies need to pay the price for their own stick. Regarding the issue of *how* to use military force, civilians tend to endorse a greater willingness to place constraints on the manner in which force is used, whereas military personnel tend to endorse a position of overwhelming force, without restrictions, or only with very broad restrictions such as the prohibition of nuclear weapons.

In 2012 the media was outraged by the action of Marines pissing on some dead Taliban in Afghanistan. The sheep have no conception of security or protection and they deplore violence even when essentially necessary. You find them dribbling over some pages of the Geneva Convention. But I have news for them: forget conventions and fairness when it comes to war because nice guys finish last. In bona fide conflicts with high stakes, such as the War on Terrorism, following the mythical Russian, Ilya Muromets, you fight in a decisive manner by cutting the head off the dragon.

Pretending to be tame or fair goes against our evolutionary past and can be terminal. The siren call for private gun ownership, however, will certainly need to be tempered with rationale restraints. The Second Amendment of the Constitution provides a citizen's right to bear arms but not arsenals or assault weapons. And there is a need for debate on the issue of the current trend of mass shootings throughout the country. I believe many Americans are contemplating the high likelihood of another civil war in the United States. Since the treasury has been ripped, dipped, and stripped (as Leo Gorcey would say, or was it Huntz Hall?), a severe economic downturn could launch such bedlam and mayhem that it will seem like a dream. Anyone who feels nostalgic about the days of the Wild West, you will not be disappointed. It's open season; ready, aim…("Hey, Slip, let's go to Louie's for a banana split." Shaadap, Satch! Can't you see I'm cogitatin?"). (Bowery Boys).

Same Sex Marriage

The recognition of such marriages is an issue of civil, political, social, moral, and religious rights in many nations. The conflicts arise over whether same-sex couples should be allowed to enter into marriage, be required to use a different status (such as a civil union, which either grant equal rights as marriage or limited rights in comparison to marriage), or not have any such rights. Religious opinion specifies marriage is only between a man and a woman and the institution has ancient roots. Although gay people have been with us for thousands of years, during the modern era they were relegated to the periphery of society, and their behavior was considered an anomaly. Recent social activism has changed the landscape and there is plenty of empty closet space, since most are now "out." Human nature has endured by the evolution of rules and values so that the goodness of a society can be maintained. Anarchy of ethics and values would result in a madhouse leading to a place we won't recognize. In my opinion, same-sex marriage is an oxymoron because it is wrong by definition. From the tone and volume of the controversy, many Americans believe the gay and lesbian population is large, but in reality it is probably only two percent.[14] We should not placidly encourage drastic changes to our culture whether they are sexual preference, the English language, or Shariah (Islamic) law.

Some issues include whether gays should have equal rights or equal inclusion and acceptance in the hetero population. Some argue for recognition but not general acceptance. More than half the states in America have voted to ban same-sex marriage as of the year 2013. The contention brings heated arguments on both sides such as the proposed hereditary basis for homosexuality versus conscious choice. They introduce supposedly homosexual butterflies and dragonflies into the debate to prove the point that the inclination is not a choice.

In 2011, San Francisco introduced an ordinance that would require nudists to cover their seats in public places and wear clothes in restaurants. The motivation for the law was *only* because it is unsanitary. Public nudity is legal in San Francisco and in recent years, a group known as the Naked Guys, have shown no shame appearing in the nude. Perhaps they need to look-up the definition of depravity because ordinary people don't like deviants of any stripe.

Although the majority of gays are very peaceful and kindly,

the minority that exhibit indecent behavior are poorly viewed. Since gay men are much more promiscuous than the heterosexual and lesbian population, this is viewed as a shortcoming. For example, a study of homosexual men published in 1978 revealed that 75 percent of self-identified, white, gay men admitted to having sex with more than 100 different males in their lifetime.[15] Many fear an openly gay person should not be enabled to hold teaching positions for their young, impressionable children. Will viewers suddenly be subjected to advertising that enables behavior which is seen as counter-productive? There is an apprehension that acceptance is a Trojan horse that is being wheeled in by questionable advocates to include the movie and television industry. The moguls of Hollywood have consistently and despicably pushed the homosexual agenda for many years to influence the credulous viewing public.

Drugs and Legalization

The U.S. has a mind-numbing history of anti-drug policy, with some of the world's harshest penalties for drug possession and sales. Proponents of the "war on drugs" believe that drugs are poison and cause addiction, crime, and family violence. Advocates of drug legalization or liberalization seek the repeal or moderation of drug prohibition laws relating to marijuana (pot), cocaine (coke), and methamphetamines (speed). Some want to see decriminalization whereby one receives a slap on the wrist or fine instead of prison. The proponents like to mention Carl Sagan did some of his best thinking while stoned. And they are most likely nostalgic about their college days when they purchased pot with their checkbooks from characters with names like Dutch or Squirrel.

In the 1970s, you could receive a shipment of *Acapulco Gold* from the postal service and no one would suspect it was other than fruitcake. But in those days the pot was *mostly* Mexican and the potency was much less than today. An uptick in drug enforcement in the ensuing decades ironically drove domestic "home-grown" cultivators in America to genetically create a superior product of higher potency. In the old college days, you could receive a shipment of crunchy cereal and cookies but the boxes might contain a baggie of LSD and purple colored pills. It's scary to imagine these are the people now running the country. They have a selective memory of a time of innocence and happiness; you could indulge and pay a small price to see Loggins and Messina with Jim Croce as the opening act, and among a crowd of only two thousand. By comparison in 2012, Bruce Springsteen played to an audience of 84,000 for a two-night concert in Chicago. Incidentally, Springsteen is from my area in New Jersey (Monmouth Country) and he has been around a long time; I saw him perform in the basement of my St. Jerome Elementary School in 1970, when I was a sophomore at Red Bank Catholic High School.

There have been some A+ advocates for liberalization of drugs to include William F. Buckley and the late and great economist, Milton Friedman. During Prohibition in the 1920s, Freidman noted, alcohol was readily available and bootlegging was common. Any idea that alcohol prohibition was keeping people from drinking was absurd. But more than that, the nation had their hoods, (like Al Capone), hijackings, and the gang wars. From an economic standpoint, there are substantial costs involved in drug prohibition and revenue gains from legalization and taxing the sales.

The famous linguist and philosopher, Noam Chomsky, claims that drug laws have historically been used by the state to oppress sections of society it opposes. Very commonly, substances are criminalized because they're associated with what's called the dangerous classes, poor people, or working people. So for example in England in the 19th century, there was a period when gin was criminalized and whiskey wasn't, because gin is what poor people drink.[16] I believe he is missing the point with that idea. Actually, the problem may not relate to the class of people, but to the class of liquor. In merry old England, they used to mix gin with turpentine, so no wonder the poor guzzlers went out of their minds. Gin is the one spirit that can change a Dr. Jekyll into a Mr. Hyde and I can testify as to never having taken a sip of gin in my life. The primitive imbibers are more interested with the effects rather than the taste. For instance, wild animals, to include chimps and shrews, have been boozing on fermented fruits for millions of years. Our caveman relatives must have tipped the gourd now and then, and the civilized Egyptians inherited the keys for the brewery from the Sumerians.

For the drugs of choice, Mexico is out of control with criminal cartels trafficking in marijuana, cocaine, and methamphetamines; the war over narcotics in Mexico has claimed more than 50,000 lives since 2006. Afghanistan is producing even more opium since the ten-year war began which costs taxpayers $1.5M per day.

While I was in Honduras during 1986 when Reagan sent the 82nd Airborne as a show of force against the Nicaraguan Contras, the people carried pistols, rifles, and machetes; but with the drug cartels today, the country is much more lethal in terms of criminal activity. For a good laugh, President Reagan's wife, Nancy, worked on a public relations campaign in the 1980s, called Just Say No—as if those fogies had any influence with adolescents or the hip-hop world of toking and popping. Some derided Nancy's approach as simplistic; liberal Abbie Hoffmann likened her campaign to the equivalent of telling manic depressives to "just cheer up."

Marijuana use among American teens is at a 30-year high in the year 2013. One of every 15 high school seniors reported smoking pot on a daily basis, according to a report released by the National Institute on Drug Abuse. Marijuana has been the largest cash crop in the U.S. for years. Libertarians are against the government telling people what to do. They say the case for prohibiting drugs is exactly as strong or as weak as the case for stopping people from overeating; it is well known that overeating causes more deaths than drugs do. You don't have to be a left-winger to observe that booze and cigarettes are legal but pot is verboten. I suspect that some of the logic behind legalizing drugs is as phony as medical marijuana. Regardless of the A+ geniuses and pundits, drug sale and use is either right or wrong.

In the Netherlands, the government tried to restrict non-citizen tourists from using pot which is available in "coffee houses." The ban on foreigners entering coffee shops was due to take effect across the whole country in 2013, limiting access to marijuana to Dutch residents. However, after intense lobbying for revenue, the law still stands, but it's now up to each city to decide how to apply it. In some respects, Amsterdam is not only a popular haunt for the British and American travelers, but it can seem sleazy with the stoners laying about the thoroughfares and parks; they can be noisy, unruly, and a nuisance. Think about the sordid aspects of San Francisco. And to add to the unpleasantness, there is a red-light district in Amsterdam filled with prostitutes in the windows for your viewing pleasure. And no, Mr. Freud, this is not a dream. It is a tourist attraction where even couples will walk through the area like a day at the mall. I interviewed one lady in the window and was humorously entertained to learn that the women have to wash the genitals of prospective clients before the business, which obviously shortens the sexual experience. I have never in my life paid for sex but, supposedly some guys, all right a lot of them, find it a timesaving endeavor—you know, akin to the drive-up window at a cheap hamburger joint. Some people want the easy way out.

Suffice to say, I would be Timothy O'Leary about legalizing drugs. Nonetheless, as a temporary experiment, the government could anoint a particular city as a free-drug zone for a period of time. Since many of the intellects warn us of the many advantages to legalization, moral to monetary, let's pick a place that could use this boost, and I propose Camden, New Jersey. I may have to change my ethical stance on this issue. But for now, my cure for the war on drugs is emphatic. No one, not even Nancy Reagan could dent this monster, but I can. If elected king, anyone caught with a quantity of hard drugs for sale goes straight to the firing squad and no questions asked. The drug war would be zipped up and carted away.

The Racial Divide

There is a simmering, festering boil on the backside of America and many other nations, and it's the notion of the racial divide. However you slice it, we just don't seem to get along, period. In America, we saw the racial divide very plainly over the O.J. Simpson verdict. As in other controversies, whites were quick to condemn, blacks were quick to defend.

But the racial divide is not only felt in this country; it is worldwide. For example, Malaysia appears more racially polarized than it has been in decades. The country's mix of ethnic Malays, Indians and Chinese has long been resentful of each other and they willfully segregate themselves. Those resentments exploded into full-blown race riots in 1969, when ethnic Malays attacked and killed scores of ethnic Chinese.

In the Philippines, the Chinese are denigrated as the stereotypical *rich Jews* of the country due to their economic resources and success.

In South Africa, there is a movement towards nationalization of the country's mines and a more aggressive redistribution of farmland from whites to blacks.

France's controversial *burka* ban became law on 11 April 2011 and sparked protests. The garment is worn by Muslim women, and in its most conservative form, thoroughly covers the face and body leaving only a mesh-like screen to see through; a fashion that would surely inspire thoughts of Darth Vader.

It may seem harsh to say that some cultures are pathetic, so I will just point toward their poor reputations. In the extreme, approximately 40 million girls have gone missing in India as of 2013. Roughly speaking, about 50,000 female fetuses are aborted each month. And about 100 million females are subject to the sex trade. The main reason for this disgusting practice is money. Families must pay high-priced dowries to marry off daughters. When a boy is born, he is celebrated because he will bring in the money, but when a girl is born, she is viewed as an expense. Since there exists a tremendous imbalance of millions more males versus females, the result is a tendency towards homosexuality as can easily be imagined. It is shameful that many females in India have the fortune of a canary in a Chinese coal mine.

China is also guilty of female infanticide especially since the one child per couple policy. There are despicable Africans who perform genital mutilation of their girls. An estimated 100 to 140 million girls and women worldwide are currently living with the consequences of this damage to the sexual area. There are other examples of undesirable places to include Afghanistan, Somalia, and Congo to name a few. The average busybodies are probably unaware that Nigeria and many of their notorious crews are synonymous with scams and scammers. Those who ignore the facts must be considered ignorant, and no my dear Doctor Watson, it isn't just ethical relativism.

From prehistoric times, for tens of thousands of years, humans have exhibited prejudice as both an innate and learned trait. The idea of prejudice is shunned in today's society; it is pilloried like a thief in the act, and yet everyone has prejudice and only the dunce or the hypocrite will believe otherwise.

Prejudice has been around since the morning of the cavemen. Yet the intelligentsia wants the masses to embrace cultural diversity as some kind of blessing. But the universal response is: NIMBY, not in *my* back yard! If you think the average American is happy about the influx of Arabs, Pakistanis, Mexicans, and Vietnamese into their country, you are sadly mistaken. There are almost as many immigrants and their children in the United States as all the immigrants who came in the 350 previous years of American History.[17] Many of these immigrants are here illegally, refuse to assimilate or learn and speak the English language, and potentially pose a security risk. The U.S. is no longer the supposed melting pot; rather, we are simply going to pot. Take for example the Muslim Yellow Pages, which has been published for over 20 years in our locale outside of Dallas. Their directory has 321 pages of business advertising for Muslims to include six pages of "Introducing Islam" as well as information on the 25 Islamic Centers in the Dallas-Fort Worth area. The Yellow Pages contains a list of 12 schools for children, but they are all Islamic and no other schools, secular or otherwise, are listed. Cheers to inclusion and assimilation in response to our welcoming country.

Many of the same immigrant commercial businesses, such as restaurants and food stores, also have a Desi Yellow Pages that caters to South Asians, which is presumably a euphemism for Indians and Pakistanis. The Dallas-Fort Worth edition contains 292 pages of advertising so they can also keep the business among themselves. Ironically, most Americans would not think of patronizing or making their purchases in this segregated manner. And it is not excusable on the basis of language since Muslims originate from diverse locales such as the Middle East, Malaysia, Pakistan, Iran, and other countries. As Pat Buchanan warns in his book, *State of Emergency*, "The crisis of Western civilization consists of three imminent and mortal perils: dying populations, disintegrating cultures, and invasions unresisted." The radio talk show host, Michael Savage, has a concise and prescient political philosophy: "Borders, Language, and Culture."

The legacy of slavery argument attributes black underachievement today to the effects of yesterday's racial discrimination. This is claimed to be a source of inequality in American society. Additionally, White and Latino Americans are deeply divided over immigration and, worst of all, speak different languages (Press 1 for English) (Hey, wait a minute, why do *we* have to press a button for English?).

Perception colors our thoughts and actions regarding the racial divide. Based on scientific study, findings indicate that while overt forms of racial prejudice may have declined in recent decades, racial stereotypes persist among many people and exert a powerful influence on the ways they view certain public policies such as affirmative action, housing, welfare, and crime. It is apparent that we have contrasting cultures. For example, blacks are a very small minority at venues for classical music, dramas, and other showcases. It seems we also speak different languages as contrasted with the United Kingdom that has diversity but a specific Queen's English.

Society has swept the problem under the carpet, and virtually no agency is capable of dealing with it in any capable manner. It has become politically incorrect to honestly address the issue head-on for a resolution. The fact remains that cultures have been clashing throughout history and there are winners and losers in every fight. For example, Africa has a history of colonial occupation as we all know, and after the treaty of Versailles during the aftermath of World War I, a man could walk from Kuwait to Cairo, turn south, and walk the length of Africa to Cape Town without leaving a British dominion, colony, or pro- tectorate.[18] But powerful nations have always dominated other lands to include the Greeks, Romans, and the Ottoman Empire. The Spanish colonization of the Americas and other locales ordained the enslavement of native people in the name of Chris- tianity. In essence, there can be no doubt that some groups or certain populations inherited a history of low class, and they are the populations that are reproducing rapidly. In Stephen Pinker's 2011 book, *Why Violence Has Declined*, he references an article by Cooney that shows many lower-class people—the poor, the uneducated, the unmarried, and members of minority groups— are effectively *stateless*. Some make a living from illegal activities like drug dealing and prostitution, so they cannot file lawsuits or call the police to enforce their interests in business disputes. In that regard, they share their need for recourse to violence with certain *high*-status people such as the Mafia or drug kingpins.

In my humble opinion, these supposed genius and wealthy apologists live in secure and crime-free, expensive, glass houses where their probability of death by violence is low compared to the average citizen.

The racial divide has become one of the many hot button issues in the war on culture. Radio commentators (conserva- tive and Republican) ardently contend that the radical Left is wrangling control of moral issues and the associated public discourse. It has become unthinkable to hold candid discussions and the current strategy is simple: when anyone expresses an opinion via the mass media, they are immediately branded as racist.

The famous American humorist, Will Rogers (1879-1935), was notable for his quote, "I never met a man I didn't like." We don't ordinarily meet someone with this sentiment and it doesn't sound quite rational, but excusable for the well-heeled and financially successful in the best of all possible worlds; it makes as much sense as the term unconditional love.

Although there are clear differences between people of different continental ancestries, there are two terms that are relevant. *Prejudice* is an attitude, a prejudging, usually in a negative way on the basis of their group membership. Is it a prejudicial belief to state that African-Americans have a higher unemployment rate than whites? Would it be prejudicial to state that African-Americans have a higher unemployment rate because they are black, or because they are lazy? *Racism* is a belief that some groups are superior to other groups. At an individual level, a person can display prejudice, but this in itself does not necessarily constitute racism.

James D. Watson will always be best known as the co-discoverer, with Francis Crick, of the structure of DNA—the famous double helix, in 1953. In an interview published in The Times of London (14 Oct 2007) he suggested that, overall, people of African descent are not as intelligent as people of European descent. Watson was vilified for these sentiments. Conversation about the controversial subjects of race and genetics has prompted some to suggest that innate differences should be accepted but, at some level, ignored. The notion that race is more than skin deep, they fear, could undermine principles of equal treatment and opportunity that have relied on the presumption that we are all fundamentally equal.

It is my contention that there are some factions who are working to cut-off any free and open discourse, and effectively pursuing a "shut up" scene. You might wonder if more people are talking to *themselves*, because we cannot talk to others in this society. One of my old supervisors, Bill Kitterman, at Army STRICOM was an old, self-proclaimed, curmudgeon who advocated that, when the management searched for scapegoats on a particular problem, he would raise his hand and testify, "I'm guilty, *now what*?" Therefore, you can attach any label you want but don't expect me to roll over and play brain dead.

The continuing controversy exists as to whether natural selection has operated on certain groups who attained superior intelligence over the course of many generations. For example, certain Jewish people are considered to have above average intelligence such as Einstein. Researchers now suggest that intelligence is closely linked to certain genetic diseases in Ashkenazi Jews, and that the diseases are the result of natural selection. Because Jews were discriminated against in medieval Europe, they were often driven into professions such as money lending and banking which were looked down upon or forbidden to Christians. For the most part they had jobs in which increased IQ strongly favored economic success, in contrast with other populations, who were mostly peasant farmers. As a result, the researchers say, over hundreds of years European Jews became more intelligent than their gentile countrymen. Let's not forget how the Jews were vilified in print over the centuries; Shakespeare's Shylock in the *Merchant of Venice*; the miserly and horrid Fagin in Dickens' *Oliver Twist*; the red-headed, fawning , and dastardly Uriah Heep in *Great Expectations*, although Dickens made some amends with Mr. Riah in *Our Mutual Friend*.

The Human Genome Project, completed in 2000, suggested that humans are 99.9 percent genetically identical across all races. At the time, the project's findings were hailed as evidence that the human genome is color-blind. But the journal *Psychology, Public Policy and Law* recently published a study that reviewed research into the differences in average IQ between Asians, Whites, and Blacks, and concluded these differences are 50 percent genetic in origin.

In *Guns, Germs, and Steel*, Jared Diamond tries to convince readers that New Guineans are, on the average, more intelligent than the average European or American. One wonders if he overdid the gourds of New Guinea moonshine while writing that silliness.

Some experts believe our biological evolution has sped up since we developed agriculture about 10,000 years ago, a sea change that led to civilization as we know it. The anthropologist, Henry Harpending, and physicist-turned-evolutionary biologist, Gregory Cochran, both of the University of Utah, make this argument forcibly in their 2009 book, *The 10,000 Year Explosion: How Civilization Accelerated Human Evolution*.[21] The human races have been evolving away from each other and are getting less alike. I am not a rocket scientist and therefore can just depend on common sense and some references, but I'm betting that intelligence has some genetic anchor along with other traits. If you don't believe the above, hearken to the typical Jewish mother: "My son the doctor—my son the law-ya!"

During my formative years, we were not familiar with any African Americans in our suburban borough. I recall minstrel shows at our Catholic school auditorium, performed by the Knights of Columbus. The minstrel show was entertainment consisting of comic skits, dancing, and music, performed by white people in blackface. The first album (long-playing twelve-inch vinyl) on my hit parade was the music of Al Jolson (1886-1950), purchased with my mother, at the local supermarket check-out counter. Jolson liked performing in blackface makeup, and I can still hear the famous echoes of the song "Mammy."

The *Fat Albert and the Cosby Kids* cartoon series was televised in 1972, based on Bill Cosby's remembrances of his childhood gang. *Fat Albert* primarily spoke to African-American kids in low-income families, and the characters were very odd indeed, but that was reality in urban slums. Mr. Cosby made public remarks critical of lower income African-Americans who put higher priorities on sports, fashion, and playing around than on education, self-respect, and self-improvement, pleading for African-American families to educate their children. He has to be one of the most beloved and influential performers of all time.

Unfortunately, on the other end of the spectrum are dreadful black leaders such as Louis Farrakhan, the Nation of Islam minister, who continually spews anti-Semitic and vicious invective to his adoring adherents. The perception towards this part of our society is dismal, to say the least.

They have been referred to as African-Americans, Black-Americans, Afro-Americans, American-Negroes, and worse, but only *they* can say that word in public—the "N-word." If it weren't sad, it would be a riot of laughter to name your children Shaniqua, Taliqua and Mohammed, but that doesn't help the youngsters in school or in the general society. The fact that African-Americans are a majority of federal prisoners on death row and a minority in the overall United States population may lead some to conclude that the federal system discriminates against African-Americans. However, there is little rigorous evidence that such disparities exist in the federal system.

The feelings are so endemic, that in the iconic 1972 movie, *The Godfather*, one of the mafia chiefs expresses his feelings about the drug business: "I don't want it near schools! I don't want it sold to children! In my city, we would keep the traffic in the dark people, the coloreds. They're animals anyway, so let them lose their souls."

Unfortunately, race relations are that bad, and although most groups grumble behind closed doors, for Cherokee Indians it is out in the open. The country's second-largest Indian tribe (Cherokee Nation) said it will banish African-Americans, who cannot prove they have a Cherokee blood relation, from its citizenship rolls. The dispute stems from the fact that some Cherokee owned black slaves who worked on their plantations in the South. By the 1830s, most of the tribe was forced to relocate to present-day Oklahoma, and many took their slaves with them. One can imagine that if this kind of action were taken by the white majority, there would be hell to pay.

In 1975 Saturday Night Live performed a skit with two famous comedians, Chevy Chase and Richard Pryor. A black man (Richard Pryor) is being interviewed for a janitor's position and undergoes a word association quiz with the white interviewer (Chevy Chase):

- Chevy Chase: Ok, Mr. Wilson, if I were to say "dog"?
- Richard Pryor: Tree
- Chevy Chase: White?
- Richard Pryor: Black
- Chevy: Negro?
- Richard: Whitey
- Chevy: Tar Baby?
- Richard: What'd you say?
- Chevy: Tar Baby?
- Richard: Ofay! (Offensive term for whites)
- Chevy: Colored?
- Richard: Redneck!
- Chevy: Spade?
- Richard: Funky Honkey!
- Chevy: Nigger?
- Richard: Dead Honkey!
- Chevy: Ok, Mr. Wilson, looks like you're qualified for the job.

The above skit demonstrates the power of humor to illuminate a problem that is usually considered beyond the pale; what we have now is a failure to communicate.

The idea of reparations for slavery keeps turning up like a bad penny, the coin with Lincoln on the face of it. It is such a ridiculous and dim-witted debate that others can waste their time with it. As many as 1.5 million Europeans and Americans were enslaved in Islamic North Africa between 1530 and 1780 but we don't generally hear about it. I find it amazing to take the train from New York to Baltimore, or comparable excursions, and gaze at the poverty out the window.

When I vacation in the Caribbean Islands, I can cut the sense of tension with a knife. There seems to be an idea that the white people should not venture past certain areas of the island, as if they don't belong there—even if it is the U.S. Virgin Islands. And crime is a real problem in the beatific parcels of paradise. Even non-white cultures discriminate based on the fairness or darkness of skin. For example, many former Spanish colonies have a social scale that favors the mother country and denigrates those of African ancestry, e.g., Cuba, Philippines, and South America.

It is astounding to realize how clueless America has been and continues to be. The fact is everyone has prejudice, and anyone who tries to refute this is either a fool or a liar. I'm sure the carpetbaggers of the bureaucracy will do the usual dirty ditty and recommend another commission to study the problem.

Mental Health

You might wonder what mental health has to do with ethics. Mental health determines how we reflect, feel, and function as we move through life. It is also serves as a barometer of how we cope with severe stress and other people. Both our mental and physical health is an interrelated mechanism. And since society and government have certain obligations as outlined in the first line of the U.S. constitution or preamble which states, "We the people...promote the general Welfare..." it seems evidence that the health of the people was in the minds of our forefathers. And moral issues have received constitutional treatment in the past such as the Amendment of Prohibition, wherein the government considered alcohol consumption as a moral hazard that negatively affects physical and mental well-being.

The requirement of Mental Health is one of the most important and yet poorly managed issues in most countries. At least one in four U.S. adults experiences some form of mental disorder at some point in their life. Statistics are probably underreported due to the perceived stigma attached to the problems which include anxiety, depression, anger or rage, and addiction, just to name a few. Across the country, we are facing massive cuts to mental health services because of staggering state budget deficits. This first-world country is woefully inadequate in addressing or treating the problem with any measure of success. And the irony is that many poor countries have much less mental distress among their population. It seems mental trauma or crisis is an assault on the brain that leaves a scar, which is everlasting; one can be repaired but when the damage is done, we have to live with it, survive and move on.

One of the problems with extreme stress is that any little straw can break the camel's back. For example, after 25 years working for the Army, I ended my government service by employment with the Veterans Administration (VA) for the last year and a half. We relocated so that my wife could live near our daughter and imminent grandchild. Unfortunately, I was ignorant of the atrocious reputation of the agency as an employer and suffered immeasurably until I was eligible for retirement. During the relatively short duration with the VA, many employees experienced similar trauma and the organization got away with it somehow. One woman worked on and off for two years, seeking relief and finally attained a disability determination and separation. I have had some terrible "pits" and "knocks" in my life, and I wouldn't wish that kind of suffering on my worst enemy. Although I am not an advocate of suicide, my wellbeing and sanity were certainly at risk.

Since music evokes memories and associations, the George Harrison song from 1970 comes to mind, "Beware of Darkness." Although I don't believe in the devil, I wasn't the only one who considered the building a candidate for exorcism. But the irony is unbelievable in that help was virtually unavailable no matter which way I turned. Medical and psychological doctors listened, nodded their heads, suggested drugs that I considered detestable, and sent me out the door with a pay as you exit smile. The chapter finally ended with the use of accumulated leave that shortened the stretch of imprisonment, and Sodom and Gomorrah were left behind with no one turning their head around for a last glimpse.

It is no secret that the health care system is a chaotic and dysfunctional entity. During my troubles, instead of receiving an orderly and structured regimen of services, my health plan allowed me to visit a plethora of different general practitioners and specialists with no game plan or coach. Of course this would not happen on a sports playing field, but it is rampant in the care of our most important asset, that of our health. You would think that the approach would include some overarching base (general practitioner) with annual visits scheduled to assess the individual's needs, with the emphasis being preventive measures rather than reacting to a crisis.

A holistic approach should be integrated to effect care of the whole person to include body and mind. Instead we have a health care system drowning in a sea of paperwork, bureaucratic regulations and policies, doctors chasing bucks to pay the exorbitant insurance premiums, and customers gulping and bending over before they foot the bill.

The inadequate and archaic system of mental health is well documented. Individuals have been treated so defectively that many former patients refer to themselves as psychiatric survivors, after enduring forced incarceration, drugs, abuse, and torture in the clutches of mental health practitioners.

These abuses have sparked Mind Freedom International, an independent grassroots coalition of activists working for human rights in the mental health system which campaigns for mental health alternatives to the one-size-fits-all medical model. A past president of MFI, Sally Clay, explains that self-help and peer support were first popularized by Alcoholics Anonymous, and were adopted by consumer/survivors as the foundation of support programs. The second most important value for consumers is empowerment. Empowerment is the idea that instead of being talked at we want to be talked with. Empowerment means that we can act on our own behalf and can have control over our own lives. Regardless of the philosophy of a mental health program, the formal treatment system carries the threat of involuntary treatment and coercion, and there is a built-in imbalance of power between professionals and clients. Self-help groups and services are not troubled by this imbalance, for they operate from a sense of mutual help and equality. The concept of recovery, which also has been in general use in Alcoholics Anonymous for at least forty years, is strongly related to self-esteem, hope, and confidence, for these are all essential to healing.[22]

Staying mentally healthy is not always easy, especially in view of the frenetic pace of our lives.

Daryl Conner, author of *Managing at the Speed of Change*, has identified five characteristics of resilient people for tough and changing times:

- Positive
- Focused
- Flexible
- Organized
- Proactive

All of the above are good attributes to attain for dealing with problems and stress, but it's easier said than done when one is looking in from the outside rather than looking out through distressed eyes. Nevertheless it makes sense to get hold of healthy ways to deal with problems such as anxiety, anger, aggravation, and fear, and reinforcing the positive passions and behaviors in our life.

Some Helpful Hints on Health

Here are some ideas to help alleviate stress in your life, although be advised, we are not trying to look like Albert Schweitzer here, nor pretend to be a guru or expert on self-help or other psychological affairs:

☐ Reading is therapeutic in that it can alleviate pain or mental distress. There is a world of imagination in books that you can vicariously experience. It's an escape that allows you to focus on something other than your own problems. The forum is so powerful and gripping that it caused Charles Dickens to lament the end of *David Copperfield* in the book preface of 1850: "I am in danger of wearying the reader whom I love, with personal confidences and private emotions. It would concern the reader little, perhaps, to know, how sorrowfully the pen is laid down at the close of a two-year's imaginative task." Reading or any type of mental activity can increase a person's longevity and long-term health. Although the new wave is to read with e-books, I will always prefer the paper copy. For many practical people, tradition and the history of the printing press are not as important because they embrace both the advantages of new technology and the mantra that "change is good." The popularity of Sudoku, a number puzzle (as opposed to a crossword puzzle), is a worldwide phenomenon. It's not my cup of tea, to stare at a 9x9 grid of numbers, but it passes the train time or subway ride. New research indicates that we lose mental acuity much earlier than previously supposed, beginning at the age of about 40-45. Additionally, improper diet damages the brain. This can be countered by active measures to eat nutritionally and keep mentally active.

☐ When I was growing up, the suburbs seemed more like rural areas compared with today. There were many more open spaces with horse farms and extensive family gardens, less traffic, construction, and consumer-driven commercial businesses. We went out to play and roamed around for hours. Change has relieved the present generation of this type of playfulness such that we are aware of the decline in outdoor activity and an increase of indoor activities such as television, computer, and video games. The sedentary lifestyle at play and at work is taking a severe toll on physical and mental health. People should take the time to get back to basics by walking more than usual. The health benefits of regular exercise and physical activity are now common knowledge. For example, my mother was able to overcome the difficulties of her mid-life crisis with a four-letter word called golf and she was admirably committed to the game. There are different strokes for different folks; the golf swing, ping-pong, swimming, and racquetball. There are the lemmings in marathon shoes and Zumba dancing crowds. The latter are mostly women who thrill for an opportunity to shake the booty, and by their devoted facial expressions, they might be related to the zombies out there. On the other hand, yoga seems to express serenity and class but it's all good. Exercise stimulates various brain chemicals that relieve stress and promote a happier and more relaxed feeling. Good habits should be encouraged at an early age because they tend to stick around as one grows.

☐ Take time for leisure activities. Take up gardening, planting, or visiting a farm in a rural setting. Plan a vacation as a reward for endurance and follow through with the get-away. Although some stress in our lives is normal, it is the unhealthy types that are dangerous. For example, employment at a senseless job (Federal government) can be very stressful because bureaucracy breeds mediocrity. Too much change can be stressful and abnormal, hence the saying, "George Washington would be rolling over in his grave" if he could see the sad state of his country.

☐ Relatives can be painful; although we evolved in small family units, this does not necessarily signify our total acquiescence to the group mentality. We often hurt those closest to us because they are the easiest targets for our moods and stresses. And the glut of self-health books on the shelves doesn't transform the makeup of human nature. I am unsure of the human propensity for forgiveness and unconditional love for instance; certain behaviors sound good in theory but contradict our nature. An online article from the Mayo

Clinic advises: "Forgiveness can even lead to feelings of understanding, empathy and compassion for the one who hurt you." Now we didn't see that in *The Godfather* but perhaps they are an anomaly. One can choose an option from the contradictory bible: either "Turn the other cheek" or "An eye for an eye." Although we hear that "To err is human; to forgive, divine," (Alexander Pope) that is not my motto when egregious harm has been perpetrated. The above saying seems to mean that we all make mistakes, but it is godlike to forgive or that we are imitating the mercy of the divine. For example, there are health professionals that insist forgiveness is the only remedy for victims of child abuse. I vehemently disagree because it goes against our human nature and common sense. A Texas father recently caught a man sexually assaulting his four-year-old daughter and punched him in the head repeatedly, killing him. You will find no one here that believes the father was not justified in his action.

I mentioned that my wife, Luchia, was a widow at age 14 while pregnant in Gonder, Ethiopia. The husband was dead but the father-in-law came to live with her family for seven months, until he could collect his one-third share of the life insurance payout by the construction company. He even took the funereal cement cross provided by Luchia's Father so that he could resell it. The father-in-law mercilessly antagonized Luchia, saying the baby would be born dead and other atrocious comments. This behavior would be difficult to excuse, but notice that Luchia's father allowed this man to live with them for many months. This is because forgiveness is important in tribal societies. Many families are related or interdependent, and conformity is the rule and not the exception. There are traditions that the tribal elders use to mediate disputes and to restore and repair relationships.

As a further example, my wife's sister in Eritrea was being physically abused by her husband. In the state where I grew up, one might think about a "Don Vito Corleone" reaction, but the father traveled to his daughter's home and mediated a peace with forgiveness. Ironically, in the case of my wife's treatment by the above-mentioned father-in-law, she swore that he would never see his granddaughter, not even in his dreams; he went blind before meeting her the first time.

I would like to briefly add that the Catholic sacrament of Confession involves the mission of forgiveness. But any priest who violates Canon Law by breaking the seal of confession and divulging crimes, no matter how heinous, will be excommunicated by the Church. Luckily, good sense prevails in some places; in 2012, Ireland's justice minister confirmed that Catholic priests are required by law to break the seal of confession to report abuse of children. In those cases, forgiveness be damned.

☐ Another suggestion for countering stress is to strive for adequate sleep. We spend about one-third of our lives sleeping and it is as important as food or drink. The trick is to determine our individual sleep needs, such as number of hours, light or darkened room, temperature, and bedding products. Although we have varying sleep needs, the magic number seems to be seven, give or take a half hour. One of the main problems for most people is "falling" to sleep. In the Old World, they "prepared" for sleep by taking a walk and a glass of wine. As mentioned elsewhere, a visit to a health spa is a restorative activity. And don't be afraid to cry occasionally if you need to. Similar to the hot sauna at the spa, crying can help to release toxins which are linked to stress. On average women cry 47 times a year and men only seven and that seems a shame. I'm not invoking the reason that women live longer than men for their crying propensity, but they have a better outlet for stress, whereas men keep their emotions bottled-up until they use the beer bottle opener. Music appreciation is inspirational and can soothe any savage beast. You can search the internet for wonderful songs such as Stevie Wonder's *Ribbon in the Sky* and *Knocks Me Off My Feet* and they are worth a listen.

☐ Can money buy happiness? Yes professor, there *are* some stupid questions. Of course money can buy happiness unless you are a miser or too dull to make the grade in style.

☐ Sometimes it may pay to give up some of our craving for control. During times of trouble, explore the possibility of delegating or handing-off some duties and responsibilities to others who can be trusted. This is opposite to the bane of modern commerce, multitasking, where workers are expected to clone their capacities and pretend to perform as multiple cogs in the machinery. If you are a perfectionist, it might be difficult to change, but give it a go. For instance, try to let go of constant righting every wrong with your house or apartment. Recognize entropy is the nature of the world; disorder and chaos are the usual and the attempt to control your environs requires too much time and effort. Limit work outside your residence since indoor air quality is much more important than the outside grass and plants, and indoor pollution can be more hazardous than the outside air. I don't know about you, but the house we live in is full of dust, everywhere and all the time. This glitch seems crucial to me since your windbag enables breathing. So indoor air includes fine dirt and particles from dust mites, animal dander, pollen, and dead skin cells. Note the things that exacerbate the problem such as shoddy construction or workmanship, household clutter, carpets, chemicals, excessive furniture, and bedding products. As you can see, controlling the air quality seems almost futile. Air purifiers do not work and the typical vacuums just blow dust out the exhaust. You can clean constantly, have the ductwork cleaned, and the dust persists. Some good recommendations include limiting carpets and installing hardwood flooring and tiles. And very expensive vacuums have a dual filtration system, both water and a HEPA filter. Going back to the subject of control, one will have less to worry about if we organize and simplify our surroundings and use time savers. This may sound ridiculous, but imagine how many hours are spent tying shoelaces and buttoning shirts in a lifetime rather than slipping on loafers and tops without buttons? Many workers have switched to wash and wear and dumped the ironing board and expensive dry cleaners. How many hours and petrol are expended bringing home the same old products from store to house, rather than buying the toilet paper and other necessities in bulk? Another very good routine is to cook nutritious foods in quantity and freeze some. There are also time wasters such as spending countless hours on the oxymoron, social networking, where strangers supposedly commune with other strangers, and the virtual world of the blog where people talk to themselves using a keyboard. And we shouldn't forget the fast food of communication, instant messaging.

☐ Better eating habits and nutrition have a positive consequence for mental and physical health. The corporate control of our sustenance is an appalling scandal that has boosted the incidence of diabetes and related problems to a staggering extent. The medical care costs of obesity in the United States are about $150 billion. For example, one of the nation's leading writers on the topic of food, Michael Pollan, suggests that consumers should be alert to the multitude of processed foods in the supermarket. In the *Omnivore's Dilemma*, he notes that there are some forty-five thousand items in the average American supermarket and more than a quarter of them now contain corn. Pollan quips "So that's us: *processed corn, walking.*" And he advises, "Simply don't buy any food you've ever seen advertised. 94 percent of advertisement budgets for food are spent on processed foods. For instance, the broccoli growers don't have money for ad budgets. So the real food is not being advertised. And that's really all you need to know." His summary advice is "Eat food, not too much, mostly plants." The corporate food providers have packaged a plethora of questionable and unhealthy choices through the years. And when research indicates the ingredients have made laboratory rats sick, they change the products since rats are our relatives. When the cheap burgers and French fries are viewed as unhealthy, they add a cheap salad to the menu. When the canned soup is discovered to be unhealthy, they change the formula to "low sodium" or "low fat." They could care less for the consumers' health; they want to maintain sales and avoid negative perceptions of their cheap products. My dad was a cosmopolitan New Yorker, and quite often advised us that no self-respecting restaurant would serve a salad with iceberg lettuce since it has no nutritional value. Most Americans are clueless and prefer this crunchy cellulose to green or red leaf lettuce. Quite naturally, a salad prepared at home cannot be matched by other than the upscale restaurants. Caveat emptor is Latin for "Let the buyer beware" (and Good Luck).

☐ In addition to the supermarket snare, millions of consumers march to the corporate beat at fast food (chain) outlets in this cookie-cutter country of ours. Although it's called "junk food," the low prices are too tempting and mouth watering to pass up, and people no longer seem to have the time and inclination to cook at home. The observation is funny that there seems to be thousands of cookbooks on the shelves but few cooks in the kitchens. The infamous hamburger joints proudly admit that roughly 245 billion hamburgers have been served to their customers' voracious bellies. And the American corporate snakes are fattening many other unwitting countries of the world. For example, the young Saudis are scarfing and slurping up the American brands of fast foods and waddling along just fine. And guess who the fattest people in the world are in 2013? The citizens of Qatar. Incidentally, the nutrition of choice should be organically grown or raised, but the expense is a consideration. As in other choices in life, nutrition should be viewed as an investment in life just as proper car maintenance will extend the life of your vehicle. One might consider buying healthy ingredients and cooking dinners for storage in the freezer. But there is no substitute for fresh food. As an example, I have made fresh fruit smoothies every morning for over 20 years as follows: Squeeze a few oranges with a citrus juicer—note that boxed juice is homogenized without the natural vitamins. An option is to use an extractor to pulverize pineapples for an additional juice. With a typical blender, add banana(s), mangoes pieces, and strawberries. You can buy and freeze the mangoes and strawberries since they will go bad in a few days otherwise. My mother was not able to provide this kind of elaborate juice but my good boy, our grandson (Danny Hailemicael) is lucky and knows a good thing through a drinking straw, even at one year old.

Since we're on the subject of food, this is a good place to mention my mother's recipe for rice pudding. This is an art and not a straight forward recipe. Take one cup of rice and boil it for 15 minutes in water. Then in a Pyrex or heat-resistant baking dish, add rice and 5 cups of milk, 3 handfuls of raisins, a smidgen of butter, one quarter teaspoon of vanilla, a small amount of sugar perhaps 1 teaspoon. Place in oven at 350 degrees and occasionally stir for the first 30 minutes of the approximately one hour cooking time, but here is the art. When the pudding has a film but still bubbling, you have to take it out and let it cool before refrigeration. Practice will ensure your Goldilocks' preference of a rice pudding that is not too wet or too dry. Enough of the schmaltz.

Consumers would be well advised to beware of nutritional supplements. It is not just a tremendous business but reaches the point of a cult following with some of the pyramid-type selling schemes. Many of the purported claims of supplements are those of snake oil salesmen in that each and every ailment can be cured with their product. They use pseudo scientific or ill defined terms such as free radicals which to my mind sounds like escaped convicts, and their antidote for sale is consequently anti-oxidants.

The corporate purveyors have a dirty little secret concerning medicines and supplements: The Placebo Effect. Many of the drugs and supplements do not work any better than a placebo or sugar pill. Some corporations are very clever and will offer free samples, because once they have you on the hook, the company automatically sends out monthly quantities of the product.

Look around and you can be fairly certain that about 60 percent of Americans are overweight. Some years ago, it was customary for Italian Americans to spend hours at the dinner table amidst many courses of food. But that was a time when they worked and expended calories by manual labor.

All across America, pizza parlors or the pizzeria can be found on every other corner. Pizza is quite tasty and so much so that people seem addicted and customarily must order this take-away every week. One of the reasons has to do with the salt content which is used in almost every ingredient of the pie; the dough, tomato sauce, cheese, and the toppings to include pepperoni, sausage and anchovies. High salt consumption is linked to problems such as stroke and heart disease; at present, 75 percent of our daily salt intake comes from salt hidden in purchased foods rather than from the use of our salt shaker at home. Frankly, you wouldn't touch pizza and the cheap burgers if there weren't the level of fat and salt in the chow.

Today we all know about junk food and lack of exercise. However, one should be wary of the various fad diets, especially the ones that initially use celebrities in the advertising followed by the average Jack and Jill in later ads. Diets tend to be short-term gimmicks that don't keep the weight off for long, and some of them are as lunatic as the supplement purveyors. There is plenty of common sense in some regional cuisines such as the Mediterranean food set which traditionally includes fruits, vegetables, pasta and rice. For example, residents of Greece eat very little red meat and average nine servings a day of fruits and vegetables. Lots of olive oil is used for cooking and a moderate amount of red wine is recommended. Bread is an important part of the diet and hummus with Arabic or pita bread is perhaps one of the best side dishes you can eat. The plate of hummus is made with mashed chickpeas, blended with tahini, olive oil, lemon juice, salt and garlic. In fact, many of the authentic Arab dishes are highly nutritious. The bottom line is take note of Michael Pollan's above advice, and when you crave the goodies, make it a practice to buy quality. For example, don't purchase cut-rate ice cream, chocolate and so forth; purchase less and nothing but the best; bon appétit!

☐ It's hard to imagine a world without tobacco because the corporate players refuse to release their grip on world-wide profits from addiction. Whether you smoke or chew tobacco, one knows the habit is extremely difficult to kick. Just some years ago, passengers could smoke within the confines of plane travel but that is now viewed as ancient history and unthinkable. As a youngster, I recall men with rapacious lungs who could drag or inhale deeply on an unfiltered butt and exhale through the mouth and nose for what seemed like minutes of time. Guys used to "bum" a smoke from other smokers in the old days, but at the current price of $15 or more for a pack in some cities, that habit is gone. Funny, a guy once told me that some GIs used to open their pack of fags from the bottom because fellow soldiers normally wouldn't bum a smoke from an unopened pack in the shirt pocket. In poor countries such as the Philippines, street urchins sell cigarettes by the piece which is not the best way to make a quick buck but rather at least a few pesos. Although the incidence of smoking has decreased in some countries, it is still a craving for millions of addicts. Incidentally, the largest tobacco company in the world by volume is China National Tobacco Company. Unlike other evolutionary tempting consumables such as sweet fruits, the corporate managers are able to lace tobacco with additional amounts of addicting nicotine and enslave millions of consumers from father to sons. People who are addicted to something will use it compulsively, without regard for its negative effects on their health or their life. The tobacco companies have very deep pockets and hefty advertising budgets to shore up their shareholder's stock and executive bonuses. For a good laugh, a cursory view of their websites will show verbiage such as "principled, innovative, and corporate responsibility," but who are they kidding? A suggestion to counter the behavior of the tobacco companies is to enlist the help of some of the world's billionaire philanthropists to expend some billions of dollars to end the psychological and physical assault on the young and older segments of the population. One wonders how this state of commerce is allowed to continue.

CHAPTER 8

The Education Fix
Class is in Session

Education of the citizen state was propelled by the printing press and paper circulation. For example, one of the most notable writers, Charles Dickens' monthly installments, later published as books, were being read by 100,000 of the common and uncommon citizens of England in the 1800s. The genius of Dickens brought awareness to authorities of the social injustices in education and child labor. During that time, many children worked 16-hour days under atrocious conditions, and with his family in debtor's prison, Dickens worked at age 12 in a Blacking Factory that affected him for the rest of his life. When visiting London, we can recommend the George Inn (77 Borough High St., Southwark), London's only surviving galleried coaching inn. Both sides of the second floor restaurant have signed photos of Dickens, although the two signatures curiously seem to be different from each other. Additionally, the moors of Cornwall in the west of England are a treasured sight. In 1840 perhaps only twenty percent of the children of London had any schooling.

The multitudes did not attend school in the early 1800s because education was not compulsory and it cost money that working stiffs could not afford. Parents had always counted on child labor as a source of security in old age. There was usually presumed to be a correlation with this and a high birth rate. It may be nature or natural selection that explains having numerous children in order to hedge against losing some along the way to retirement. The idea was to have a lot of children, or as many as the mother could stand, but to keep them either in the dark or at least down on the farm. This is just good old common sense. My wife's parents in East Africa had nine children and it is a mutual aid society. In the modern era, a newfound awareness, coupled with rising prosperity and invention, became the impetus to form an educational system. The Industrial Revolution was the kick-off event for this magnanimity as the barons of business reluctantly realized the need for an educated workforce to run the cogs in the wheel of fortune.

It is at a particular point in time that the school or classroom became the occupation for the young in lieu of laboring on the farm. With rising standards of living and increasing productivity, the economy could afford to excuse the young people to molt into pupils. Evidently an educated pupil will morph into a better and more profitable employee. Consequently the laboring class was making inroads into the realm of the rich and privileged who generally avail themselves of a private education, involving considerable expense, with a supposedly corresponding elevation of learning and advantage. Some of the more obvious aspects of a private education include: (1) You usually get what you pay for; (2) Smaller class size provides more individual interaction; (3) Discipline allows focused attention; (4) Higher expectations and reward for results; (5) Wealth meets wealth. For example, there is no comparison between Jesuit teachers and the typical public school.

Let's go to the head of the class and skip the humdrum lessons taught by the antiquated headmasters of confusion and obfuscation, i.e., the school boards and superintendents. The fact is education in modern times is a boring and broken system. The school system had the upper hand, and ruled up to the 1970s, but the good old days were characterized by discipline with the muscle and jaw breakers to back it up. The student could be good, bad, or indifferent, but punishment and the fear of god or nun was never far away for the Good, the Bad, or the Ugly. President John F. Kennedy gave a famous speech with the line "Ask not what your country can do for you; ask what you can do for your country." The masses were not to question authority since the individual was to produce and ask no questions. In other words, you were to "do-or-die" and better if you like, "Theirs but to do *and* die" (Alfred Lord Tennyson 1854). It was a strict system, holding up fairly well after we dusted the Fuehrer from the scene in World War II, through the ensuing prosperity from victory, but showing a little fraying at the edges with the simmering disenfranchisement of black people and the civil rights protests in the 1960s.

It is one of the ironies of history that the American founding fathers are considered the intellects of their time, and yet they were also smart enough to own slaves from West Africa. It is generally established that Thomas Jefferson, the third president of the United States, kept one of his slaves, Sally Hemings (1773-1835), as his mistress and had several children by her. American society largely dismissed the claim for almost 200 years on moral grounds, until a DNA analysis in 1998 indicated the reality of the liaison. What a lasting legacy they bequeathed to the United States and other countries that continue to simmer and fester like the step child that no one wants to acknowledge. But a burgeoning population of immigrants and other clucks in the broth of America led some reformers to standardize and homogenize the masses, and consequently increase expenditures to square-away and fortify the developing brains in the fortress termed the system of education. And a mammoth system it became of dollars, school boards, bureaucracy, regulation and the unions—full of systemic inoculation to further the indoctrination of the Good, the Bad, and the Ugly. But regardless of the shop talk, the U.S. has a low literacy rate compared to other developed countries while ranking below average in science and math.

I only wish them good luck training the great unwashed in this chaotic and frothing sea, as the ship founders with the captain missing; and the occupants keeping their seats warm in the changeless classrooms, droning "rote-rote, row your boat, gently down the stream–merrily, merrily, merrily, merrily–life is but a dream," and gathering endless bits of unrelated and irrelevant facts, facts, facts: when was the Magna Carta signed? (1215 AD); where is the country formerly called Rhodesia? (Zimbabwe, Africa).

Rising expectations led instead to a dreary mediocrity. Educate the people? Novel idea that, but rather, wouldn't it be more convenient and profitable to occupy them? The way to subdue the masses is to "fool them and confuse them." This is when a system shines, such as the venerable examples of the teachers unions and the public school system for instance. Make the vulnerable young get up at an ungodly hour, and while they're fuzzy and confused, feed them a processed food item, and cart them off to the cold, cruel world. Remand them to the lockup for the remainder of their youthful days and may God save their souls. Keep in mind that to be cynical is not always a bad thing and as Einstein said: "The important thing is not to stop questioning."

Once in the system, it is hoped the pupil will steer clear of rebellion, and crank-out the dreary lessons. Try to fit in, and memorize "just the facts, ma'am" Who discovered America? (Christopher Columbus in 1492); what is Evolution? (Never mind, go back to sleep). The main concept of the educational system is to learn enough to become employable and keep the cogs oiled and turning in the wheel of fortune.

Depending on various objective and subjective parameters, students are graded and categorized as smart to obtuse by a simple alphabetical regime or adjective:

- A = very smart
- B = above average
- C = average
- D = below average
- E = dunce
- F = beyond hope

Various other grading systems have run the experimental gamut such as the pass/fail system where smart-to- thickheaded are lumped together and are distinguished from the lot termed pathetic and beyond hope. This is the egalitarian idea of marking most pupils in a feel-good way, a philosophy of "I'm OK, you're OK" although it always falls out that some are not so OK. The system has also used a numerical scheme, and similar to the A-F dodge, where for instance:

- 90-100 = very smart
- 80-89= above average
- 70-79= average
- 60-69= dunce
- Below 60= pathetic

Engineers are noted for favoring the numeric scheme since it is more exacting and boorish, for example 95 is very smart but not M.I.T. material. Yet the artistic types enjoy the simpler and refined letter scheme of A-F which has some flair such as the humorous "you get an E for effort." I normally categorize myself as a B+ type of person based on various Catholic grammar school report cards that are verifiable. As Johnny Cash sang "I don't like it but, guess things happen that way." In my opinion, B+ is the best of all possible worlds; neither a boorish genius nor in the dunce and thick-as-mud category. Sort of reads like a Libra horoscope, has balance, uses the right hemisphere of the brain, with artistic flair etc. My Catholic elementary school at St. Jerome in West Long Branch, New Jersey, employed a wily set of nuns who added an extra grading scheme. To the regular subjects such as arithmetic, using the A-F scheme, they took a grim pleasure in assigning additional praise or barbs in the "character" section for appearance and attention span etc:

- S = satisfactory
- U = unsatisfactory
- I = incompetent

This was a slight attempt to submarine the little wise crackers who consistently tested above-average but could use a little figurative saltpeter in their soup. During fourth grade, I supposed that Sister Joan-Marie could not remember my name because she kept calling me *Baccalà*. It was only later that I found out that it means "dried fish." If I could go back in time, I would reply "Wait a minute! I resemble that remark!" and would bark like Curly of the Three Stooges while rubbing my crew-cut head. On second thought, maybe I wouldn't have the "nouve" (as the cowardly lion explained) because she was a pounder and probably could have gone a round or two with Mike Tyson. This was the same nun who demonstrated the impression of any student's failure to move on to Catholic High School after her eighth grade class; with a symbolic action, she stood on a chair, took the crucified cross off the wall and proceeded to place it in the garbage can.

The need to grade people, to categorize and pigeonhole is a function of how the brain works and has been evident from prehistoric times and hence the adage "gut feeling" or "sizing up a person in a flash." Most people on the planet are of the "C" type mentality. The typical consumers are very average in the department of ruminants and are surrounded by a modicum of genius and dunce. As everyday experience confirms, the majority of your encounters are with the dumb and dumber; there's just no way to avoid it or lend excuses. You see them at every turn; feeding the pigeons on the Atlantic City boardwalk or Trafalgar Square. Some of them watch never-ending soap operas where the men are all beautiful and the women handsome. Many of them drive on the freeways in Dallas. Quite a few sit on juries to acquit murderers and other psychopaths—you know, the garden variety knuckleheads. This quote from Oscar Wilde, a cast-off character with that yin-yang but tragic genius, is something to the point: "We live in the age of the overworked, and the under-educated; the age in which people are so industrious that they become absolutely stupid. And, harsh though it may sound, I cannot help saying that such people deserve their doom."

Bias is Part of Our Nature

For purposes of survival, early humans had to make relatively swift decisions such as (1) If he looks different, and not from our clan, apply a club over his head. (2) If you stumble upon a woman, your clan or mine, drag her home. Later in history, humans employed the handshake ostensibly to show that no weapon was ready for employment. Most humans are right-handed, and to be left-handed was thought to be evil hence the term *sinister*, a word derived from the Latin meaning left as in left-handed.

Like many archaic and boorish traditions, the handshake endures, and even females have adopted the gesture, but I for one care less for it. It is as useful as twirling a basketball on your index finger. On occasion, though, even I robotically fall for the action involuntarily when embarrassment would otherwise ensue. But every day, people shake hands with ardent criminals and saints alike. They will tell you that the handshake puts the individual at ease and is a practical and physical way to connect to human souls. I say, "Rubbish," especially in the grip of an oily and slimy paw and the various nefarious overtones that go hand-in-hand with the deed. The too close to your body-space shake, the too long and never ending grip, the bone breaking vise, the evil smirk on the face shake. And just try handing over a jellyfish handshake to your opponent and watch them drop it like a hot potato! The handshake is a compulsory action that is also used to size-up your opponent's strength or weakness and should go the way of greeting cards and disappear. We will see it go the way of the dodo when the "Bird Flu" epidemic comes to a town near you.

We drag along weary customs. Why do they have New Year's resolutions on one day only? I can see changing your clock and smoke alarm batteries on one particular day, but why can't they curb their vices all year long? Many of our behaviors are puzzling. For example, we all think to ourselves every minute of the day, but it is considered taboo or disturbing if someone thinks out loud. It is alright to do so by yourself but not around other people. Similarly, men have worn ties since the 1600s as part of a uniform or to signal group membership, but I have not donned a tie for the past 15 years, and will never wear one again.

There's no way around it, we have our manners based on customs and what is expected. To thine own self be true. But we must categorize, its biology, and yet to have "bias" has become the bane of human behavior. How dare anyone have an opinion, especially an unfavorable one, formed with rudeness?

Just as there seems to be an element of truth to joke-telling—George Carlin for instance—there is some modicum of truth to ideas concerning bias. That the Irish are blotto seems somewhat harsh and not their objective and real situation, and yet the Irish have been known to—well, they occasionally tip a glass—well all right a few glasses—OK, OK, they're loopy. My mother's brother, Uncle John Mulhern, was the classic G-man (government man) from the days of J. Edgar Hoover (1895 -1972) the first Director of the FBI in the United States. John was the typical black Irish—tall, tough, with that pointed nose slightly angled to the side like a prize fighter, and the eyes of a hawk that you'd better recognize as an Irishman not to fool with. John did his duty with the U.S. Coast Guard during World War II and was noted for his involvement in the capture of the most famous Russian spy, Colonel Rudolf Abel in 1957. Unlike the current crop of leakers, they never divulged any information of import, not the J.F. Kennedy assassination or any other security event and secrets were just that. Like most of our Irish kin, Uncle John was a drinker, and when we visited their clan in Scarsdale (Westchester county of Yonkers, New York), John was invariably sitting with a glass of his favorite cocktail, a Manhattan, which was bourbon whiskey with a tiny splash of vermouth. This was his ritual morning, noon, and night when not at work. And he let us view his Smith and Wesson .38-caliber revolver on the closet shelf so we were in awe. His wife, Aunt Gertrude of German descent, was a knock-out, with similar good looks as my mother.

Uncle John came to visit one Christmas holiday, and I mentioned my involvement in a karate class at university. We were outside at the street between our two huge evergreen trees, and John probably had a few drinks and proceeded to test my abilities, but my mother came outside to our wrap-around porch and starting yelling to her younger brother. "John, stop it! I don't want you hitting Billy!" Even though he was in his late 50s and I was twenty-something, he could have made mince-meat of me and my mom knew it. If I could go back in time, my advice would be: "Pal, you don't find rainbows in the bottom of a glass"... but that might be too much of the pot and kettle and besides, he could throw me for a loop. Since Uncle John drank at all hours, I consider that a character flaw and generally don't imbibe before sundown.

Speaking of comedy, I went to Atlantic City some years back with my brother and sister to see the one-of-a-kind comedian, Don Rickles, and after we tipped (bribed) our way to a front row table, we watched Rickles expertly slam into the nearby audience with every prejudicial joke for Whites, Blacks, Jews, and Asians. Rickles is known for his sarcastic put-downs and aims at his audience for target practice. Finally, he turned to me for what I supposed was my undeserved roasting, but he only asked my name and listened as I gulped and stammered "humanah, humanah, on leave from Saudi Arabia" and he nicely remarked, leaving no wounds. I was relieved. Here was the master (Rickles, not me) who could insult any race, color, or creed. He could make you slink under the table with his wit or have you and the audience roaring with laughter and it's all about bias, and about people, and how we are all different, funny and often pathetic in our thin skins, donated by nature for the express purpose of well, being able to watch Rickles in Atlantic City. At the end of the performance, I was clapping like crazy in appreciation, and Don took his bows on stage but looked down at me and said, "Thanks Billy." Now there's a class act!

The Mentality of the Masses

Apart from the humor and subtleties of bias, there are more serious and threatening aspects of the issue which are not acceptable, such as violent attacks which were heroically opposed by the famous American, Martin Luther King Jr. But if a society forbids free thinking, all will be lost. We have to strive to do better than average in order to sustain ourselves. After all you could be among the great unwashed but for the grace of God, Buddha, Allah, luck, ad nauseam. During a recent holy Hindu festival in India for example, 30 million humans washed their bodies in the Ganges River. Sounds rather quaint to some, but I wouldn't think of tiptoeing in the Ganges River, never mind with 30 million other sets of toes. Talk about dreadful practices that might make one green about the gills to think about, but this is a good representation of the mentality of the masses. Dickens had a talent in describing the rat race of life, and in *Hard Times*, he writes about a place called Coketown:

> *It was a town of red brick, or of brick that would have been red if the smoke and ashes had allowed it; but as matters stood, it was a town of unnatural red and black like the painted face of a savage. It contained several large streets all very like one another, and many small streets still more like one another, inhabited by people equally like one another, who all went in and out at the same hours, with the same sound upon the same pavements, to do the same work, and to whom every day was the same as yesterday and to-morrow, and every year the counterpart of the last and the next."*

For thousands of years, men such as Plato (c. 427-347 B.C.E.) discussed aspects of political philosophy and how government should be run. In spite of the idealism with which he is usually associated, Plato was not politically naive. He did not idealize, but was deeply pessimistic about human beings. Most people, corrupted as they are, were for him fundamentally irrational, driven by their appetites, egoistic passions, and informed by false beliefs. If they chose to be just and obey laws, it was only because they lacked the power to act criminally and were afraid of punishment.

Nevertheless, human beings are not vicious by nature. They are social animals, incapable of living alone. Living in communities and exchanging products of their labor is natural for them, so that they have capacities for rationality and goodness. The quality of human life can be improved if people learn to be rational and understand that their real interests lie in harmonious cooperation with one another, and not in war or partisan strife.[4]

Plato and other intellectual giants believed logical reasoning leads to the conclusion that the masses cannot govern themselves and therefore only the intelligent should be at the helm of the ship of state. The ideal nation is one guided by principled leaders with values that promote society to higher civilized levels. Unfortunately since the human race is very primitive, the nations on earth have been led by men of lower intellect, to include pirates, tyrants, and fools. By analogy, the global report card indicates that most humans score a "C" grade and thus are average in awareness, wisdom and intelligence. This biological and evolutionary bell curve sums up the history of the race and its present situation. Nasty attempts have been made to alter the face of human-kind such as Hitler's Aryan mad house. And the present posse of gene splicing scientists is no longer the fiction of the imagination that might someday be able to tinker with an ideal human form.

The good old days weren't so great, but life was certainly more manageable. Humans were a more humble lot in the preindustrial era, and if lunatic barbarians didn't police the population, the black plague and various diseases kept a steady check on the numbers. The planet lacked a supervisor with no one in control, until modern man rebelled against his lack of creature comforts, and with righteous indignation, flayed the earth to gain his due. In a blink of an eye, humans have evolved on the earth, and in a primitive fashion, have raped, polluted and destroyed other animals and the environment. We are temporarily stuck on planet earth and we will not be capable of escaping any time soon in our primitive condition. Therefore you would think that humans would live and learn (education) as well as live and let live. Perhaps there are too many fools who believe in an afterlife, the Great Escape. Apparently it's not the gods who must be crazy. Along with my two-year old grandson, I have logged innumerable hours watching the Mickey Mouse Clubhouse and Barney, the overbearing purple dinosaur; they make much more sense than the afterlife aficionados. Can't the dogmatic institutions set an example and realize it is time to hang up the gloves? Muhammad Ali balked at retirement and was punched for so many additional rounds; Abbott and Costello lingered *way* after they ceased to be remotely amusing. Former presidents, with the exception of George W. Bush, who disappeared for several years incognito or in hiding, generally refuse to quit the limelight. Even George Carlin, albeit with his fantastic wit, but with wispy pony tail and raspy voice, might have considered early retirement but he probably needed the money.

Grand ideas do not come from average thinkers. Truly monumental human strides are generated from the intellectuals such as Copernicus, Galileo, Newton, Einstein and a set of other giants of intellect. Instead of being recognized as the first string among men, thinkers are sidelined in favor of vapid characters such as actors, sportsmen, and other celebrities. Entertainers have a place in society but not on a pedestal for worship. Life's authentic heroes are those who perform real work that inspire us such as the scientists and social workers.

The human dilemma is our ability to annihilate most of life on Earth, with the exception of bacteria which will outlive us all, while a majority of humans continue to mumble over their Korans or Bibles with glazed eyes and outstretched hands. Humans have failed in the brains and education department. For example, nearly 42,000 of government schools in India operate without a building![5] And India has one of the lowest female literacy rates in Asia.[6] Then again, a radio program on 7 August 2006 mentioned that the bottles of the two famous American colas produced in India contained pesticides; one hopes they learned to get the kinks out. In China, more than half of the population is engaged in agriculture, and more than 70 percent of its rural population lives on less than two dollars a day.[7] The media tries to convince us that the combined population of India and China (about 2.5 billion people) are all educated but only a small percentage exceed the American brain power. Unfortunately, though, as the current world Super Power, it is shocking that the United States is churning out some very dumb citizens, and in various cities, the high school dropout rate approaches 50 percent. Foreigners account for about half of all engineering Ph.D. holders working in the U.S., and a large fraction in math and computer fields.

Parents are so apathetic that most of them have never walked the hallways of their kid's school to observe their daily rituals. The adults may be afraid of what they will see. In many schools, even the teachers are afraid of violence and intimidation. In America, the people have been sold a bill of goods about political correctness so that it now seems distasteful to speak the truth. The schools are not allowed to teach the negative consequences of the Muslim part of the world. For example, in August 2006, a Muslim plot to explode ten planes flying from the UK to the U.S. was foiled, and as a consequence, all non-Muslim passengers were banned from carrying liquid items (water, toothpaste etc.) on future flights. Students are taught (brainwashed) that it is politically incorrect to watch Muslims or for the police to profile any particular group of people. Although most terrorist activity is perpetrated by Muslims, we shouldn't single them out for close scrutiny.

For the Western youth, tattoos and piercings on various body parts are a commonplace practice and so widespread or trite that I consider it conformist. In previous centuries (when there were ships of wood and men of steel), tattoos were adopted by drunken sailors who copied the Polynesians (visions of naive swaying torsos and palm trees come to mind) and other *primitive* cultures. The wearing of a tattoo, or an earring by men, goes back to ancient times but there was a purpose in mind such as status symbol, appeasement of the gods, or even punishment. For the current crop of conformist teenagers and their aged counterparts, many will regret the body decoration in a few years. In the meantime, the conformists must abide by the stricture of wearing the earring on the right side (a sign for homosexuals) and hence the dictum "left is right, right is wrong."

Wearing long hair in the 1960s was a male sign of rebellion or individualism although others often saw it as faggy or effeminate. By the way, there should be a rule that, at the first sign of gray or male pattern baldness, the long hair goes. This does not apply to silver pony-tailed bikers with missing teeth perhaps. For my fashion sense, long hair is far more preferable than the current fad of body piercing, which the adorable youth are indulging to include the nose, belly, nipples, tongue, and you can guess where else. Our world is changing so fast that the educational systems are woefully behind the times. John Lennon, an icon of the famous Beatles, once said, "I'm not going to change the way I look or the way I feel to conform to anything. I've always been a freak. I'm one of those people." Talk about creativity, anti-establishment, and non-conformist. John Lennon was that and so much more. And when I looked at the John Lennon biographies, I was astounded to observe the many pictures of the man, and each one is a different looking individual. Although I'm no conspiracy advocate, I found it strange that he was shot dead (8 December 1980, New York City) in view of his activist leanings to include an anti-nuclear bias.

To sum up my feelings on the educational system, I have a saying "Never let schooling interfere with your education." There is a lot of meaningless and less than useless information going through the classrooms of the world and it is analogous to the internet in that a wealth of information is not always enriching. There are some uses for the computer and there are times to shut it down. Wisdom does not move by osmosis into tender brains without proper instruction, in spite of years of rote memorization and loads of impractical facts. Schools are rather baby-sitting institutions or better yet prisons and no wonder the inmates are revolting!

The Fix for Education

Here is my shot, crack, or stab at a fix to the educational system; a suggested course or a partial pardon from the warden:

AGE:

5	KINDERGARTEN
6	GRADE 1
7	GRADE 2
8	GRADE 3
9	GRADE 4
10	GRADE 5
11	HIGH SCHOOL 1
12	HIGH SCHOOL 2
13	NATIONAL SERVICE
14	OJT On the Job Training
15	COLLEGE 1
16	COLLEGE 2
17	COLLEGE 3
18	IDEPENDENT STUDY/TRAVEL

The above education schedule is a suggestion or starting point for discussion on how to rescue education from obsolete practices and practitioners. The education system is in need of radical change because society is paying too high a price for little return. And don't expect the problem to be fixed by a government committee with the usual suspects; *you* know from experience how effective those groups are, especially when the committee is stacked with the average dumbbells. We need the intelligent and talented people like the crew in the corporate world. We all know that corporations are experts at slicing and dicing through a problem (with ethical repercussions perhaps) to maximize profits and stabilize the enterprise. The education problem is a similar takeover target because schools are producing dropouts, illiterates, and the unproductive. The progressive dunces in the current system even plan to delete penmanship from the typical curriculum. The master key is to recognize an idea that was attributed to Einstein. "Everything should be made as simple as possible, but not simpler."

Enlightened education will positively affect our living standard, and if we retool the system, there will be new and improved learning centers in lieu of lip service. The physical structures should not be just schools but Learning Centers that engage both youth and adults. Parents should be more involved in the course, rather than the occasional report card or parent-teacher conference. One of the unfortunate consequences of advanced knowledge is a growing disrespect for parents. Since the child is handling computers and other gismos from an early age, they realize parents can be ignorant of these tools. Technology has a way of advancing so rapidly, that it can leave older people, with their lagging brain power, in the dust. For example, the electronic product manuals have become so onerous that they are only available online. Parents should be encouraged to actively pursue an educational tie-in to the proposed learning centers. Since a large percentage of employees receive some type of continuing education at the workplace, we might arrange a program that permits the parent to visit the learning centers for workplace training. This would enhance the educational bond in the family.

Parents should have a foot in the school door rather than dismissing the child at the bus stop and accepting negative peer pressure. It is a known fact that peer relationships are important contributors to the quality of children's development. Fellow classmates and friends have far greater influence on what teens think and how they act. There are too many working, single mothers who use day care as substitute parenting, and although this may be unavoidable, some kind of amends might be considered. Perhaps the system can assist with arranging more quality time for the available hours. It is a shame to have children for nights and weekends only. Education begins at home where the parent or caregiver teaches everyday activities from speech to tying shoelaces. There are some parents that want to shift the young ones to an institution as soon as possible, sort of off the breast and on to the formula. Children should be able to play at home for as long as possible within the first few years of life as enjoyed by the "baby boom" generation. There is time enough for formal training, and the home-provided sense of security will last a lifetime. At age four, parent and child could both attend some periodic classroom sessions that are analogous to training wheels on a bike. The child would have a more positive view of socializing with unknown people, and it would be less stressful. At the age of five, kindergarten is the place where the young sponge is deposited for time to play, socialize, have cookies with milk, and nap. It is a mild indoctrination to the eight long years of elementary Boot Camp to follow.

The educational routine includes an eight year stretch, with four high-school years for good behavior, and four more years of college, with perhaps a sprinkling of postgraduate study for the professional student (absurd in many cases). The elementary school should be reduced from eight years to six and high school should be reduced from four years to two. For a change there could be one or two different periods of National Service at the elementary and high school level, and the service could be performed instead of a summer vacation. In lieu of sitting around listening to boring lectures, or memorizing countries whose names will probably change soon, the student would actually get into the real world and work towards achievable goals. Likewise the nation would benefit from the activity performed by all these energized youth. Instead of sitting around and whining as idle youth are want, they could make a difference and contribute to society, rather than play the typical sponge who soaks up the taxpayers' money. We could get them off their backside in the hope of a payback to society. If there is a lot wrong with today's youth and method of schooling, odds are the system is dull and lacks the ability to inspire and motivate their customers. What was expected from the older generations does not cut it now; the times have changed and with it the population of sponges, who are prodded like cattle to the brink of mediocrity.

The story of young students and adolescence is only understood since the advent of brain imaging technology. Our brains take much longer to develop than we had thought. Scans show that brains undergo a massive reorganization, or wiring upgrade, between our 12th and 25th years.[9] Teens are known for the traits of excitement, novelty, risk, and peer pressures. These are now recognized as adaptive qualities, and not just the idea of "doing foolish new stuff with friends." Researchers now believe this adolescent behavior, over the course of evolution, has provided an adaptive edge to the human race. It has allowed our people to leave a safe home, move into unfamiliar territory, and populate the world. On the other hand, for certain dysfunctional groups, such as the black American community, a relatively significant percentage of their population will be incarcerated due to the inability to maintain a nuclear family unit. The take-away message seems to indicate that when parents engage and guide their teens with a light but steady hand, the children generally do much better in life. With this recognition of neuroscience and brain development, both parents and teachers must take a different view of adolescents and their supposedly idiotic behavior.

Counterintuitive steps and other decisions need to be made in regards to education:

- Cut education budgets. There is egregious waste in all bureaucracies. The term "Fraud, Waste, and Abuse" is simply lip service and not taken seriously. Government offices habitually spend their budgets and request more. For example, many departments such as the military are directed to spend millions even if the work is unclear. Get the money on the contract regardless of any need or facts. Use it or lose it.
- School funding should be changed. Property taxation pays

for almost half of public elementary and secondary education. The policy of state funding is viewed as outdated and not very resourceful. The disparity of poor versus rich schools, such as Camden (NJ) and Freeport (NY) respectively, is a function of the county property taxes. As property values decrease, there is no link for a drop in the school tax. And in many cases, the wealthy districts are subsidizing poor ones i.e., a redistribution of wealth. If you send your children to expensive private schools, the public school taxes are still compulsory.

- Tighten up on discipline. Society in general is a free-for-all and there are just so many millions you can send to the lock-up. Consider a Boot Camp (light) type of training in the schools especially for the delinquents, duds, turkeys, and lemons. Experience shows that Boot Camp works to instill discipline and responsibility. Consider a one to two week camp for students in the second year of high school. Instill the work ethic of previous generations because some of the current crop does not know how to work. Not to beat a dead horse, but only to show a work habit, here is a list of the author's 25 jobs worked during a lifetime:

1. Painting, Mr. Hilton, NJ—
2. Lawn mowing, various, NJ—
3. Rug installer, Assistant—
4. Snow shoveling, NJ—
5. Bowling alley, NJ, Janitor—
6. Holiday Inn, NJ, Dish Washing—
7. Bahr's Restaurant, Highlands, Bus boy—
8. Newspaper Lenzakis, Racetrack, Selling—
9. Sullivan Bros., Monmouth Park, Printing—
10. Harry M. Stevens, Monmouth Park, Dish washing—
11. Diner, George Papageorge, NJ, Dish Washing—

12. Mead Data Corp, Proof reading, Dayton—

13. University of Dayton, Janitor—

14. University of Dayton, Gardener—

15. L.M. Berry Yellow Pages, Dayton, Admin Ass't—

16. Newspaper Zenia Gazzette, Ohio, Ad Sales—

17. Tax Assessor's, Long Branch, Admin—

18. Radio Shack, NJ, Manager—

19. USCG, Boatswain's Mate—

20. Army, CECOM, NJ, Contracts—

21. Army, Saudi, Contracts—

22. Army, STRICOM, Florida, Contracts—

23. Army, Qatar, Contracts—

24. USCG, North Carolina, Contracts—

25. Veteran's Administration, Dallas, Contracts—

☐ Provide a course entitled Organization-101 that will instruct students how to maintain an orderly and logical mindset.

☐ Teach the ability to listen which seems a rare skill. It is a common problem to forget someone's name within ten seconds of introduction. Focus on personal relationships. Most people only know approximately 50 to 100 others and this reflects ancient human nature; just look in most personal address books. Therefore, young people should understand the misguided fixation with social networking and the possible negative cost versus benefits.

☐ Encourage student participation in salesmanship to defray expenses such as school trips. Sales by students should be relatively free of permits, taxes, and other burdensome restrictions. Enlist the support of local businessmen to mentor various revenue generating activities.

- [ ] Create a documentary film on comparative religions and philosophies for viewing in high school. The purpose is to demystify indoctrination of extreme choices of belief.

- [ ] Shorten the school day for youngsters and gradually lengthen the period as the pupils grow.

- [ ] Reduce the influence of teacher unions and tenure. (Good luck!).

- [ ] Provide more tutors to underachievers. Enlist philanthropy, donations, and donators to raise the bar of competency.

- [ ] Use English only. And don't be ridiculous.

- [ ] Determine to what extent school buildings can function after hours as dual use so that another tenant can defray expenses.

- [ ] Consider separating the sexes for a two year period before puberty. Boys and girls develop physically and mentally at different ages. I'm thankful that my parents didn't send me to an all-boys school but I'll admit to a lot of daydreaming in my co-ed Catholic classes.

- [ ] Create a first class reading list. *Lord Jim* (Conrad) and *Captains Courageous* (Kipling) are fine reading, but the old, vanilla list should be sprinkled with some practical and out of the ordinary books such as: *Guns, Germs, and Steel* (Jared Diamond), *The Omnivore's Dilemma* (Pollan), *The Hidden Reality* (Brian Greene). You know it is a challenge to reach consensus and compile a decent and brainy reading list. Therefore, the committee should avoid dumbbells and their dense selections. You read poems about slavery on your own time. An appropriate list should not be driven by either diversity or homogeneity. Upon viewing the average suggested reading list, it seems apparent that many are as boring as a nude beach. The proposed list might be different than the following question suggests: if you were stranded on a remote island for five years, what 10 to 20 books would you like to have? Would one of these be the novel *Shogun* by Clavell, rīdā-san? I would also like to have the classics from Robert Louis Stephenson to include *Kidnapped* and *Treasure Island*, but what about *Robinson Crusoe*?

☐ Reduce indoctrination and social engineering. Stop or reduce taking on the roll of parent, teacher, confessor, psychiatrist, soothsayer, sage and former financial adviser to the Greek government. For those old enough to remember, there was only one *Carnac the Magnificent* and his name was Johnny Carson. We recognize there are goals to education such as preparing students for work and to think. But what cultural values are being taught and just whose values are represented? Values reflect a person's sense of what ought to be. They were originally broadcast in small communal settings, but with the Pandora's Box of diversity now prevalent, people must recognize that different cultures maintain a hodgepodge of contradictory ethics and values. We are required to wade through that situation and find a decent balance. But since various religious organizations cannot correspond with each other, we need a secular approach to what is right or wrong. Values were customarily taught in the home. Now there are not so many homes, just houses. So, there is a need for another channel to deal the cards of values. The question remains who or what committee will adjudicate which values are the ones we should adopt and uphold.

☐ Consider scaling back sports activities in schools. Yes, children need physical activity in the daylight. No, there is nothing terribly wrong with competition among youngsters. But the activities could be geared to the average student rather than making stars or heroes in the usual baseball, basketball, and football exercise instruction. Professional sports are generating billions of dollars in revenue. Today the fans have been fooled by the total commercialization of their favorite pastimes and the exploitation that has ensued. Worse yet, there is criminal activity in sports. For example in 2013, European police officials revealed widespread match-fixing of soccer games in recent years, with 680 games globally deemed suspicious. Since most sports have amateur players far outnumbering the professionals, the pros use the younger players to restock the farm. You might say that academic athletics are subsidizing the corporate board of sports. For example, if you identify as a nerd like me, you were hard-pressed to participate in school sports regardless of the unfair and unwanted competition. As a 92-pound high school sophomore (Red Bank Catholic), they used me like a mop on the wrestling mat, so I was not the epitome of Spartan athleticism. But the point is the groomed athletes typically graduate from elementary, secondary, and college institutions; ready for the talent scouts looking for a new crop in the field of dreams. So, in a sense, if you have a golf team at your school, the taxpayers might be subsidizing the payroll for the next $100 million sports celebrity. It's all about the money in college sports. Many institutions of higher learning are more recognizable for their sports team than academic appeal, e.g., Notre Dame Football. They pull in billions of dollars and, once again, you (the taxpayer) are subsidizing a portion of this *not-for-profit* business. In conclusion, curbing sports in schools will starve this obsession and counter the ubiquitous soccer moms and batty dads who live vicariously through their children. Most alarming is the fact that 300,000 (sports related) brain injuries occur each year in the United States. In fact, the latest fad in 2013 is the number of lawsuits brought on behalf of thousands of former (professional) ball players, such as Tony Dorset, for previous head injuries. It is ironic that the purpose of education is to develop the brain and yet we watch on the sidelines as the children get drilled, tackled, pummeled, and wacked for the sporting life.

Dumbing Down

It is noticeable that the potential of youth has catapulted over previous generations due to technology and information advances. With a progressive standard of living, even physical advances have developed in the present-day youth. Might this have something to do with the growth hormones injected into the force-fed cattle on corporate feedlots? Compare the physique of girls today with those of women from the movies of the 1940s. However, emotional development has not kept pace due to dilution of culture and the so-called dumbing down of the population. Examples are numerous such as the fanatical interest in violent sports or entertainment instead of the benevolent pursuits such as classical music and the more refined arts. Some of the effects of dumbing down include:

☐ Loss of morals and values due to greed and materialism.

☐ The agenda of Political Correctness obscures human differences and turn "equal opportunity" into "equality for all."

☐ General apathy of the society due to disillusionment and fear inspired by the size of institutions and government.

☐ A propensity to push for "social justice" with unlimited entitlements for the great unwashed.

☐ Young people recognize and imitate fleeing from the world's problems, leaving it to the next guy or the next generation (like a budget deficit or global warming).

It only takes one nuclear detonation to establish the ultimate dumbing down of the population, and how primitive and uncouth we can become. Using a tiny portion of the brain's ability, it is not hard to imagine that education should be the priority on the planet. We particularly need to train the Muslim fanatics since they are the candidates for riding a suicide nuclear car bomb through our metropolis. The righteous minds can debate and argue, but only intelligent persons realize that people are a problem and therefore we need less of them and not more of them. The English Economist, Thomas Malthus (1766-1834), noted that unchecked populations increase at a geometric rate so that when you feed the starving populations, you severely increase the misery. This was graphically depicted decades ago in the renowned National Geographic Magazine. The path to hell is paved with good intentions, which means that the so-called do-gooders will step on your head to get to their heaven. I'm sure the Spanish Inquisition started out in a fraternity of good intentions. Likewise, the Christian missionaries spread their creed and the Spanish language, along with a good dose of diseases. And millions of unwitting natives with no immune defenses, however uncouth, were wiped out. Thus the expression "no good deed goes unpunished." If it is true that a significant portion of the general public is mentally unfit, then how do we induce nations to recognize and adopt an effective educational structure? Daunting challenge indeed! In his 2011 book, *The Beginning of Infinity*, physicist David Deutsch writes:

> *Setting up self-sufficient colonies on the moon and elsewhere in the solar system — and eventually in other solar systems — will be a good hedge against the extinction of our species or the destruction of civilization, and is a highly desirable goal for that reason among others."*

My comment or question:

How many Oxford or Cambridge academics does it take to screw in a light bulb in intergalactic space? —We have enough problems back here on spaceship Earth which requires our focus and imagination. — Merrily, merrily, merrily, merrily, life is but a dream, and people are the "stuff" dreams are "made on.

CHAPTER 9

Superstition and Progress
Believe and Belief

The past can be imagined as a wobbly wheel that rolled humanity along a clueless and ignorant path. And ignorance is bound with superstition which promotes the metaphysical or paranormal for the purposes of control. It has been suggested that humans are programmed to believe in the supernatural as a sedative to the self-conscious knowledge of death. This belief has a survival advantage because for lack of control in life, the unsuspecting can fall victim to nature's sticky web. Ancient superstitions are like today's urban legends; false stories that sound plausible and purposely spread among an audience to proliferate over many years. Modern humans are just as gullible and ill-bred as their ancestors and find it difficult to distinguish truth from fiction. The Old World throngs, however, lacked the scientific bases to comprehend reality and therefore were dependent on tales, myths, and legends to construct their world view and rationalize existence. Just as the likes of Mark Twain are few and far between, plausible story tellers of the gifted and entertaining type represent a minority in the population who could provide meaning and inspiration in an otherwise fearful and confusing world. Such talent would be coveted, sponsored, and controlled as Galileo was in 1633. The "father of modern science" was placed in house arrest for the remainder of his life after crossing the views of the Catholic Church.

Before advancements in science, superstition reigned and humans held the following beliefs.

- [ ] The idea of cause and effect was vaguely understood such that an earthquake was seen as the gods' displeasure rather than a geological phenomena e.g., plate tectonics. My mother explained thunder as the "angels bowling in heaven" and that was good enough for me.

- [ ] Power can derive from the gods in the animal world and thus wearing of bear skin or leopard claws transforms the wearer. Medicines made from animals often purport to have properties which are associated with the animal. Many aphrodisiacs either incorporate the penises of other animals or are shaped like penises. For example, dog penises from Thailand are sent to China and Taiwan, where they are consumed as energy boosters.

- [ ] Sacrificing unsuspecting humans and animals will propitiate the gods of weather.

- [ ] Do unto others before they do unto you.

In keeping with the animal kingdom, the ancient human system was regulated by brute force, imposed by the rulers with the fear of pain. The inducement to fealty and obedience is easy to promote among the cowering masses. In every time and place can be found a con artist with the associated schemes, and magic and magician have always found a secure foothold in the life and imagination of the ancient and modern alike. If you can fool most of the people, most of the time, you've got a leg up, and coupled with old fashioned force, that is a commanding combination to secure a community or kingdom. It has always been a fairly secure occupation or career path for the high priest, witch doctor, medicine man, and the like, as popes and kings have understood for many centuries. Even in the modern age, many countries have been ruled by such tyrants as Fidel Castro, Idi Amin, Saddam Hussein, Muammar Gaddafi, and Kim Jong-Il. It is astounding that just one man can control millions of his oppressed subjects. The operative idea of control is paramount for any organized entity to survive. Chaos and anarchy are fun concepts but generally not good for business, as any despot worth his salt can attest to. We take electrical power generation for granted, but what happens in urban streets when a blackout occurs? Wondrous anarchy and chaos as the mobs rampage through plate glass windows for television sets and appliances in belly laughing, riotous good cheer. And sometimes they even burn down their own neighborhood, and lucky for you that they don't think and burn down your neighborhood.

The Brain is a Man with a Mission

The relationship of consciousness and the brain is not fully understood, but steady progress is underway. Cognitive neuroscience correlates the study of the brain, mind, and body. The human brain is slowly revealing its secrets, so we can understand the chemical and electrical processes that constitute the mind and consciousness. The brain has approximately 100 billion nerve cells or neurons interconnected by trillions of connections, called synapses. It is the thinkers of the world who are trying to discover how the brain produces the elusive ideas such as conscious thought and dreams. In fact, researchers are currently mapping neurons to detect how memories are stored in the brain. After all, one of the main attributes that define you and I are our memories. You are the entire set of memories accumulated in a lifetime. But it will take some decades before a substantial part of the brain's neural network can be mapped and analyzed.

The brain is a cranky, old gismo, and it allows us to deep-six bad memories to the delete file so we generally remember the good times like the wellspring of our youthful indiscretions, and not the bad times like most of our existence. Some memories are outstanding like a film that I recall from the age of six: The 1956 Russian epic, The Sword and the Dragon, directed by Aleksandr Ptushko. It's a story of Ilya Muromets, a 12th century, sword-wielding warrior and his exploits of strength and valor. The film is widely claimed to hold the record for most people and horses ever to be used in a film, a cast of 106,000 and 11,000 Horses!

Poor memories are often the product of ineffective initial encoding, which usually occurs because little attention is paid during the initial encoding and processing phases, where no emotional linkages are established. When asked to identify the only accurate picture of a U.S. penny on a page with nine other choices, very few people can make the correct selection from the sheet with nine imposters. Although most adults have likely seen and held over 10,000 pennies during their lives, few can pick the correct picture. The reason for this is simple: we don't really care enough to memorize what an exact reproduction of a penny looks like since a penny has such little personal value. With over ten thousand exposures to the stimulus, the response is still inaccurate without a personally motivating linkage to details in the coin. There are two groups of people who can make an accurate identification of the penny. They are either professional coin collectors or penny-pinchers. When there are emotional "hooks" planted for the learner, the probability of subsequent recall increases dramatically.

It is possible that thoughts are composed of a type of physical field, and like all fields such as the gravitational and electromagnetic fields, there are particle constituents, for example, gravitons and photons respectively. They are the messenger particles for these two particular force fields. For example, when you see something, you can think of it in terms of a waving electromagnetic field entering your eye and stimulating your retina, or in terms of photon particles entering your eye and doing the same thing.[2] Just as people can swim through waves of water, we are continuously immersed in a sea of electromagnetic fields from the technology of radio and cell phones. Electronic devices allow signals or information to be broadcast and received to include television programs. In like manner, developing technology allows brain signals to be decoded so that paralyzed patients can control external devices; we will be theoretically able to read minds and so we won't need a "penny for your thoughts." The implications are mind boggling but the know-how is far in the future. If thinking is related to a physical field, it would indicate that what we call spirit is not a separate essence or soul-type entity but an integral part of the physical brain, which would upset the metaphysical belief systems of the world. There is no spirit that moves on because once it's pronounced dead and the brain is finished, that's the end of the line.

It might be possible to create a conscious brain if the specifications become available. After all, is this not one of the aims of science? For instance, Artificial Intelligence (AI) is a domain of computer science that explores whether machines can solve the types of problems that human beings are well known for. If we consider that life has been evolving on Earth for about 3.5 billion years, imagine what a conscious human engineer could do in a fraction of that time.

But we will not see a conscious machine anytime soon, in this budget-busting world. Although simulation has been a buzz word for many years, you only have to observe the primitive state of the activity in the government-industrial sector. For example, at the University of Central Florida (2005), admittedly not the apex of academia, their simulation department had a sorry excuse of a small, tinker-toy robot roaming the hallways. The football budget is undoubtedly much larger but the simulation "travel" budget is well funded for the usual getaways. At the adjacent Army simulation agency, they operated like a business, charging and collecting a profit from work performed for other agencies. The bonanza was used to fund delightful travel for "conferences" in Alaska and Hawaii. The payoff for simulation has been relatively paltry to include procuring some savings from flight simulators, weapons simulators and the like. So, serious scientists are making attempts to simulate the brain or simple neural networks. But you can imagine solving the puzzle of such complexity, which involves innumerable connections and billions of simultaneous transmissions that coalesce inside the brain in order to form a thought, is no easy assignment.

Neuroscience may confirm that we have an innate or intuitive sense of right and wrong that surpasses even the commandments of God. Ethics, not godly revelation, is the primacy of human affairs. To think, rationalize, and believe, is enabled by our brain—a functioning, evolved organ that is too complex for the average human to grasp, and beyond the present grip of scientific understanding.

To think, wonder, or imagine is unique to the brain which seems to control the constituent parts of the body for survival and gene propagation. Keep in mind, the development of the modern human brain is a recent arrival at the party that has been raging and raving for over 4 billion years.

In the days of the cave man, the brain was a mere toddler. Consider that the anatomically modern humans of 100,000 years ago showed no signs of modern behavior.[3] Their activities were of limited scope, such as foraging for food, clubbing thy neighbor on the head, and womanizing. Within small enclaves, humans stayed together, much as chimpanzees do, to form primitive societies as a unit for survival. After tens of thousands of years of star gazing, beings were bound to learn something such as astronomy or storytelling, and it might have been the development of language that propelled humans towards the continuum of advancement. Wisdom could be written down in various symbols. You know how the story changes by word of mouth, so writing was a major advancement. Life became more interesting since ideas could be discussed, written down, passed along, and the creatures now had a reason to hang out together. Finally stories and fairy tales could be conjured to the delight or trepidation of the new group of beings—called an audience. You can imagine the odd and primitive notions of the "cavemen" ancestors such as belief that thunder and lightning was the almighty God. To them, the world was fearful. Today the world is scary. Cranial development is the puzzle-solving process of increasing control in the world of entropy. That's the obvious difference between all the other animals and the brainy humans who could control their environment and bring some kind of order to a perceived chaotic universe.

Humans gained control of their dominion with the rise of

civilization by a combination of factors:

- [ ] Shared/common interests.
- [ ] Steady food supply.
- [ ] Adequate means of defense.
- [ ] Stability of system with rulers.
- [ ] Punishment for rocking the boat.

Humans are like the man with a mission due to their unique brain that fosters wonderment and the need to find purpose for existence. Civilizations are distinguished from a band of chimpanzees by some differences such as brain, posture, and amount of hair. Although we share 98 percent identical DNA with the chimpanzee, humans forged ahead by the impersonal chance of an evolved brain and more advanced cognitive ability in comparison to a monkey. Nature's process of selection has fine-tuned the brain with the distinguishing traits of consciousness and awareness. The brain thus has some interesting attributes so that even if it does not know the exact answer to a life question, it will take a guess—in some cases an educated or fairly intelligent guess and in other cases a brainless and unrewarding one. It also has the capacity to think and use reason which results in famous one-liners such as "I think therefore I am"—Rene Descartes.

If man formed civilizations then why aren't all members intelligent? As with other hereditary traits, such as blue eyes and blond hair, higher cognitive ability or intelligence is passed to the select minority of offspring. But wisdom and intelligence derived from heredity is not an automatic proposition because even if the brain power is received, it must be used to a capacity or exercised and that can only occur by nurturing the body that houses the delicate organ. A tribe that discourages individual thinking while promoting aggression/violence will dilute the pool of brain power in the population. In a primitive hunter-gatherer society, the strong survive (natural selection) by action of brute force while the brainy sensitive types tend to avoid conflict by use of the educated guess and running in the opposite direction. This saves them for another day, but the appearance of flight is a drag on the respect and affection from the fair maidens of the tribe, and another cause for dilution of the community bank of brain power. Imagine a discussion around the tribal campfire and which topic would win the attention of the animal-skin-clad group:

A – Let's listen to the music of the wind through the trees.

B – Let's strangle that howling meat for tonight's barbecue!

Life on the savannah involved competition for resources, for a leg up, and for willing or unwilling mates. The game of competition still plays out as it did then— "Winning isn't the only thing, it is everything." (Vince Lombardi). Psychology 101 teaches young students that the average personality will put down another to buoy or advance their feeling of self-worth. We are all guilty of the act of gossip where personal or sensational information is revealed in a grapevine-like fashion and when, for example, people attend parties, what is the first thing that they do upon leaving? They talk about the other people, it just seems natural. What better path to self-promotion than by destroying the competition.

The effective way to rule the unruly mob is to instill fear and deal harshly with enemies and disloyal subjects. Recognizing that the occasional brainy and sensitive dissenter may raise his head, a quick retaliation will be a lesson to keep one's head low to the ground. Enough lessons of this sort will cause brainy heads to be kept quiet. Basically it is easier to command a group of consumers if the population isn't overly brainy, ambitious, and sensitive. So, if that element can be deliberately weeded-out or diminished, the prospects are better for a secure grip on the reins of power.

The power brokers are very clever psychologists and keen observers of human nature which supports their control of the crowd. We are all familiar with the herd mentality such that just being the center of attention is an inherently stressful situation. Many social events involve some type of stage fright and even standing up to introduce ourselves is a predicament for most people. For example, Barbra Streisand, after forgetting some lyrics during a 1967 Central Park concert, stopped performing live for almost three decades. We can be easily led because of our innate fears that we have little control over.

It doesn't take a lot of imagination to realize that people can be controlled with a simple story, and the more frightening the tale, the greater the effectiveness. For example all humans have lived in the light/dark cycle of which we now understand as the rotation of the earth with respect to the sun. But imagine the primitive campers with fear of the dark, especially among children, and the belief in ghosts or the bogeyman, yikes!

I recall an assignment from my college professor, William Frost, in a course on Demons and Exorcism (University of Dayton Ohio). For homework, he challenged four students to sleep alone that night, and in the dark to call the devil. Some had to turn the lights back on. My response was that I had no intention of calling the devil. Professor Frost offered his congratulations and explained how the brain can play funny or not so funny tricks on the unsuspecting and unwitting mind.

Human beings have a capacity for self-deception and psychologists know they have to be careful when they go poking around the human mind because you're never sure what you'll find there. Psychosis, contrary to the conventional mainstream view, is most often not merely the manifestation of biochemical aberration or a "broken brain," but a fundamentally psychological phenomenon. And, as such, it demonstrates the dangerous degree to which the human mind is capable of massive self-deception. None of us are beyond deceiving ourselves. Such self-deception, which in its most extreme and pathological forms we deem delusional, is much more pervasive than most imagine.

You are Saved!

It's easy to see how fearful life must have been for early humans who had their fill of Murphy's Law, lack of scientific knowledge, and nowhere to run in the night except away from the campfire and into the darkness. What could be the answer to these dreadful problems (snare drum/cymbal) SALVATION! Just as a child can be soothed by a lullaby, humans are mesmerized by creative fictions that pluck us up out of the muck of earthly existence, and plunk us down near the throne of an almighty puppeteer who relieves us of our load. Just as proposed at my workplace, if you don't know something, make it up, that's the trick learned by primitive wizards to explain the rudiments of life:

☐ If there's lightning, the gods are unhappy. **Solution:** sacrifice human or ill-favored dog.

☐ If you're sick, you must be guilty. **Solution:** exorcism; like modern pharmaceuticals, possible side effects include death.

☐ If the hunt for food is successful it's an obvious side effect of last night's sacrifice. **Solution:** repeat same tonight.

☐ If you capture a foreign virginal female, there must be a god **Solution:** be thankful.

Human societies of all stripes labeled certain actions as taboo, i.e., proscribed by society as improper or forbidden. It seems to me that the idea of taboo is problematic or at least mysterious, and because there are no universal taboos, then they are just another rule or idiosyncrasy of a particular group. Even incest is not universal which reminds me of my favorite sister-in-law who used to say, "Incest is best." In some cultures for instance, the ins and outs of the body's bowel movement is taboo. It is the subject of endless jokes, euphemisms, and metaphors, but it is a plain natural movement. Just like many other mechanisms, for example, a plant takes in CO_2 (carbon dioxide) and excretes O_2

(oxygen). An automobile takes in gas and spews out exhaust. A cosmological black hole takes everything in the event horizon and turns it into chopped liver or worse. The human body you know takes in all kinds of rubbish, and turns out some ghastly things. The body requires nutritional input and here comes the output! Not to be too serious, there's that old saying "my shit doesn't stink" and usually you see this as "My ---- doesn't stink" since to speak or write plainly is taboo. The arrogant phrase refers to the stinky actions of others. The famous comedian, George Carlin, had a lot to offer on this and other taboo subjects, and this is only a portion of his routine:

"Consider: You can be shit faced, be shit out of luck, or have shit for brains. With a little effort you can get your shit together, find a place for your shit or decide to shit or get off the pot. You can smoke shit, buy shit, sell shit, lose shit, find shit, forget shit, and tell others to eat shit and die."

There seems to be a lot of funny, neurotic, and Freudian things going on with the subject. Fred Zwicky, the scientist known for the theory of Dark Matter, was noted for a similar expression; he used to call other astronomers at the Mount Wilson observatory "Spherical bastards." Why spherical? "Because they were bastards when looked at from any side."

You're toilet trained at some tender age and then you're on your own! Don't want to hear about it, don't want to see it or smell it, abominable! Some cultures have customs that deal with food versus toilet. The Arabs and East Africans eat communally, from one platter as opposed to separate plates for each person. They eat with the right hand only; to do otherwise is an insult since they use the left hand for the toilet business. This is customarily not discussed in polite company. Other than doctors and nurses, few outsiders are witness to our personal hygienic problems, i.e., when the body is not working properly. Why is the topic of stool verboten when it is a useful gauge of the plumbing system? No, the public would more likely consider reading tea leaves.

Compare men and women's public facilities. The men have to stand at a urinal and, like the New York subway system, pretend to ignore each other. Women, on the other hand, enjoy enclosed privacy in a stall. Some guys take the newspaper with them (sports section of course) and I have a word of advice for them; if you need that much time on the 'throne,' you'd better change your crappy diet. (Taking care of business!). The Western world makes a big deal out of the event from the infancy stage of diapers with mother's comments about "the package" through toilet training when they send you into a closet with sage advice such as "just do your thing," and no wonder some people are confused. It's become a hush-hush affair, the subject of innuendo and definitely not a topic for polite conversation at the dinner table. When I saw a bidet in Saudi Arabia, I didn't have a clue as to what it was. It derives from a French word meaning trot since you ride it like a horse. Modern society has sanitized nature to the extent that we live in a sterilized world. The modus operandi is that, as long as I don't see something, it doesn't exist.

We live among a plethora of microscopic bugs to include those residing in our body. But if bugs are visible, they must be eradicated with pesticides that are ironically harmful to humans. When I first visited my wife's family in Africa (Eritrea), there were hundreds of flies around the mud hut when food was being served. At any given time, there were ten of the little buggers landing on me, and I'd grown up detesting even one fly in the house. Similarly, life in the countryside involves a lot of the flying pests. When I visited the Ohio farm area, they were in grand attendance at any picnic. And my co-worker Homer O'Krepki from Binghamton, New York, said he could sense a great spring day by the loud drone of thousands of flies on the side of the barn. Our gut is residence for bacteria that are friendly and needful and yet we toss antibiotics around our environment in the hope that the bad bacteria does not develop immunity to the drugs (and that the good bacteria will not suffer consequences).

We deodorize our bodies and manufacture scents for our homes and cars. But there is dichotomy to consider; sometimes people need to freshen up: Just try riding in a Pakistani taxi in the third world and you will sniff the drift. The western world has quite a few unnatural habits such as hiding natural bodily functions, and ignoring the fact that all systems of the body have immense importance and are barometers of the health of the individual. People would do well to expose the fallacies of certain taboos such as derision of the human waste system. Another example that comes to mind is the taboo of sex, a behind closed door affair, other than to emphasize the blatant advertising of the glitzy, glossy, sugar-coated side of the business as opposed to the messy details of reality.

Discussing Religiosity

Belief systems or religions are customs that characteristically serve one principal master: humans. As Michael Shermer asserts in his book, The believing Brain, "Religious faith and belief in God have equally adaptive evolutionary explanations. Religion is a social institution that evolved to reinforce group cohesion and moral behavior."[5] The aware and conscious brain has evolved, but contrasted with other creatures, the human brain is able to think and believe, and in many cases people believe what they're told. A celebrated example in the West is the child's belief in a Santa Claus who comes down the chimney and brings presents. The Tooth Fairy is a useful fantasy that provides comfort to children when they lose a baby tooth. In like manner, the idea of a supernatural realm became grist for the mill or a crutch that filled the void in an otherwise inhospitable and mystifying world. There are differences, however, in contrasted beliefs. The brain's notion of Santa Claus is easily dispelled at a certain age. For example, with four older brothers, my belief in Santa was disabused at a young age. The older siblings already knew Santa had flown the coop, and therefore I should follow suit in lockstep. Figuratively speaking, the brain's shelf for belief in Santa is a no-brainer and effortlessly sent to the dust bin of neuronal circuits. But the belief in Satan, on the other hand, with all the religious accessories, is not easily dispelled. This is serious business that hangs around for a lifetime. You can profess to be an agnostic, but the brainwashing from early childhood, with the cast of characters, deity, icons, and leviathan paraphernalia, leaves an imprint that is mighty indeed to shelve behind the counter. You could say that religious or spiritual memes have a long shelf life.

Brainwashing is an effective way to control and influence people. The formula reads: Employ a number of time-tested tools such as fear, intimidation, and reference to authority. Divide and conquer is another old strategy whereby groups are encouraged to oppose each other rather than the subjugator. Some effective tactics to control the population include: Stifle free thinking. Render certain words and ideas taboo such as racist or criticism of the government; and setup a two-party system with labels such that Democrats are liberal while Republicans are conservative. An English-speaking citizen with a Russian accent might assert, "This is like Soviet Union!"

In prior ages, there were a lot of unknowns in the physical world that could not be understood in the absence of science. It was only natural to attribute the mysteries to the gods and follow the controllers. There have been various sightings of the gods to include burning bushes in the bible through supernatural images (the Blessed Virgin Mary) even appearing like Rorschach Inkblots on windowpanes of office buildings in New Jersey. Just as children can be quite inventive, humans have conjured a motley crew of gods of varying faces, styles, and severity to include benevolent gods, malevolent gods, and quirky, unpredictable, temperamental gods. Richard Dawkins asserts that "Blind faith can justify anything. If a man believes in a different god, blind faith can decree that he should die—on the cross, at the stake, skewered on a crusader's sword, shot on a Beirut street, or blown up in a bar in Belfast."[6] Faith is such a successful brainwasher in its own favor, especially a brainwasher of children, that it is hard to break its hold. It is a state of mind that leads people to believe something—it doesn't matter what—in the total absence of supporting evidence.

All of us experience sensations such as pleasure and pain. Feelings are stimulated by our environment from which we form beliefs and values. Brain research reveals that a group of chemical cocktails are associated with feelings. These neurotransmitters can motivate or sedate, excite or calm us. For example, dopamine is associated with feelings of pleasure; endorphins behave like morphine to assuage pain. Certain foods, such as chocolate or chili peppers, can lead to enhanced secretion of endorphins. The chemicals produced in the brain are quite extensive and include serotonin, which regulates mood and appetite, and provides a feeling of well-being.

To put the puzzle together, let's consider several aspects that comprise the source of human actions and behavior. We have brain architecture such that various structures contribute to the whole, and it is like a grab bag of parts for various functions. For example, there isn't one part of the brain dedicated to processing the divine, although the pineal gland was once thought to be the seat of the soul. Instead, according to recent research, religiosity is dislocated and strung out along a neural network comprised of the frontal, parietal and temporal lobes. If religiosity operates in specific parts and chemicals of the brain, then its origins might be written in the blueprints of life, our genes. A genetic origin of religiosity might stem from an evolutionary drive toward inclusion. In this way, learning a society's religion, like learning its language, is hard-wired into humans through inherited genes.

Science tells us that we are creatures of accident, clinging to a ball of mud hurtling aimlessly through space.[9] The belief systems were conceived to answer the weighty questions of the day such as why are there floods and droughts. Why is there a Murphy's Law? Where do my ancestors go when they die? (To a garage in Buffalo, New York, according to George Carlin). Why does the earth shake and spit fire into the sky? And countless other unsolved mysteries. It is in our nature (common sense) to conjecture and solve the puzzles because the brain is focused that way. When you see a magician's show, you don't leave your seat before you've said or wondered "how did he do that?" The brain seeks patterns or order in nature and it looks for answers to questions.

Rituals are an important part of religions. They are actions or ceremonies that were originally performed to appease the gods but continue in importance for social bonding. One thinks of fertility rites which must have been extremely important for the ancient, small clans of hunter-gatherers. Abraham Maslow developed a hierarchy of needs. People must first satisfy the basic needs of food, shelter, and clothing. Therefore one would suppose rituals were performed for these initially. Higher needs include social and psychological ones such as love or belonging, and perhaps associated rituals for these came later. We tend to forget how many current rituals we perform all year. Some mundane examples include praying in church, holiday parties, marriages, and even the hand-shake. More esoteric examples are rituals belonging to the masons, college fraternities, and satanic cults. Religious rituals are some of the most prevalent and time-honored. Arabs kneel down, facing Mecca, lean forward and touch their foreheads to the ground. Jews bob and weave before the Wailing Wall in Jerusalem. Catholics apparently change bread and wine into flesh and blood which they term 'transubstantiation.' That reminds me of the biblical account of Jesus transforming water into wine during the Wedding at Cana. Apparently, the party ran out of cheap wine, so Jesus delivered, and the waiter made a remark about departing from the custom of serving the cheap stuff last; lip smacking Chateauneuf-du-Pape! Most of us have seen the National Geographic photos of Ethiopian women with "lip plates" the size of basketball hoops. This ritual of body modification by lip-stretching is considered a sign of beauty, but these women have trouble speaking normally and often drool since they essentially have no lip or teeth on the bottom of their mouth. Another extreme ritual relates to Jesus on the cross. Devotional crucifixions are common in some countries such as the Philippines. Worshipers drive thin nails through the palm of the hand and the ritual might include whipping and wearing a crown of thorns.

Humans have genes that predispose us to indulge in rituals. Notice that repetition is the norm for rituals. Practice makes perfect as in dancing, and rituals are geared for group participation since conformity is an ancient trait of humans. Take for example the Macarena phenomenon, a worldwide hit in 1996. Many believe that a world record for group dancing was set in that year, when a crowd of 50,000 people danced the Macarena in Yankee Stadium. This is the ultimate in conformity, to go along to get along. Rituals use music extensively along with gestures and dancing. The performance and appreciation of music goes back at least 50,000 years ago as evidenced by bone flutes for instance. The origin of music is speculative but we entertain several theories to include the evolution of a mother-child bond, or the need for men to attract sexual partners. Music is universal to all human cultures, and as to the chicken or egg theory, music most likely preceded language.

The main function of music is to enhance social coordination and it proved to be both emotional and spiritual. Examples include the gut-wrenching ballad from Sinatra's failed marriage to Ava Gardner, All My Tomorrows, from 1958, to the black gospel song by Aretha Franklin, Precious Lord Take My Hand, from 1956. Music involves rhythm, melody, structure, and repetition that literally stimulate the human body. What a legacy! From the humble beginnings of ancients banging logs with sticks, to the orchestral works of Rimsky-Korsakov played by the Philadelphia Orchestra, conducted by Eugene Ormondy: Scheherazade and Russian Easter Overture. Bomm, bom-bom, Bom-Bomm! We would raise the volume on the Hi-Fi while dad conducted the orchestra from his chair in the living room. If the Russian music doesn't make your emotions soar, then you are not aware of how to live. This is possibly the most significant insight of this book. (Bomm, Ta-Da, Ta-Da-Da!) (Don't worry, Dad; I got it). Such power, intensity, and sophistication that classical music provides. You can look at a painting, but it won't sweep you away like the string section.

Orchestras were once a symbol of high-brow entertainment, but that changed with one particular genius. Leonard Bernstein was able to popularize the classics in a way that no previous musician had ever done. An entire generation of Americans was drawn to great music through his television shows. Anyone who attended a Bernstein concert left feeling the profound wonder not only of music but of life itself. Incidentally, there is some slight etiquette involved in listening and applauding classical music. The undergraduates should learn that the audience claps only at the end of a selection; there may be two or three "movements" or sections to a piece (check the handout or playlist provided) and the audience should refrain from clapping until the end of the last movement. It's awkward and embarrassing because many concertgoers of the current generation are not aware of this custom. Similarly, I find it humorous that one can't attend a jazz session and fail to clap with every riff. You cannot minimally applaud at the end of a piece but are expected to clap for every instrumentalist for every tune.

With a few exceptions such as classical music and jazz, many listeners seem to prefer a vocalist or singer along with the in-strumentalists. There is something about singing that lights up our brain circuitry and is considered ancient and universal. Like anything else, there is talent. Frank Sinatra was referred to as The Voice (among other nicknames) because he had the attributes for inspired singing to include, pitch, timing, timbre, phrasing, and rhythm. It's simple really; take another look at Frank. People enjoy the guitar and piano, but we prefer singing, blue eyes and a great smile. One cannot imagine listening to the Rolling Stones without Mick Jagger. I like to mention for aspiring singers, that if you can do Over the Rainbow as made famous by Judy Garland in the Wizard of Oz, that is a great test for talent. Here an associated trivia question must be included: In the 1939 Wizard of Oz, who had the most roles and what were they? The answer: Frank Morgan had five roles in the movie to include the carnival huckster Professor Marvel, the gatekeeper of the Emerald City, the carriage driver for the horse of a different color, the guard at the wizard's hall, and the Wizard of Oz.

My wife and I were fortunate to hear Luciano Pavarotti in Qatar (of all places) several weeks before the Iraq War. Opera can seem problematic if one does not comprehend the Italian language, but in Luciano's case, it's not relevant. Although the conductor of Russia's Bolshoi Symphony Orchestra had to help the heavy opera star on and off the stage, one cannot easily match his arias with a musical instrument.

Actually science is learning a lot from birdbrains; researchers have discovered that birds with vocal learning abilities (songbirds and parrots) have brain structures for singing, and learning to sing, embedded in areas controlling movement. It was also found that areas in charge of movement share many functional similarities with the brain areas for singing. This suggests that the brain pathways used for vocal learning evolved out of the brain pathways used for motor control. The results from birds are consistent with the hypothesis that spoken language was preceded by gestural language, or communication based on movements (one of several competing explanations for the origin of spoken language). Both humans and chimps gesture with the limbs while communicating, and young children gesture even before they begin talking. "Gesturing is something that goes along naturally with speech," according to Erich Jarvis, associate professor of neurobiology at Duke University. The brain areas used for gesturing may have been co-opted and used for speech.[10]

Music has been used as a manipulative tool all too often. For example, advertisers know that vocal music permits the passage of a verbal message in a speechless way in order to sell more products. A pitchman can resolutely sing a message which would sound corny if spoken from a page of ad copy. The Christian church tried to monopolize music by restricting it to vocal chants and hymns in the absence of instruments because with the former, they could control the message, such as the "Mighty Fortress is Our God." Instruments were associated with the sensual heathen cults and instrumentals tended to be entertaining and distracting at liturgical services. Gregorian chants continue to represent some of the most inspiring music to date and for 2000 years of changelessness and supposed permanence, in vaulted cave-like structures, the echoing sound was both monumental and ominous indeed. In New York City, visitors can experience this majesty at one of the largest (in use) cathedrals in the world, St. John the Divine, located at 1047 Amsterdam Avenue & 112th Street. You can check the schedule for visiting chorale groups. On the other hand, the ancient pipe organ was an excellent counterpart to religious vocalization. For instance, the Monastery of Winchester England built an organ with 400 pipes that could be played with two monks at the same time, but only when 70 monks would work as wind makers. The music was so loud that it could be heard in the entire city.

At the other end of the spectrum of music, the current crop of rock and roll concert-goers will gladly pay dearly to sit with 20,000 other fans and are expected to sing-along with the performer which conserves the star's voice for the next gig on the road. Even though they are paying to attend to the entertainers, the crowd will sing along en masse. The performers should keep in mind that we are paying them to entertain the crowd, not the other way around.

Music is second nature for me. I can remember at age three, sitting before the huge, booming, antique Hi-Fi console as my dad would play Harry Belafonte singing the Banana Boat Song: "Day-o, Day-ay-ay-o, Daylight come and me wan' go home... Its six foot, seven foot, eight foot BUNCH!" And the baby would laugh at this point. I have been humming the sounds of music for over five decades, at least since the age of six; move over family Von Trapp and Jackson Five! People consider you a 'happy person' if you hum or whistle in public places, go figure; it's just the way it is. My mother pushed all her boys onto the stage at an early age with a smattering of red lipstick and rouge to make us look livelier.

When I was nine years old, my mother sprang for guitar lessons for one of my older brothers, and I tagged along. Nick Mascolo was a master of the guitar, violin, and piano, with hands as tough as leather and that sharp-pointed thumbnail. I could smell the tomato sauce that his wife was cooking in the kitchen on Melrose Terrace in the predominantly Italian section of Long Branch. He charged only $3 per half-hour, and at the end of the session, I would accompany both of them on the drums and tap dance as well. My mother purchased an antique, pearl colored, Slingerland drum set from Mr. Mascolo for $90 and I made a lot of noise, but Ringo Star got the job instead.

When I later took guitar lessons from Mr. Mascolo, there were no 'Fab Four' sheets of music, only polkas that did not resonate or motivate, but he used to say to me "William, I'm gonna make-a you rich." Yeah, but how do you get to Carnegie Hall? Research by Hambrick and Meinz indicates that intellectual ability matters for success in many fields such as music. It's not just the 10,000 hours of practice, but basic abilities, such as short-term memory capacity, which are known to be substantially heritable, also contribute to performance differences. You could say that the cream rises to the top.

Six of our brood attended high school at Red Bank Catholic in New Jersey, which has a superb musical tradition. I was fortunate to participate in the Chorale Club and in several of Broadway's best such as Guys and Dolls and Man of La Mancha; the musical directors included some of the pros in the business to include Ruth White, Robert Hebble, Mary Woods Kelly, Robert Wilson, and Anthony Polistina. Instruments never sat well with me but I have sung in an amateur status in many states and countries; I can belt out Sinatra's New York, New York like you wouldn't believe.

The beat goes on; and that is the heart beat that so many drum sounds imitate. Could the caveman grunt on key? Of course they could and they had music teachers in the bird songs playing all around them. They may have imitated the sound of the wind through the trees with primitive flutes. Even monkeys can play the drums by banging on dead logs. They might not do as well as Gene Krupa or John Bonham, but they get the message across. For example, my wife's musical heritage from Eritrea includes just a few instruments such as a handheld, five-string, harp-like instrument called a kirar and a hand-held drum suspended from the neck with a rope loop. The kebero is a large drum with an animal hide skin on each side of the drum. Not to appear unduly biased, but each song sounds the same to me. That's the funny thing about music depreciation as Slip Mahoney would say.

As previously mentioned, the Eritrean drumming is a constant and unchanging beat that might be reminiscent of the human heart beat. Besides the singing by men, many songs include piercing, high-pitched female vocalizations that, like the Tigrinya language, derive from the back of the throat. The Eritrean traditional dance is unusual also. In large gatherings, several hundred people will move in a circle around the dance area to the rhythm of the music. But their movements are quite restrictive and conservative. Dancers shuffle along in the circle with arms down and at their sides. It is customary to jerk the shoulder muscles during the dance and there are various stylish performers who might jump or bend their knees along the circle.

The song continues for what seems an eternity to outsiders. During the last minutes of the song, the musical tempo increases and dancers cease the circular motion and dance in groups of twos or threes, facing one another until the end of the song. Due to my dental background, I hardly ever smile. One crooked tooth as a youngster made me that self-conscious, and I wasn't trained to act with a fake British-type smile. But you have never seen such smiling as naturally occurs on the Eritrean dance floor— and they have such a flawless, bright white and enviable set of teeth. Their communal happiness during this dancing ritual is picture perfect.

Mirror Neurons

Although genes profoundly influence behavior, researchers at UCLA found that cells in the human anterior cingulate, which normally fire when you poke a patient with a needle (pain neurons), will also fire when the patient watches another patient being poked. The mirror neurons, it would seem, dissolve the barrier between self and others. V.S. Ramachandran calls them "empathy neurons" or "Dalai Lama neurons."

Humans display sophisticated social abilities. The human brain has multiple mirror neuron systems that specialize in carrying out and understanding not just the actions of others but their intentions, the social meaning of their behavior and their emotions. "We are exquisitely social creatures," according to Dr. Rizzolatti, one of the discoverers of mirror neurons. "Our survival depends on understanding the actions, intentions and emotions of others." Mirror neurons provide a powerful biological foundation for the evolution of culture. Until now, scholars have treated culture as fundamentally separate from biology. But now we see that mirror neurons absorb culture directly, with each generation teaching the next by social sharing, imitation and observation.

"When you see a spider crawl up someone's leg, you feel a creepy sensation because your mirror neurons are firing." Without them, we would likely be blind to the actions, intentions and emotions of other people. The way mirror neurons let us understand others is by providing some kind of inner imitation of the actions of other people, which in turn leads us to simulate the intentions and emotions associated with those actions. When I see you smiling, my mirror neurons for smiling fire up, too, initiating a cascade of neural activity that evokes the feeling we typically associate with a smile. I don't need to make any inference on what you are feeling, I experience immediately and effortlessly what you are experiencing.[13] The research is leading some professionals to link autism with a deficiency in the mirror neuron system since many autistic children have difficulty with imitating other people's actions. If the brain is wired with imitation inducing mirror neurons, this suggests the negative consequences of violent movies, television, and video games.

We should consider what types of programming are being watched by impressionable children. The television has sponsored Flash Gordon, Superman, Spiderman, Bionic Woman, and other manifestations of unrealistic, and perhaps unhelpful, role models. Children see these larger than life figures and often try to emulate them. But they cannot be faster than a speeding bullet, or able to leap tall buildings. Unfortunately, many sports can be viewed in the same light. During the past few decades, many athletes have used performance enhancing drugs such as steroids and the list of sports celebrities would be long indeed. For example, after years of denials, Lance Armstrong finally admitted in 2013 his seven wins in the bicycling Tour de France involved drugs. In 2006, Baseball giant Barry Bonds, who holds the all-time Major League home run record, allegedly lied under oath about steroid use and failed a test under the league's amphetamine policy. Unfortunately, the children are deceived into believing this is the way the game is ordinarily played. Of course you can be faster and stronger with the supplements of champions and as the man said, winning is everything. Perhaps the best way to tackle the superhero problem is to allow children to play, but make them aware of limitations and extremes.

Most of us intuitively believe monkey-see, monkey-do. Media violence provokes imitation. We also understand that the U.S. is a fairly violent country and some of our sports mirror this: Boxing, Kick-Boxing, Wrestling, Ice Hockey, Football, and Cock Fighting (Si podemos) (Yes we can). After a three-year investigation ending in 2012, a national football team received fines and suspensions for a bounty system of payoffs to deliberately injure opposing players—and the name of the team ironically, The New Orleans Saints. Regarding criminal and unethical activities, this is the iconic tip of the iceberg one might imagine. The only idiotic sport we don't have is Bull Fighting, but its introduction wouldn't surprise me at all. I don't care how pretty Muhammad Ali was, pathetic describes a sport with the aim of bashing each other's brain. Some scientists advocate that we are a pack of neurons, so have your neuron call my neuron about this business of violence in America.

Richard Dawkins is known for the idea of memes. He believes in a fundamental law that all life evolves by the differential survival of replicating entities. The gene or DNA molecule is the replicator on our planet. But a new replicator, the meme, conveys the idea of a unit of cultural transmission, or a unit of imitation. A ritual is an example of a meme. Just as genes propagate themselves in the gene pool by leaping from body to body, so memes propagate themselves in the meme pool by leaping from brain to brain via a process which, in the broad sense, can be called imitation.[14] For instance, the idea of God has been around for a very long time because it has high survival value, similar to a lullaby, and satisfies our psychological needs. You might agree that the meme for Elvis Presley will be replicated for many hundreds of years in the future.

So how the mind works involves heredity and culture or both nature and nurture. Note that a fad is distinct from memes. For example, the Macarena dance mentioned above was a fad. Generally fads fade out; they are continually dreamed up, and then the participants move on to a new one in a relatively short period of time. For example, almost all American men wore a hat before 1950. There were various styles through the years to include the fedora worn by Humphrey Bogart and the most coveted head, Frank Sinatra. In recent years, white boys imitate the black gangstas from L.A., by wearing a baseball cap backwards. When we were kids, sunburns were possible at the beach, but we didn't know about skin cancer; we do know about it today, and for us melanin-challenged people, its good advice to keep your shirt on and wear a hat. But bear in mind, the older generations had brains to cover up; they used hats for sun protection, to keep the head warm, and like Frank, to cover a bad hair situation.

CHAPTER 10

The Demise of the Gods & the Meaning of Life
Ready, Set: Indoctrinate!

The single most negative impact on human activity is organized religion. It's like organized crime, but much worse. The reach of the Mafia is only regional in extent and the criminal activity has been mitigated by prosecution and arrests. But the religious institutions have long tentacles and their impact, for good or ill, is suffered for millennia. As to the difference between a religion and a cult—one of them has tax exempt status. It's a matter of degree like the difference between being curious and being nosey. In my opinion, bringing up baby in one of the dogmatic, conventional religions is child abuse. That may seem harsh but is similar to an Atlanta radio show that proposes the same for sending your child to public school. Although this is serious business, you can't help but laugh at some of the religious parities of the past. For example, we were entertained with the Don Imus shtick of the fictional "Right Reverend Billy Sol Hargis, pastor of the First Church of the Gooey Death and Discount House of Worship" where this week and this week only, you can make a five-dollar donation for just $2.98, but you get credit with Him for the full five dollars. Say Hallelujah. Parenting does not require a license, but you need one for just about anything else in life.

The parent-child relationship often involves indoctrination; a process of instilling one's ideas which discourages independent thought as well as acceptance of other opinions. I suppose most people, whether intelligent or ignorant, would want to download the software or junk from the shelves of their brain if they could.

But they can't, so socialization and/or indoctrination are the choices, which represent a time-consuming and dicey prescription. We have all heard, "Don't do as I do, do as I say" and "We learn from our mistakes" (supposedly the adviser wants you to learn from his or her mistakes, not your own). Since people generally conform to expectations, religious lobbyists rubber-stamp their children to the congregation.

In 2011, an Orthodox rabbi, and supposed mystic of congregation Shuva Israel, was the subject of missing funds. Millions of dollars in donations to the rabbi's congregation that was intended for his charity could not be accounted for according to his consigliere. In cult-like fashion, people would lineup for hours to receive his blessings. In New York, the Rabbi's base of operations was located in a building purchased for $28 million, financed largely by donations from followers. You just can't make this stuff up, and it is better than fiction! Stop and think a minute. Why do you feel it necessary to pass along the same religion to your carbon copy? Many will argue that a child needs to be raised with some kind of religion, which they can go with or discard as an adult. The religious promoters will tick-off a list of benefits derived from devotion; among them are piece of mind and the prospect of everlasting life, so it acts as a pacifier. But why not use a system that excludes dogma and meaningless rituals?

Our upbringing was Catholic and the rituals were drastically changed in the 1960s. The mass was said in Latin which sounded like gibberish and the priest conducted the service with his back to the audience like a third-world shaman. They used to preach "fire and brimstone" but decided to cool-it because it's otherwise better for business. The spectators had no say in the proceedings other than to shell out the pocket money. Several members of our clan were altar boys but we didn't get paid for it, and we had no clue why we were doing it. And they would dust off the sermons on each occasion that were repetitious and uninspiring for the most part. My mother was a staunch adherent and I wish it were possible to bottle and sell that kind of devotion. How she thought that rigmarole would rub off on me, I don't know. In the grand scheme of things, I had my share of second hand clothes, so don't try to pawn off these used goods, please.

In primitive times, organized religions were yet to be invented, but humans were well on their way to the big leagues about 50,000 years ago in what Jared Diamond terms the Great Leap Forward.[1] It is possible that evolutionary processes permitted increased brain function and speech so the two-legged ancestors were off and running. Humans finally got a handle on the use of stone tools, and advancement was right around the corner at the end of the last ice age, about 13,000 years ago.

The idea of a system or organization blossomed at this time when humans developed food production by domesticating plants for crops and animals for various uses including food and labor. Up until this time, all humans were hunter gatherers, living the gypsy life of foraging for food and moving on to the next feed. Without wheels they only had capacity to carry the baby, a few stone tools and not much else.

Food production allowed a ready supply of grub that permitted steady employment—the nine-to-five job and a settled existence. Heretofore life for all animals was a dog-eat-dog world but it became a human-eat-dog world. We ate certain meats from the cow, pig, chicken, or animals that were bred for the purpose, such as we do today with roses or tomatoes, and selecting the ones we like for taste or color and growing those specific varieties.

We also breed dogs to bring forth certain desired qualities as pets. So, with a full belly and tools in hand, humans were well on the way to becoming the deadliest of predators and they only lacked a system or organization. As Francis Bacon said (1561-1626) "Knowledge is power" and when writing was invented by the Sumerians around 3000 BC, humans could now catalog knowledge in a concrete form, rather than just by verbal means. This ability to write on clay and later paper-like materials meant the birth of bureaucracy and hence hierarchies, power structure, rules, ruling class, henchmen, despots, and greedy pigs—an organization or system.

A settled lifestyle requires some form of governance over the multitudes of recruits in the newly established communal society that humans evolved into, otherwise anarchy would prevail. The majority of subordinates are subservient to the professed king, ruler, or despot who controlled the machinery of food production, accumulation of wealth, as well as the belief system of faiths and superstitions. In the hunter gatherer community, all were necessarily involved in the mundane routines of the day. But in a settled lifestyle, the competitive human nature spawned an era of rulers, inspirational killers (like Alexander the Great), who would convince the masses, by fair means or foul, that they hold the power of the gods, or at the very least are the middlemen in the commerce of heavenly pursuits. In order to hold the attention of the populace, you either need a good game (scam) like the man behind the curtain in the Wizard of Oz, or you have to use threats and force, and it helps to combine the two.

When you're on the run as a hunter/gatherer, there is not a lot of time to think of the unknowns and there's little need to. But in the settled community, there's time to reap and sow, to accumulate possessions and wealth, and to load the backs of the lower classes and other beasts of burden to full capacity. The thread that holds this societal fabric together is the arcane belief system that there are gods to pacify and other mystifying aspects of life that can only be explained by the intermediaries and high priests up in the palace. And they kept a tight hold on the people because to let them wander like sheep from the fold, well, you never know where they'll end up, although most likely in some other camp with a more inviting scheme and devilish bag of beliefs. The early settled life was pockmarked with crude subsistence and occasional bedlam, so belief systems tended to be flexible in honor of the invading infidel of the month. When an empire grows very powerful and defensible, though, a belief system hardens into a strict and dogmatic religion that prohibits criticism or change, for example the Pharaohs of Egypt, the Christian fanatics in the Bible belt, or the Islamic fascists.

Humans were a wandering and clannish lot from the Caveman to the Bedouin. It is generally considered that humans evolved from African apes starting about seven million years ago. Actually researchers suggest that sociality emerged about 52 million years ago. The earliest primates sought safety by being solitary and inconspicuous, moving only at night. It seems that when they shifted to daytime activity, they sought safety in numbers.

At some point, humans beat tracks out of the Dark Continent and moved up and out. According to some accounts, 50,000 years ago, in the northeastern corner of Africa, a small group of people left their homeland. Much of Africa had been depopulated and the ancestral human population had dwindled to a mere 5,000.[2] Those leaving, a group of perhaps 150 people, had many risks, to include confronting previous emigrants such as the Neanderthals. Clans stayed together, and as they wandered to different localities (the grass is always greener somewhere else), adapted to their environment. For example, humans who lived in present day Europe, over long periods of time, evolved white skin, since they no longer required the sun-protecting attributes of dark skin, and they also lost the ability to dance evidently.

In addition, this separateness of lineages made for distinct and different languages and customs. For example, of China's 1.3 billion people, over 800 million speak Mandarin, and some 300 million others speak seven other languages.[3] There are biological reasons for the uniqueness of different cultures, and the traits of the people, such as the typical hair and eye features of Orientals. However, the human population as a whole share many common attributes. From a short time after birth, humans can already detect subtle facial differences and know their parents to the exclusion of every other face. Hence a baby can often be hushed by the sight, smell, and feel of the mother. This behavior of humans is programmed in the brain and is the direct result of the DNA being passed through the generations. It is a fact that related species have similar social structures, presumably because the genes for social behavior are inherited from a common ancestor. This spells trouble for ecological explanations but in humans, cultural variation hides both the social unity of humankind and its biological foundation.[4]

In like manner, human adults fear and are suspicious of others who we term strangers, foreigners, aliens etc. Russian xenophobia comes to mind. Today, young children are cautioned not to take candy from a stranger. Humans were usually afraid of strangers for good reasons; remember the painful club over the head.

People can be insular and they don't like to rock the boat because they might fall out as the bait for bigger fish. For example, the Japanese kept White barbarians out of their country up until the 1850s. Clans that prospered and flourished did so for a reason. They had a system. And by and large all systems are similar in that there's somebody in charge who has the money or power to get everybody else moving and following the leader.

The fledgling early empires variously consolidated their power and extended their range of influence merely with brute force. The basic strategy was roam, rampage, rape, ruin, and rebuild. Exceptions to the general rule included a more sophisticated approach such as the recent emergence of the Kingdom of Saudi Arabia. Their original King Saud consolidated his power by roaming among the various tribal tents in the region. And in the grand sperm-bank style, the sum total of the deposits and withdrawals resulted in hundreds of progeny, and that's called beating your enemies from within. As another outstanding example, the infamous Genghis Khan was the master who dumped his DNA into a good portion of Mongolia. As history revealed, the great empires of Greece and Rome took the baton of power from their predecessors in the wondrous rat race of life, the expanding drive to conquer and civilize with the support of government. It's not difficult to imagine how one persuades the pack to unite for war to face brutish and bloody battlefields, to hack and kill from town to town. There are rewards in roaming and rampaging for the master that are called the spoils of war, and not only wine, women, and song. But after the fires are doused and rebuilding is finished, how do you keep the occupants in line? That is accomplished by selling an ideology and rooting it in a dogmatic religion—"Onward Christian soldiers!"

Looking backward, many of the gods appear as dull as the conjuring humans, and a multitude of gods have been thrown overboard, keelhauled, shipwrecked or marooned on desolate islands never more to see the light of day. And many a god has jumped with the rats, as the ship of state, with too many barnacles on the hull, slinks into the murky depths of a cold, cruel world.

An estimated 100,000 belief systems have existed in history, and many have fostered ethnic and tribal wars. [5] In the name of the gods, millions have been slaughtered, burned, roasted for dinner, mutilated and tortured for god's sake. The notion of a god served a decent purpose in so far as humans need a story to satisfy psychological or psychically related experiences of the brain and its environment. It was expedient, like thumb sucking, in assuaging our many fears and anxiety. Although you would expect the infant or juvenile mentality to grow up one day, nevertheless humans have dragged their ancient, dog-eared beliefs with them from the Stone Age to the Space Age, because the averages are ignorant of the many benefits and successes of science that call into question the need for a father figure, God. Einstein wrote about cosmic religious feeling in the New York Times Magazine in 1930. By this he meant the awe inspired by our ability to think and speculate about the Universe. "The religious geniuses of all ages have been distinguished by this kind of religious feeling, which knows no dogma and no God conceived in man's image; so there can be no church whose central teachings are based on it." This was obviously a sensible individual.

The ticket to an afterlife has been an enticing prospect from the time of the caveman since existence was perceived as a bowl of pits versus cherries; life is a bitch then you die and like sentiments you won't find in Chinese fortune cookies. Since religious consciousness emerged, perhaps among Neanderthal communities, there have been thousands of Primal Religions as mentioned, but the majority of these are unknown because they existed in pre-literate times. We do, however, know about several hundred such religions from the work of archeologists and anthropologists.[6] Today we have a whole smorgasbord of religions of various flavors according to taste to include Christianity, Islam, Buddhism, Hinduism, Judaism, just to name a few. Over one-third of the world population adheres to a form of Christianity. Latin America has the highest number of Christians, most of whom are Roman Catholics. Islam is practiced by nearly one-fifth of the world's population, most of who live in parts of Asia, particularly the Middle East. Judaism, though a major world religion, has fewer followers than Hinduism, Buddhism, and various other religions practiced primarily in Asia. Atheists and those who consider themselves nonreligious make up more than one-fifth of the world's population.

All Aboard the Soul Train

At some point in time, the concept of a soul was conjured as a means to an afterlife. Even Neanderthals buried their dead with some kind of ceremony, and they probably wondered: "She's dead, now what?" Did he consider her as a soul mate? Not likely—next in line! Is there such a thing as a soul mate, then or now? (They didn't have Greeting Card companies back then).

The Neanderthals died off with some controversy surrounding their disappearance, but it's a fair bet that the sneaky humans (Homo sapiens) had a hand in it; as in the story of David and Goliath, the bigger they are the harder they fall. If our descendents weren't genetically superior to the lunkheads and they were still around, what a problem we would have in the arena of social programs and income redistribution, plus we would have to teach them how to dance, shucks (insensitive brutes). The immortality of souls became a soothing remedy to the death dilemma. As with God-based views, naturalist critics offer counterexamples to the claim that a soul or immortality of any kind is necessary for meaning. Great works, whether they are moral, aesthetic, or intellectual, would seem to confer meaning on one's life regardless of whether one will live forever.

Plato explained soul as a concept related to the body which

is a clump of matter with no essence. It receives its essence from being endowed with an immortal principle which exists through eternity in the realm of the perfect ideas of the beautiful, the true, and the good. It should be noted that the concept of an immortal soul is totally foreign to the bible, the Old and the New Testament. St. Paul held that the belief in an immortal soul is of the pagans. Although the church integrated the immortality of the soul as official teaching, John Calvin admitted that the understanding of the soul's immortality can be better found in Greek philosophy than in the bible.

Invention of the soul was the ticket to an afterlife because it presupposes there is more to life than meets the eye, and that the body is just a contract carrier of the universal, mystifying spirit that simply moves on like the good guy in a bad Western movie. If you buy that ticket, you're well on the way to heaven. Are we eternal souls with a short-term lease on our physical body or is there some other explanation that has nothing to do with supreme clock winders? This sense of transcending the body and achieving union with some immortal, timeless essence is unique to humans. To their credit, apes are not preoccupied with theology and religion.

Humans have been prospecting for an afterlife like greedy miners on a California mountain. A belief that heaven or an afterlife awaits us is a "fairy story" for people afraid of death, Stephen Hawking has said. But many similar pictures come to mind, whether in the hills of Columbia or Philippines, where the great unwashed, wallowing like sheep in the mire, toil for precious gems and gold for the master. With stoic, mindless acceptance, they work towards their final reward while holding to the icons and relics of the martyrs and saints with the hope of another life in the hereafter. Various afterlife scenarios include the idea of a stream of consciousness that all humans are plugged into, and like cow's milk from udder to pail, we finally fade back into. Some belief systems propose the idea of reincarnation as in India. They have a recycling program of living where you may be a prince in this life and a toad in the next or vice versa. One can envision that, while pondering their reincarnation, they keep busy flipping through a copy of the Kama Sutra to bone-up on a new position. If you didn't know better, one might view it as a good excuse for bad behavior in this lifetime. And just who cares if they come back as a cockroach? It's absurd.

The Christian scenario envisions a post-game paradise that includes the resurrected body inclusive of tattoos, piercings, and all the other artificial trimmings. Muslim and Jewish religions similarly believe in a heaven and hell afterlife. Visionaries and God sightings are unfortunately few and far between which makes you wonder. Belief in multiple gods, polytheism (the more the merrier) has been the norm for most of the world's religions from ancient Egypt, Greece, and Rome to the current day. At some point in time the various cast of characters were percolated down to a manageable number—one god or monotheism of the desert religions such as Judaism, Christianity, and Islam.

As you might have imagined or experienced, the dry, inhospitable desert is a very boring environment and not conducive to multiple gods from the supernatural realm; one might expect multiple gods in more plush surroundings like a rain forest. In an austere and unforgiving locale, common sense suggests that it is challenging to advertise and sell the services of a multifaceted or multi-faced troupe of gods. In a time is money standard of living, the KISS system works more effectively...Keep It Simple Stupid! Even the Christians boiled down the works to three: Father, Son, and Holy Ghost—although the nebulous ghost has been shelved as unsellable. Their cup runneth over with this glop and the thirsty are still slurping it up. In a steady stream manner, the sales pitch was cast upon the waters and the bait has been taken: – for the single clock winder who created man and his minions. There is no need for sightings of a deity because the brand is stamped on the brain case of the average human, with pithy, unquestioning, faith-based zeal. Ironically, there are superior numbers of UFO sightings today compared to supreme being sightings and those who see a UFO are called eccentric but one whose spies a deity is accused of "smoking something that ain't exactly legal" (as Leo

Gorcey quipped in a Bowery Boys movie from the 1950s).

It is astonishing and ironic that each religion claims to be the one and only true faith. Catholics say that all non-Catholics are heretics or lost souls. Muslims view others as infidels. Jews claim to be God's chosen people and others are schmucks. These parochial beliefs are like languages in that each group has a different one and the communication is virtually impossible, and certainly frustrating, because everybody is babbling gibberish in different tongues. Similar to other aspects of human endeavor, each religion would like to eliminate the competition. Protestants routinely kill and maim Catholics in Ireland. Moslems pray the Jews will be flushed away once and for ever. For example, if you travel to Jordan, you either say nothing good about Israel or you keep your mouth shut. Generally, the houses of worship are a store front for the world's hypocrites and it gives them a place to go at the end of the week for a meet and greet.

The extreme example was portrayed in Mario Puzo's The Godfather, where the Mafia chief sits in church while his orchestrated executions are occurring simultaneously. How many sanctimonious perpetrators lurk in the Houses of the Holy is anyone's guess, but I would say there is standing room only. After all, if God is everywhere, why don't they pray at home instead of going to some building and donating money?

Did somebody say money?

I recall in (childhood) disbelief when the Catholic Church warden would visit our house to petition my dad for a ten percent (tithe) of his income. With seven children to feed, he would tell them "I have to see a man about a dog." One of the principles of tithing is: give back to the Lord in gratitude a portion of everything God has given, whether through paychecks, dividends, unexpected windfalls, Social Security payments, allowances or gifts. Funny, it doesn't mention funds through graft, gambling, or bootlegging, although they should be entitled to a cut off the top.

As far as religious attendance goes, perhaps there are worshippers in the flock who attend for romance and fantasy since you don't always get that at home. Then let's not forget that some of the deepest sleep and dreams can be the reward for the more pious insomniacs. Religions are flawed institutions. Or as Oscar Wilde said: "It is only the auctioneer who can equally and impartially admire all schools of art."[11] I'm not sure if that quote applies here but there it is.

There are no Close Encounters with Aliens, None!

The gods are not UFOs, but they both wear the Vaudeville hat and cane in their act. Many humans have claimed to observe alien beings and just as we say sex sells, UFOs are a steady income for the hucksters and con men among the sheepish rubes of the population. At least several hundred thousand (estimated) UFO sightings have been documented over the last 50 years, and the total number of UFO sightings is estimated to be in the millions. According to Carl Sagan, "Humans view aliens as god-like and keep searching for them in the hope that they will provide a religious experience and save us from ourselves."

To describe the probability of alien sightings, we need to rationalize the extent of the universe. Since we humans are mentally deficient, it is difficult to grasp the immensity of the universe with our limited capacities. For example, according to some models of inflationary cosmology, if the entire cosmos were scaled down to the size of earth, the part accessible to us would be much smaller than a grain of sand.[13] It is theorized that, early in its history, the universe expanded by a factor of perhaps 10^{30} and that would be like scaling up a molecule of DNA to roughly the size of the Milky Way galaxy, and in a time interval that's much shorter than a billionth of a billionth of a billionth of the blink of an eye. We keep hearing about the search for extraterrestrials.

The spooky phrase, "We are not alone" seems superfluous; of course we are not alone! And there are seven billion other people who are not alone, not to mention the billions of other animals that we are rapidly sending to perdition. For example, in 2011, poachers in South Africa have killed 443 rhinos, more than ever before as demand for their horns continues to increase in Asia. The street value of their horns, which they use as medicinal cures, has soared to around $65,000 per kilo, making it more expensive than gold, platinum and, in many cases, cocaine.

If there are aliens tuning in to earth, we do not have the ability to decode their message: "Don't call us, we'll call you." And we can probably forget about attempts to contact aliens by radio transmission or other signals because of the inverse square law—the farther a wave travels, the weaker it becomes (signal degradation) until it is unrecognizable.

In answer to the question of life on other planets, the answer is possibly yes, due to the immensity of the universe. Actually there is a way to calculate the number of alien civilizations in our galaxy using the Drake equation, but it is not very precise. However, due to the huge size of the universe, it is only logical to view the probability of alien life as very high. They are definitely out there; but the probability of a human seeing an alien life form is slim to none. The reason is the vast distances involved. If the closest alien is 50,000 light-years away, the probability of our meeting is extremely unlikely even given their advanced technology. Consider that the Earth's most powerful radio signals have by now expanded to fill a sphere only 65 light-years in radius. The Pioneer 10 spacecraft, launched in 1972, was last heard from in 2003 and is generally headed for the star Aldebaran. Even though Aldebaran is only 68 light years away, it will take Pioneer 10 over two million years to reach it.

There are Earthlings who want to meet and greet the aliens of outer space. For example, SETI, (the Search for Extraterrestrial Intelligence), is an exploratory organization that seeks evidence of life in the universe by detection across interstellar distances, using methods such as telescope arrays and radio frequencies. I don't want to accuse these types of groups of being frauds but perhaps they may be called misguided. Their jobs are similar to Federal government positions—it's like unemployment, but you have somewhere to go every day. There is a SETI organization that sends out small portions of data to millions of home computer users around the world. The distributed computing project uses the average citizens' computers during the idle time of the machines in the search for alien transmissions. If you have time to waste and nothing better to do, fine; look and listen for UFOs. Humans need to clean up the mess in their own back yards before bothering the advanced aliens. Or perhaps these voyeurs are dreaming of advanced military technology. Humans think nothing of swatting flies, so what do they expect from the aliens? Stop being a pest! The probability of a visit to earth by aliens is the fanciful dreams of Hollywood movies and other hucksters. The universe is approximately 14.7 billion years old, and regardless of our dreams or imaginings, this insignificant planetary rock called Earth is cruising through space-time with a crew of mental midgets on board.

I pose an interesting question to guests concerning the possibility of alien close encounters. If an alien spacecraft were to land in your backyard, and they gestured for you to go off with them, would you leave Earth? Consider there is a chance that you may never return. My answer: yes.

It doesn't take a rocket scientist to distinguish the gods from UFOs. For some strange reason, many humans are desperate to get off this rock at least mentally and have conjured stories that maintain humans are descendants of aliens who landed on Earth thousands of years ago. They laud the idea that much of human technology came from alien visitors and that they are still in the neighborhood. One of the best examples comes from the books written by Shirley MacLane, the Hollywood actress. Her views on UFOs and reincarnation would be considered laughable, but due to her celebrity status, the viewers will sit on the edge of their seat to listen. Phenomenal sightings such as ghosts, gods, and goblins have titillated and terrified audiences in the circus of primitives and moderns alike. Not only can the human brain be easily fooled, but we are stamped with a fear of the dark and cannot navigate the uncharted regions of the mind.

The Meaning of Life

There is a need for balance and thoughtful concern for where we are and what actions humans should pursue to sustain a viable existence. Obviously the present course is on shaky grounds. Does it matter? Does anything we do matter? It might; since we are in the game, we may as well see where the parade will take us. This is part of our programming; we are thrust into consciousness and need to throw our chips onto the table just for the thrill. It is our gambling nature and naiveté to think we have the odds on our side to win the jackpot in life. Lucky for us, we are cuckolded to think as we do. Otherwise, like the emperor with no clothes on, our gang would be viewed as a failure if we let pessimism rule the day. Yes, we all end up in the same old sorry state: Nowhere. But we plod on against the odds because it is the only game in town. It's easy to declare the heck with it and nothing really matters, but I say "so what?" We are not so special that the outcome of the poker game is somehow more important than playing the cards how they fall.

It may be that we are only star dust with the obvious attributes and then some. But there is nothing wrong with being comprised of mechanistic matter with attendant propensities to float and swim through time and think brilliantly on occasion. So we finally die?

I don't think that life is pointless, as in debating the superiority and influence of American versus British music, Elvis or the Beatles for instance. That topic is futile because there is no reason to choose one over the other. The fact that a child (and a majority of adults) has no clue as to how your computer operates, in theory and practice, does not negate the computer's meaning; one simply doesn't know. But it surely is not pointless. Will we ever know the meaning of life? The answer: Not in this lifetime (or in any other one). The age-old programming keeps us going with egg-timer efficiency; it is both laughable and sad at the same space-time, but we slog on as best we can, nod to Darwin, and move on.

We are all unfit, it's just some of us are more unfit than the rest but that's not the point. To the individual, this lack or shortfall of meaning leaves one as just another unsatisfied cog in the wheel of life, but don't take it too seriously. On the superficial level, pain and suffering are never desirable and we are programmed to bathe in our own remorse. But on a different level, even this shall pass, meaning better days are ahead. For the disciples of Darwin, the end game of life is to pass along genes to another generation, and move along.

This is the purpose of life but not the meaning of life. All life forms from plants to humans struggle and connive to successfully reproduce. The goal is to handoff one's DNA to the next relay runner (offspring), and make a splash into the gene pool. This is a programmed and mechanistic action. It's as if one can mate, reproduce, and smugly sit back with a job well done. Many of these kinds of notions are patently human but on the other hand, does a bird or plant experience the same conceited appreciation for their role in life? The plants and birds don't have a conscious idea of the meaning of life and this is our conundrum to think we should have some sort of ultimate meaning for our existence beyond the obvious mechanistic, assigned role. If there should be any meaning to existence, it can only be relevant beyond individual pursuits and aspirations. And even then it appears to be problematic and unknown at this time.

Our parochial occupations are mere window dressing for the larger picture of a cosmos that appears coldly impenetrable to primitive perspectives. Throughout human history, there have been individuals that might be thought as enlightened or higher beings, the relatively few of high intelligence. They have lived through the ages but often in the background with low status and thus unable to influence societies to a great extent. Our everyday experience shows that brains and brawn are often mutually exclusive; it seems that brute force can muscle the smart fellow into the background. We have to work in order to change that attitude.

Just as ethics or morals seem to take a back seat to greed and corruption, the ambitious find it more preferable to sacrifice the Virgin rather than standing up for what is right and decent. This sad state of affairs is condoned and perpetuated because there is a lack of direction and focus on education. The history books are filled with great men and tremendous misdeeds and the general population in effect is slightly schooled, pitifully educated, and terribly unrefined.

But the bottom line is this: The nurturing and education provided to a developing person will help determine the payoff in terms of great expectations. (A wine maker does not cultivate and produce a fine wine by using sour grapes). Unfortunately the history of the world indicates a shipwreck and a giant genetic pool searching for a life boat. It has not been the fault of the flock that their existence is a chain-link of being born, branded, bedded and be gone; beggars can't be choosers. They are a product of the folly that preceded them; and the same lack of awareness will inevitably follow, unless we launch a revolution in our schools and in our minds.

Mankind has been pondering a question for ages "What is the meaning of life?" and one poignant answer is that you are not supposed to know. About this question, Charles Darwin noted, "I feel most deeply that the whole subject is too profound for the human intellect. A dog might as well speculate on the mind of Newton." The size and scope of the known and unknown universe is indeed so mind boggling that primitive life forms such as ourselves are swaddled in an atmosphere that permits only ostensibly reasonable answers to unreachable questions. And the ultimate meaning is for now elusive. If you could have asked Einstein the supernatural question, "Do you believe in God?" Odds are he would evade a yes or no answer; more likely, in a diplomatic way, Einstein would espouse some opinion about the mysterious nature of the universe and its laws that represents the concept of God. Firstly, he was a famous and often-quoted celebrity, and secondly, he was a Jewish immigrant to the U.S. and may have been reluctant to bluntly state an opinion on the ultimately sensitive topic during the early decades of the 1900s.

When I was a child in 1966, there was the controversial Time Magazine article with the title, "Is God Dead?" The magazine caused a hue and cry that was equaled only by John Lennon's offhand remark that the Beatles were more popular than Jesus Christ. Here we are more than 40 years later, and the record player needle is still skipping and popping the same line: "I'm just sitting here watching the wheels go round and round" (John Lennon).

If the majority of the world is wrong about God, that would not necessitate a huge despairing cause for concern. The top will keep on spinning and wobbling whether the proprietor is in or not. You often hear that the absence of a Divinity will lead to chaos and riots in the streets; but I'd like to know, what do we have now? Everywhere you turn, someone is lamenting that the world is "going to pot" because God has been put out to pasture. No! Since the dawn of humans, every generation perceived their world as a downward spiral and it is the human condition to complain. Once again it is not the absence of God in our lives that is the problem; it is the presence of educational systems that are failing to provide a 'money-back guarantee' on the schooling product.

The take away message in the context of life's meaning is that humans are in charge of this venture of life, and as stewards of our destiny, we must humbly accept our responsibilities and obligations. We must work to solve our predicament which is that people are vulnerable to their power, passions, and false impressions. Just as an oncoming train can only be ignored or denied for so long, there are warning signals that indicate a different track must be taken if we are to continue to live with integrity and sanity intact. Even the average citizen can sense the loss and confusion in present society as we contend with a host of negatives such as poverty, pollution, and a degraded lifestyle. Therefore it appears necessary to cast off our delusions and misconceptions because there is no referee or divinity that will step in and take charge or act as the conductor of our journey.

If one recognizes the futility of the status quo and the need to alter course, then what are the available options or choices to consider? Naturally various opinions and commentary proliferate through electronic media. One of the hottest topics around is the idea of a One World Government. This conspiracy theory has gained popular support because various wealthy and connected powerbrokers seem to be running the show like a wizard behind the curtain, able to influence the global, political, economic, and social landscape. Foremost among these include the World Trade Organization (WTO), International Monetary Fund (IMF), Federal Reserve Banks (FRB), the World Bank, Bilderberg Group, and the United Nations (UN). At the other end of the spectrum are the outliers and anarchists of various protest movements such as Occupy Wall Street. They are fed up with the seeming corruption and thievery that is endemic in the world at large. Many people now believe in income or wealth redistribution where money is taken from the rich and given to the poor. Are these the best solutions to the world's problems?

I would like to suggest that education is the most telling candidate to adopt as a rejoinder to the perceived problems in the world. You can feed and medicate all the impoverished people around the globe, but the population will unsustainably increase beyond the current seven billion. You don't make much headway, that way. Hence this is one of the most important ethical issues of all time. It would be a very difficult decision, however, to justify withholding sustenance or capital from certain populations, due mainly to their weak institutions, to save the planet. But surely we are at the point where humans must consider the role of playing God in order to secure our continued existence here. There needs to be a concerted effort to apply maximal resources and full steam to effectively educate the population at large. Perhaps with some luck and expert tutoring, we can curb the bobbing and weaving in the houses of worship, in the boxing ring, on street corners—and leave it on the dance floor. Violence and veneration were carted in humanity's bag of tricks that brought us to the current millennium, but what the world needs now is more respect, awareness, and awe.

Awareness is best thought of as mindfulness. By contrast, if "ignorance is bliss" (Thomas Gray 1742), which implies that some are ignorant, then knowledge and awareness are somehow viewed detrimentally. But intelligent thinking, although uncomfortable at times, is one of the preferential attributes of the human condition. Gray's poem "Where ignorance is bliss, 'tis folly to be wise" was written in the context that it is better for man to be blissfully ignorant of his fate, because "Sorrow never comes too late, And happiness too swiftly flies."

There are many cute attempts in the web of writers, throwing ideas like darts at a dartboard, such as awareness is described as the witness whereas the thinking brain is the judge. Suffice to say, common thinking is often the simple rote of restating previous insights without much understanding, critical reasoning, or creativity. There is the phrase "Standing on the shoulders of giants" made famous by Isaac Newton in a letter to Robert Hooke in 1676. By this we comprehend there is really nothing entirely new under the sun. Despite that, advances in science are built on previous foundations. Therefore awareness is being able to see the big picture. It is not just living in the moment as some contend or sitting in a meditative position. An example of awareness is to recognize that a superpower has sent the Calvary to Bosnia and Iraq but ignored the slaughter in Rwanda and Darfur (Sudan) of Africa. I suppose we are always learning throughout our lives, but intelligence is about a foundation of wisdom, awareness, and understanding. Whether on the phone or in person, I frequently say: Hello, I am ready to ask my first stupid question of the day (Yes, teachers: there are stupid questions). This is awareness albeit on a humorous level. So, how do you accumulate wisdom and awareness? It is not my place to suggest Yoga or Zen however laudable such activities may be.

Awareness can be learned like anything else, but one must have some modicum of intelligence and it helps to have a source, benefactor, or tutor for this exercise. If it can be learned, the obvious source would be the school rooms of the world. One cannot usually acquire phenomenal attributes from ignorant relatives, peers or exotic gurus. Thus a radical change to education is considered worthwhile. We must recognize that an enormous amount of good money is thrown away on celebrities or other suspects, and the school systems squander reams of funds in a mindless manner because many culprits are on autopilot in the cockpit of the brain. Awareness these days is represented by wearing 'pink' on the backsides of casual shorts for breast cancer awareness (silly), and jogging marathons for various causes or promotions. In recent years, the fad of wearing "awareness wristbands" has emerged that represents advocacy for diseases or a charitable organization. Consumers can show off by wearing their virtue on their sleeve with a colored, silicon band. The awareness colors include Gray for brain cancer (I get it, 'gray matter'), colorectal cancer is Brown (what else?), Green for depression (not blue?), and headache is Burgundy (too much red wine?). The trend is just as popular as phony friends on the internet but I suppose it's easier than carrying a billboard or picketing for any old 'just cause.' And ironically, the fashion was started in the year 2004 by the quintessential phony and cheater, Lance Armstrong. "Think of how stupid the average person is, and realize half of them are stupider than that" (George Carlin). Such activities are well intentioned advocacies, but the big picture needs to be appreciated and framed as crucial to our general well being. Too bad there is no patent formula for acquiring wisdom and awareness as sold in the pill and supplement markets. It requires hard work and mentoring by those with experience.

A final comment about awareness of a different sort: A random internet search for spiritual awareness reveals a disciple of Paramahansa Yogananda in the form of The Center for Spiritual Awareness in Lakemont, Georgia. The spiritual director, Roy Eugene Davis, includes the following guidance on the website: "What is our real purpose for being in this world? It is to awaken to knowledge of ourselves as spiritual beings in relationship to a Reality which, not confined by space, time, or relative circumstances, is infinite. When we are fully enlightened while expressing through a body, our awareness extends beyond the sense-perceived environment to include all planes and dimensions of the cosmos and beyond them, to eternity. It is only the soul's confinement of awareness to an erroneous belief of independent selfhood that limits it. The truth is, because the soul is a unit of God's consciousness, it is infinite."

Ok, that's interesting.

They say "life is short" or that "youth is wasted on the young."

The basis for these reflections is that humans take many years to mature due to the evolution of the brain and the need for extended parental care. Whereas flight school for ducklings is just a matter of weeks, humans acquire both genetic and cultural information but require several decades to reach full mental maturity. In the ancient world, life was short and humans were evolved to pay close attention to the near term. In the present day, life would seem short to those who have been coasting along without awareness or a focused sense of our place in the biosphere. If you are not a thinking or educated person, life does seem to pass you by. We can no longer afford our insatiable and unfathomable habits to spend and consume, idly and complacently turning a profit as a means to a mindless end. Since the formative years are crucial for cognitive development, proper education must be viewed as an investment in the stock of human welfare. The legacy of the Enlightenment is the belief that entirely on our own we can know, and in knowing, understand, and in understanding, choose wisely.[14] Therefore it seems evident that the world desperately needs a crash course in decision making and a long-term commitment to learning and education, and it has to be top-down as well as grass roots or all encompassing.

"Billy, eat your peas; there are millions of starving Chinese in the world."

"Mom, if they were here then I would gladly give them my peas."

I hope or wish my parents were paid back for their sacrifices. I hopefully held their hand, each in their turn, and helped them during their final days and said goodbye. My mother, what a trooper! She endured five operations for cancer with chemotherapy, radiation, and never a peep out of her in complaint. I requested the morphine that allowed her to float away to sleep, and eerily, with many of her children in attendance, she called 50 times to her friend, Margaret O'Reilly before she left. During our childhood, my mother often expressed her wish that, upon her decease, we have an Irish wake or party. That didn't happen and the elders didn't understand I suppose. You know, Mom, a house is not a home when you're not sitting there. And thanks for those preschool peanut butter and jelly sandwiches with milk that you would set on the little table, on the back porch of that cracker-box house, so I could watch the world go by. I'm still there and waiting for you even if you don't show.

My wife's country of Eritrea has a custom similar to an Irish wake. Actually, there are other similarities between the two countries that go beyond my ken. The Eritreans gather for 12 nights at the house of the deceased and prepare a tent for a large gathering. They tell very funny jokes, and if a man falls asleep, they might paint his nails with polish; for a sleeping woman, they may paint her face with lipstick. Upon awaking, a judge will convey some small fines that will be donated to the grieving family. Some visitors might tell fortunes with seashells for a small stipend with the same purpose. The intent of the gathering is to make the family laugh and provide some relief. For those not able to attend, one must pay their respects when visiting, even after one or two years.

Comparable to the Irish, if you know the deceased, one must cry or wail, otherwise they will carry a grudge. On the 12th night in Eritrea, the family will pay for the preparation and cooking of a sheep or a goat if they are not well-off. This is to show gratitude for the mourners' help and attendance. Don't know about you, but I can't stand the idea of tip-toeing to death or crawling on my hands and knees to keep the wheel rolling. I want to leapfrog into those cold, dark waves, make a hell of a splash, and then when I open my eyes, to see Jackie Gleason at the pearly gates holding two (single malt) double scotches. Life is like a smile, it's temporary. So make the best of it.

There are no aliens or bogeyman under the bed, so hush, don't worry my darling, and just go to sleep. Just go to sleep.

REFERENCES

1. E.O. Wilson, Nature Revealed, John Hopkins Univ Press, 2006, pp. 223-226.
2. David Bohm, Thought as a System, Routledge, 1994, p. 112.
3. Niles Eldredge, Why We Do It (New York – London, 2004), p. 30.
4. Stephen J. Gould, Rocks of Ages, (New York 1999), p. 4.
5. Brian Greene, The Fabric of the Cosmos, (New York 2004), p. 156.
6. Frans De Waal, The Age of Empathy, (New York 2009), p.21.
7. Dawn Starin, Bug Buffet, American Museum of Natural History Magazine, Oct 2011, p.16.
8. Noam Chomsky, The Acquisition of Syntax in Children, Cambridge, MA: MIT Press, 1969.
9. The Orlando Sentinel, 29 Nov 1998, p.A-15.
10. G.Viamontes and B. Beitman, Mapping the Unconscious in the Brain, drbeitman.com/ papers/ psychAnnals..
11. Sarah Stein, The Pursuit of Plumes: Jews, Ostrich Feathers, and Modern Global Commerce, 2008.
12. Bloomberg. 12 March 2009.
13. Leon Levy, with Eugene Linden, The Mind of Wall Street: A Legendary Financier on the Perils of Greed, 2002.
14. J. Edgar Hoover, The Man and his Secrets by Curt Gentry, (New York 1991), page 84.
15. Steven Pinker, The Better Angels of Our Nature, Why Violence Has Declined, (New York 2011), p. 696.
16. Sandra Steingraber, The Whole Fracking Enchilada, Orion Magazine, September 2010.
17. Royal Society of Chemistry, rsc.org, Mar 2005.
18. www.leas.ca, Labor Environmental Alliance Society, Jan 2007.
19. Evan Schwartz, Waste Management, Wired Magazine, 24 May 2010.
20. E.O. Wilson, The Future of Life, (New York 2002), p.90.
21. Arms Without Borders: Why a globalised trade needs global controls, Control Arms Campaign, Oct 2006
22. EmotionalCompetency.com, Developing Social Skills.
23. Richard Dawkins, The Selfish Gene, 30th Ed 2006, (first pub 1976), p. 198.
24. Frans De Waal, The Age of Empathy, (New York 2009), p.187.
25. Frans De Waal, The Age of Empathy, (New York 2009), p.187.
26. Ernst Mayr, What Evolution Is, Basic Books, (New York 2001), p. 118.
27. Letter from Darwin to Asa Gray, 22 May 1860.
28. Stephen J. Gould, Rocks of Ages, (New York 1999), p. 198.
29. Paul Ehrlich, Human Natures, (New York 2000), p. 308.
30. http://www.comw.org/pda/0310rm8exsum.html, Project on Defense Alternatives, Carl Conetta, 20 Oct 2003.
31. Charles Darwin, The Descent of Man, New York: Appleton and Co., 1883, p.609.
32. Scott Atran, In Gods We Trust, Oxford University Press, 2004.
33. Michael Hoffman, The Japan Times Online, 27 February 2011.
34. Michael Hoffman, The Japan Times Online, 27 February 2011.
35. http://goto.bilkent.edu.tr/gunes/zen/zenphilosophy.htm
36. http://www.media-awareness.ca/english/parents/marketing/advertising_everywhere.cfm
37. NY Times Online, Business,You For Sale, Natasha Singer, 16 June 2012.
38. NY Times Online, If Smart is the Norm, David Dobbs, 22 October 2012.
39. New York Times, In Good Health, Gina Kolata, 13 June 2012.
40. Walter Isaacson, Einstein, (New York 2007), p. 543.
41. Brian Greene, The Hidden Reality, (New York 2011), p. ix.
42. New York Times, nytimes.com, Dr. Jack Kevorkian Dies at 83, Keith Schneider, 3 June 2011.
43. efmoody.com/estate/lifeexpectancy.html
44. V.S. Ramachandran, The Tell-Tale Brain, 2011, p. xv.
45. William P. Frost, Abortion Perspectives & Issues, Univ of Dayton, p. 56
46. Heritage Foundation, D. Muhlhausen, Death Penalty Deters Crime, 28 August 2007.
47. William P. Frost, Abortion Perspectives & Issues, Univ of Dayton, p. 39
48. Scientific American, Sep 1979, p. 116.
49. Mark Cohen, Vital Signs, Discover Magazine, March 2012, p. 32.
50. ucsusa.org, Union of Concerned Scientists, 30 October 2002.
51. Gelpi and Feaver, American Political Science Review, Vol. 96, No. 4 December 2002.
52. The Atlantic Online, G. Franke-Ruta, Americans Have No Idea, 31 May 2012.
53. Bell and Weinberg, Homosexualities: A study of Diversity, p. 308, NY: Simon and Schuster, 1978.
54. Wikipedia, Noam Chomsky.

55. Pat Buchanan, State of Emergency, 2006, p. 244.
56. Pat Buchanan, Churchill Hitler and the Unnecessary War, 2008, p. 100.
57. Steven Pinker, The Better Angels of Our Nature, Why Violence Has Declined, (New York 2011), p. 84.
58. Nat Geo News, James Owen, Did Discrimination Enhance Intelligence of Jews, 18 July 2005.
59. Peter Tyson, Are We Still Evolving, PBS.Org, NOVA, 14 December 2009.
60. Sally Clay, Mindfreedom.com, 2002
61. Michael Pollan, Omnivore's Dilemma, 2006, p. 19.
62. The Victorian Web, David Cody, 14 Oct 2002
63. Wikipedia, the free encyclopedia, Education in the U.S.
64. Charles Dickens, Hard Times, Dover Thrift Editions, 2001, p.16.
65. The Internet Encyclodedia of Philosophy, W.J. Korab-Karpowicz, 2006
66. www.infochangeindia.org, 2006
67. Victoria Velkoff, Women of the World, 1998.
68. Education in China, www.internationaled.org/publications/ ChinaDelegationReport, Seo 2005, Page 6.
69. wikiquote.org/wiki/Albert_Einstein.
70. National Geographic, Oct 2011, p 36.
71. David Deutsch, The Beginning of Infinity, Penguin Books, 2011, p. 63.
72. William Shakespeare, The Tempest, Act 4, Scene 1.
73. Kenneth Wesson, Memory and the Brain, Nais.org, Spring 2002.
74. Brian Greene, The Fabric of the Cosmos, (New York 2004), p. 254.
75. Nicholas Wade, Before the Dawn, 2006, p.71.
76. Stephen Diamond, Evil Deeds, Psychology Today Online, 30 November 2008.
77. Michael Shermer, The Believing Brain, St. Martin's Press, 2011, p. 186.
78. Richard Dawkins, The Selfish Gene, 30th Ed 2006, (first pub 1976), p. 198.
79. Richard Dawkins, The Selfish Gene, 30th Ed 2006, (first pub 1976), P 330.
80. BigThink.com, Neurological Origins of Religious Belief, John Cookson, 14 September 2010.
81. Paul Ehrlich, Human Natures, (New York 2000), p. 214.
82. Science Daily, Bird Brains and Vocal Learning, 11 March 2008.
83. V.S. Ramachandran, Mirror Neurons and the Brain in the Vat, edge.org, 10 January 2006.
84. New York Times, Cells That Read Minds, 10 January 2006.
85. Scientific American, Mirror Neurons, Jul 2008.
86. Richard Dawkins, The Selfish Gene, 30th Ed 2006, (first pub 1976), p. 192.
87. Jared Diamond, Guns, Germs, and Steel, 1999, p. 39.
88. Before the Dawn, Nicholas Wade, 2006, p. 10.
89. Jared Diamond, Guns, Germs, and Steel, 1999, P. 323
90. New York Times, Nicholas Wade, Genes Play a Major Role, 19 December 2011.
91. E.O. Wilson, Consilience, 1998, p. 266.
92. Albert Randall, Religion as Faith in Transcendent Salvation.
93. Michael Martin, Microsoft Encarta Encyclopedia, 1998.
94. The Meaning of Life, http://plato.stanford.edu/entries/life-meaning, Stanford Univ, 2007.
95. William P. Frost, Abortion Perspectives & Issues, Univ of Dayton, p. 46
96. V.S. Ramachandran, The Tell-Tale Brain, 2011, p. 282.
97. Wikipedia.org, Oscar Wild, The Critic as Artist, May 1891.
98. Carl Sagan, The Varieties of Scientific Experience, p. 128.
99. Brian Greene, The Fabric of the Cosmos, (New York 2004), p. 285.
100. E.O. Wilson, Consilience, 1998, p. 325.